# The Skeptical Economist

# The Skeptical Economist

## Eli Ginzberg

WESTVIEW PRESS
BOULDER AND LONDON

Copyright © 1987 by Conservation of Human Resources, Columbia University

Published in 1987 in the United States of America by Westview Press, Inc.; Frederick A. Praeger, Publisher; 5500 Central Avenue, Boulder, Colorado 80301

Library of Congress Cataloging-in-Publication Data
Ginzberg, Eli, 1911–
  The skeptical economist.
Bibliography: p.
  Includes index.
  1. Economics.  2. Economic policy.  I. Title.
HB71.G53  1987      330      87-2165
ISBN 0-8133-7372-7

Composition for this book originated with conversion of the author's computer tapes or word-processor disks.

Printed and bound in the United States of America

6    5    4    3    2    1

To my fellow board members
and the staff, present and past,
Manpower Demonstration Research Corporation,
1973–
in collegial appreciation

# Contents

*Acknowledgments*                                                              ix

**Part One: Economics in Disarray**

1   The Long View                                                             3

2   The Education of an Economist                                            10

3   Sources of Skepticism                                                    22

History Versus Theory, 22
The Limits of Theory, 24
The Depression and the New Deal, 26

**Part Two: Economics Triumphant**

4   The Institutionalization of Economics                                    35

The Heyday of Economists, 35
Disillusion with Economics, 38
The Post–World War II Era, 43

5   We Are All Keynesians                                                    50

The New Economics, 53
The Reagan Approach, 58
Alternative Theories, 59

6   The Economics of the American Nobel Laureates                           64

General Theory, 65
Methodology, 70
Money and Finance, 76
History and Policy, 81
Overview, 86

7    Changing Times, Changing Theories                              88

The New Era, 88
The Internationalization of the U.S. Economy, 90
The Revolution in Money and Finance, 92
Human Resources, 93
The Push for Equity, 95
The Not-for-Profit Sector, 97
The Laureates and the Real World, 99

**Part Three: Economics in a Lower Key**

8    Research in Human Resources                                    109

Focus on the Unemployed, 109
Occupational Choice, 112
The Eisenhower Studies, 113
The Talented, 116
Macro-Studies, 118
A Half-Century of Human Resources Research, 121
Human Capital Versus Human Resources, 122

9    The Policy Arena                                               125

Women and the World of Work, 125
Educational Preparation for Work, 127
The Challenge of Race, 130
Health Policy and Programs, 133
Technical Assistance Overseas, 137
The Armed Services, 143

10    Toward Realistic Economic Policy                              148

The Reality of Change, 148
The U.S. Political Process: Some Lessons, 151
Earned Income and Income Transfers, 155
Unprepared for Work, 157
The Shortfall in Jobs, 161

11    The Value of Skepticism                                       166

*References*                                                         173
*About the Author*                                                   176
*Index*                                                              177

# Acknowledgments

This book—which is not the one he wanted me to write—has been much improved by the care with which my good friend, Professor Moses Abramovitz of Stanford University, went through the first draft. He found a great many places where corrections and emendations were required, and he often suggested the specific rewrites. I am greatly in his debt for his careful reading; I absolve him from any and all responsibility for the shape and content of the final version.

My long-time friend and close collaborator, Professor Sar Levitan of George Washington University, asked to see an early draft, and as a quid pro quo, gave me some helpful suggestions and corrections.

Two members of my staff, Thomas Bailey and Dean Morse, read the manuscript and made suggestions that I followed.

Anna Dutka of my staff performed a major service by filling in all of the holes in the first draft and also checked and corrected many facts and figures. Her assistance was invaluable.

My wife, Ruth, despite her discomfiture about my writing such a personal book with so many autobiographical details, nevertheless did her best to sanitize and simplify my prose, for which I thank her.

Sylvia Leef prepared the first typescript from my difficult-to-read yellow pages, and Shoshana Vasheetz put the first revised draft on the word processor and oversaw the successive revisions.

*Eli Ginzberg*

# PART ONE

# Economics in Disarray

The late 1920s was not a propitious period for a beginning student to be exposed to economics. The U.S. economy was presumed to have entered a New Era characterized by "perpetual prosperity," an era that mainline economics could not explain or illuminate. And shortly thereafter, the Great Depression, with the most dire consequences for output and employment, occurred in the United States and most of the developed nations. Once again, mainline economics was left at the starting gate, unable to explain what had happened or what governments should do to extricate themselves from the ever-deepening depression.

Small wonder that some of us became skeptics. What is inexplicable is that most of the young professionals did not lose their faith.

# 1

## The Long View

This book, more than most, requires that the writer set forth his intent and design and describe how he plans to develop his argument. My intent is to look back on my more than half-century as researcher in human resources and as policy adviser in order to extract some lessons, particularly with reference to the potential and limitation of the discipline of economics. I was originally trained in economics but early became estranged from that discipline. During the fifty years that I have taught, pursued research, and served as a policy adviser, economics has experienced wide-ranging fluctuations in the way it is viewed by its practitioners and by the public. Only a small minority can recall the conditions that existed sixty, seventy, or eighty years ago. Those who can have what economists refer to as a "comparative advantage," that is, if they know how to use their perspective. If I am alive in 1989, as the actuarial tables predict, my seventy-eight years will cover about 40 percent of the total history of the United States since its formation as an independent nation.

One may ask, "What has time and perspective to do with economics and economists?" The answer is either very little or a great deal, depending on one's posture. It was the view of John Maynard Keynes that most statesmen pursue economic policies that reflect the outmoded ideas of academic scribblers of earlier generations. How can one fault this generalization? Newborns may be tabulae rasae, but by the time individuals leave their parents' homes, surely by the time they graduate from college or university, they have had at least twenty-two years of indoctrination. Fortunately, not all teachers and not all of the influential persons who have had a part in their indoctrination have proffered the same view of the world or shared the same values. Adolescents have to fashion their own syntheses, but all are under inexorable pressure to adopt one of the models to which they have been exposed, modified to some degree by their developmental experiences and preferences.

An observation of Albert Einstein complements that of Keynes. Einstein stated that even the greatest scientists are capable of only one revolution: They can turn the theories of their teachers aside or on their heads and offer an alternative theory more consonant with reality. But even the brilliant investigator can do this only once because the person who has made a breakthrough inevitably becomes a captive of his or her own theory.

If we trace the beginning of economics to the publication of Adam Smith's *The Wealth of Nations* in 1776, we can identify two mainstreams of inquiry, possibly three if we count the combining of the two. The first consists of model building of competitive markets; the second seeks understanding from the ordering of historical experience. Occasionally, a major synthesizer combines the two, as did John Stuart Mill, Karl Marx, Thorstein Veblen, and, in this century, John Maurice Clark, Joseph Schumpeter, and Gunnar Myrdal.

The dominant model-building approach rests on the implicit and explicit assumptions that in competitive markets, changes in prices will establish an equilibrium between demand and supply. Of course, equilibrium will be possible only in the long run and may merely be approximated and never realized, but both static and dynamic models enable analysts to ignore institutional complexities and explore new and important relationships based on a series of simplifying assumptions.

Empiricists also need simplifying assumptions. They cannot possibly order and elucidate all the facts but must select among them and seek to generalize their meaning and significance.

What then distinguishes the model-builder from the empiricist? The difference lies in their respective attitudes towards institutional change. The model-builder believes that because competition has been the dominant mode of organizing economic activities in Western Europe, North America, and Japan throughout this century and even longer, models that seek to refine the analysis of how competitive markets operate can yield important new knowledge that will add to understanding and contribute to policy. The empiricist contends that to attempt to understand the developed economies of the twentieth century without consideration of the changing roles of central banks, trade unions, defense industries, multinational corporations, large-scale research and development, higher education, the economic role of women, the revolution in communications, metropolitanism, and strivings for equity is to deal with "empty boxes."

A long perspective can be an asset or a liability. In the 1960s, as a member of an informal advisory council to a Wall Street investor, I was responsible for commenting at quarterly meetings on employment and labor market trends, about which I was reasonably informed as a result of ongoing research as well as my chairmanship of the National Manpower Advisory Committee. At that time, my colleagues with few exceptions were strongly optimistic in their appraisals of the economy. I kept looking for and introducing warning signs that the economy might become straitened, if not in that quarter, then in the next, or the following quarter. There was no evidence of labor market strain, wage escalation, or costly strikes. But I was uneasy about the long uninterrupted period of economic expansion, covering a quarter of a century with only an occasional break. The memory of the Great Depression of the 1930s was still with me. I could not shake off the belief that sooner or later the economy would again falter, and I kept looking for the incipient signs of the reversal.

As the mid-1960s turned into the late 1960s, I became more wary. I taught basic macroeconomics at Columbia University's Graduate School of Business and often indicated skepticism about Washington economists who said they had learned to fine-tune the economy. As the 80th month of the boom turned into the 90th and the 90th into the 100th, I did not waver; but successive classes of students understandably were not impressed with my repeated warnings to wait and see. It was not until the 106th month that the expansion ended, and by that time most of my students had lost interest in the issue.

The question has been asked in the past whether it is possible to ignore the changing contours of modern economies while we attempt to learn what makes them tick and to sort out constructive from injurious policies. An inspection of any of the ten or twenty leading economic journals provides a ready answer. Most academicians are busy elaborating one or another model, usually with the help of sophisticated mathematics but with scarcely a bow in the direction of the changing institutional framework. There are, of course, many articles based on econometrics that try to assess the causative factors in different markets, although the data sets are frequently inadequate.

A principal aim of this book is to examine economics at its best and to explore the extent to which the most advanced theories are able to illuminate the changes that are occurring in the real world and to point directions for policy.

A parallel aim is to set out the intellectual and emotional forces that led me to question the dominant tradition in economics: the commitment to the premise that economics is a science and that through dedicated work one can capture the complexities that govern the behavior of men in their pursuit of material gain.

There is little point in criticizing the assumptions, methods, and results of the leading group of talented and conscientious scholars who are in the mainstream of contemporary economics unless one offers an alternative approach, if only in outline, to heighten the contrast between the appraiser and the appraised. Accordingly, I have outlined the scope of my research work in the field of human resources and have discussed how I have used it in my role as a policy adviser, primarily to the federal government.

The book is divided into three parts. In Part One, I summarize the disarray that overtook mainline economics during the Great Depression, when leaders of the profession could explain neither what had occurred nor why, and discuss the profession's inability to focus on what should be done to halt and reverse the unraveling of the economy.

In Part Two, I set out the major developments that changed economics, both as a profession and as a discipline. The much expanded role of government during the New Deal and World War II created a strong and continuing demand for economists, and the profession's strength grew, the more so because Keynes's *The General Theory of Employment, Interest, and Money* (1936) had provided a new analytic approach and new policy directions whereby depressed economies could be turned around.

The long period of sustained economic growth in the United States during the next quarter century was interpreted by observers both in and out of the economics profession as testimony to the advances of the discipline and as the translation of the new doctrines into public policies.

In the concluding two chapters in Part Two I review the contributions of the thirteen American Nobel laureates in economics, who by definition, have been among the leading contributors to the development of the discipline, and I consider whether and to what extent their work was grounded in the evolution of economic thought or in the realities of economic development. A much foreshortened answer is that the Nobel laureates were for the most part inner- rather than outer-directed.

In the four chapters in Part Three I set forth briefly the focus of my research into human resources and discuss how this research guided my activities as a longtime policy adviser to the federal government, with primary involvement in the areas of womanpower, race, economic development, military manpower, and health care policy. In the penultimate chapter drawing on my expertise in employment policy, I suggest how the United States, confronted by disturbingly high unemployment, should act to protect and strengthen its long-term commitments to equality of opportunity and the work ethic: It should provide, through a federally financed job-creation program, second-chance opportunities for disadvantaged youth who reach adult status unprepared for the world of work.

In the concluding chapter, drawing on earlier analyses, I call attention to the constructive uses to which skepticism can be put both in assessing the relevance and potency of economic theories and in designing and choosing among different policy interventions.

This book is out of the mainstream because the coincidence of my years of graduate studies with the Great Depression made me skeptical about the potential of economics to become a science and, even more so, to serve as a guide to simplistic public policy. I could not accept the psychological assumptions with which mainline economists worked, namely, that all persons were driven in the marketplace to maximize their economic gains; that the dominant apparatus of demand, supply, and price could explain the myriad transactions that occur every minute of every hour of every day; and that efficiency and equity would be enhanced if governments restricted themselves to enlarging the domain of the competitive market.

I had been taught a lesson in my graduate student days by my teacher and mentor, John Maurice Clark, that stood me in good stead. I had written a long paper on some of these methodological issues. When Clark returned my paper with a few kind words and a few critical marginal notes, he suggested that I put it in a desk drawer and leave it there for a year. After that, if upon rereading I still thought it had merit, I should clean it up and submit it for publication. I followed Clark's advice and the paper remained in the drawer.

Then why this book? There is no simple answer, but I will do my best to call attention to some of the reasons that led me to tackle it. First was my longtime distancing of myself from the work of mainstream economists. The journals that I continued to scan had become increasingly mathematical and esoteric. I wanted to acquaint myself anew with the best of the work in economics, hence my selection of the thirteen Nobel laureates.

Second, whereas the past ten to fifteen years have not witnessed a replay of the devastation of the early 1930s, it has seen mainline economics toppled from its leadership position. I was led to look more closely at what had happened. How could one account for the hubris of economists' thinking that they could fine-tune the economy? Why, once the phenomenon of "stagflation" had come to dominate the developed economies, had economists been stymied in their understanding of the phenomenon and, more importantly, in suggesting how it might be overcome?

There was a third impetus. I know that although the academic leadership had captured all the levers of power—faculty appointments, editorships of key journals, membership on research grant committees, and other positions that gave them tight control over the discipline—a large, possibly even a growing number of younger economists (and some older ones as well) were questioning what had happened and were increasingly restive about the future. While I had no illusions of being able to alter in any significant fashion the balance of forces between the mainliners and the dissenters, I thought I owed it to the latter to make what contribution I could by drawing on my long involvement in the discipline, if only from the periphery.

I hold the conviction that individuals who have had the good fortune to have had long and interesting lives should reflect on their experience and seek to extract some lessons from the vantage of their lengthened perspective. Even if one accepts, as I do, that history is open-ended and that the future will always be different from the past, one should still probe beneath the surface of the past in the expectation of learning something important about the behavior of men and women in their earlier struggles for existence. Clearly, it would be foolish to apply such lessons uncritically to a new and different present and future, but in an evolving world in which humans must make their own way, even imperfect markers from the past may prove useful. In fact, in the absence of other guideposts, these markers from the past are all we have.

As I look back on the past five to six decades, this is what I observe about the relations of economics to the changing economy: The dominant neoclassical theory of the 1920s had little to offer by way of support or criticism of the prevailing view that the United States had entered a New Era characterized by perpetual prosperity. The same neoclassical theory proved itself to be largely irrelevant with regard to the Great Depression: It could not explain what was happening or what should be done to arrest and reverse the losses.

Although some people believe that President Franklin D. Roosevelt's New Deal programs, which succeeded in halting the decline, were informed by the new Keynesianism, there is at best only limited support for tying the two closely together. The support is curtailed further if one remembers that as late as 1940 the unemployment rate had not dropped below 10 percent.

The long period of the post–World War II expansion of the U.S. economy and later of the economies of all developed and many developing nations is conventionally tied to the triumph of Keynesian theory. There can be no argument that the theory captured and came to dominate contemporary economics. What can be challenged is the extent to which this long-sustained growth cycle was initiated and maintained by governments pursuing Keynesian policies. My reading of events suggests that the tie was much looser than most believe.

The most recent period of stagflation and the post-1982 recovery of the U.S. economy present another conundrum. I noted earlier that economics had little to offer by way of explanation of the causes of stagflation and even less advice for the cure. Moreover, the recent U.S. expansionary cycle has called forth a number of conflicting theories, from "supply-side economics" and "defense-Keynesianism" to the emergence of an international capital market in which investors pursue both short-term interest differentials and long-term security objectives. A skeptical economist would conclude that more time will have to pass before a selection can be made among these alternatives. But even at this early date, long before we have the necessary perspective to understand the most recent period of Reaganomics, it is a safe bet that we will find few linkages between the economics of the academy and the arena of public policy. If this proves to be the case, then the record will be firmly established. For six decades, mainline economics has gone its own way with only an occasional and minor impact on economic policy. In the face of such a record, there is room for a view that is skeptical about the scientific pretensions of economics and that looks anew at what happened and why.

# 2

## The Education
## of an Economist

In 1922, my parents took my sister and me to Europe so they could visit their relatives and friends. We spent most of the time in Germany, the remainder in Holland and England. When we arrived in the middle of May in Bremen, the German mark was trading at the rate of about 275 to 1 U.S. dollar; when we left Germany at the end of August the rate was almost 1,000 marks to the dollar. This was my first exposure to rampant inflation.

In the 1930s, a family friend who owned a chain of inexpensive men's retail stores in New York City reported that his store in Yorkville had been denuded of inventory in the early days of the New Deal. At that time, Yorkville had a large German population. Because these people had lived through the uncontrollable inflation of 1922–1923 in Germany when the mark lost almost all of its value, the neighborhood clientele was determined not to be caught again.

In June 1985, a banker who had recently returned from a visit to Argentina introduced me to a new concept: staying ahead of "physical" inflation. He described a race between the customers taking goods off the shelves and the clerks scurrying around to stamp higher prices on them.

There had been other lasting impressions from my 1922 visit to Europe, some of which became clear only in retrospect. I had been in a section of Berlin where twenty-four hours later Walter Rathenau, the Jewish foreign minister of the Weimar Republic, was murdered by the precursors of the Nazis. On the train trip from Berlin to Wildbad (in the Black Forest), we shared a compartment with a colonel in the Reichswehr who told us that he had spent the past year training German recruits on Russian soil!

We visited my aunt in Amsterdam. One morning she seemed to go suddenly berserk; with great speed she removed from sight many gold, silver, and porcelain items that had been on display in her living and dining rooms. A few moments later a man rang the bell, was admitted, walked around the recently stripped rooms, made some notations on a piece of paper, and left. I later learned he was the tax assessor responsible for estimating the property tax that my relatives had to pay.

One more impression of that trip abroad. We spent time in Cardiff, Wales, where my aunt's family lived. South Wales was not doing well in 1922, and my uncle's music shop was not prospering. It struck me that there was not much difference between the situation of the Germans who had lost the war and that of the British who had won.

In my senior year at DeWitt Clinton High School, I had to take a one-semester course in economics. Although the textbook was dull, the subject intrigued me and I considered changing my interest from history to economics. I sensed that such a shift would give me a broader choice of careers. I knew one thing: I did not want to follow in my scholarly father's footsteps. I recognized that his constricted life-style, working from morning until evening in his library, except for going out to lecture twice a week, would be too confining for my tastes.

My freshman year at Columbia College in 1927–1928 was exciting, especially the course in contemporary civilization, the backbone of the first year's curriculum. The following years were even more exciting. During my second year, my father decided to spend his sabbatical (the only one he ever took) at the Hebrew University in Jerusalem. My sister lived with our relatives in Wales, and I enrolled at Heidelberg University. When relatives and friends inquired what I was studying and I replied "Economics," almost without exception they would make slighting comments. Economics was not a serious subject for a serious student, except possibly as an adjunct to the law, but not as a field in its own right. As a matter of fact, I spent more time studying philosophy, history, and law than economics. I studied with Heinrich Rickert, the leading neo-Kantian scholar of his day; I listened on occasion to Karl Jaspers; Otto Debelius gave a wonderful course on Hellenism and Christianity; Eugene Taubler lectured on Rome and the history of ideas; Gustav Radbruch and George Jellenick were my professors of law; and my principal economics teacher was Emil Lederer, who was assisted by Jacob Marshak, both of whom achieved worldwide fame. When time permitted, I listened to Karl Mannheim.

Max Weber had moved to Munich in 1920 and died shortly thereafter, but his presence still dominated the University of Heidelberg. His theories were widely accepted there, not only in sociology and throughout all of the social sciences, but also in law and humanities.

The prevailing mood in Germany was somber. Many of the students who had completed their work for the doctorate could not find jobs.

The daily press reported constant and ever-worsening brawls between the Communists and the Nazis. In retrospect, one could see that the Weimar Republic had lost its way.

I spent the spring vacation of 1929 traveling through Switzerland and Italy, going all the way south to Sicily. And when the second semester was over, I went to Grenoble for the summer session.

These seventeen months in Europe left an indelible impression on me. I would never be able to deal with any economic issue except within a larger societal context. History, politics, culture, and class clearly were factors that had to be included both in analyzing economic problems and in seeking solutions.

When I reentered Columbia College in the fall of 1929, I enrolled in some graduate courses in economics open to selected undergraduates, as well as in courses in philosophy, history, sociology, anthropology, and even biology and physics. I studied with Frederick J. Woodbridge, William L. Westermann, Robert MacIver, Franz Boas, and Ruth Benedict. In economics, I took E.R.A. Seligman's course on public finance the last year that he taught it and H. Parker Willis's course on money and banking. Willis had been Senator Carter Glass's principal consultant in the drafting of the Federal Reserve Act. Wesley Mitchell, the founder and leader of empirical economics, once remarked that Willis's views on inflation had not changed since the two men were fellow students in the 1890s in Chicago! The history of economics, about which contemporary U.S. economists know so little, has not dealt kindly with either Seligman or Willis. But they left their mark on me if only because their academic work was balanced by their deep involvement in public policy.

The lack of knowledge about their own discipline that characterizes most contemporary economists and their conviction that their ignorance needs no defense never cease to surprise and upset me. Thorstein Veblen, John B. Clark, Frank H. Knight, and my teachers Wesley Mitchell and John Maurice Clark are neither read nor quoted, and many doctoral candidates probably could not even identify them. I doubt that even a small minority of present graduate students have read Adam Smith's *The Wealth of Nations* or Karl Marx's *Capital*. When Willard L. Thorp, the author of *Business Annals* (1926), was asked on his oral examination at Columbia about David Ricardo and replied that he hadn't read Ricardo, Mitchell adjourned the examination.

Let me quickly add, however, that instruction in economics at Columbia in the early 1930s was uneven. The department was in a period of transition. It had recently lost three of its senior professors: first Henry Moore, an early mathematical economist, then Seligman, and last, Henry Seager, a labor expert, who had died while on a trip to the USSR. They were replaced in 1931 by Harold Hotelling, Carter Goodrich, and Leo Wolman. Several younger faculty members were added at the same time.

The range and quality of teaching were inadequate. Mitchell gave two courses: "Current Types of Economic Theory" (which had earlier been transcribed by an entrepreneurial student in two volumes with a sales price of $5 per volume) and "Business Cycles."

John Maurice Clark, who had been bid away from the University of Chicago in 1926, also taught two courses, both on selected aspects of current theory. His lecturing style left much to be desired; therefore, it was our wont to divide the listening chore among several of us.

The other key members of the department were V. G. Simkhovitch, an economics historian who had written an interesting book on Marxism vs. Socialism and who repeatedly expressed his disdain for economics and for economists. He excepted only his former classmate from Halle University and present colleague, Wesley C. Mitchell; James Waterhouse Angell, a Harvard-trained monetary economist; and Robert C. Haig, who had succeeded to the McVickar Chair when Seligman retired. Both Frederick C. Mills and James C. Bonbright were on School of Business appointment lines, but they were also members of the Graduate Department of Economics.

Most doctoral students in economics at Columbia University at that time were exposed to little or no systematic training in neoclassical theory, and the majority took only a first course in descriptive statistics. The formal requirements stipulated mastery in seven subjects: four, including economic theory, on the oral examination, and three by certification. I certified in statistics, money and banking, and business cycles (with Mills because Mitchell was visiting at Oxford) and was examined by Clark in theory, Simkhovitch in economic history, Wolman in labor, and MacIver in sociology.

The degree requirements also stipulated that candidates complete a dissertation; the degree was conferred only after a publisher's contract had been signed. My dissertation, *The House of Adam Smith* (1934), was the first book-length study in English of Smith. It reinterpreted Smith as a left-of-center economist who believed that the broader dominance of the market would result in a higher rate of economic growth and a more equitable distribution of income, to the disadvantage of the landlords and the large merchants and manufacturers. The dissertation also traced the "subversion" of the theory at the hands of the classical economists and modern conservative leaders, specifically President Herbert Hoover and Pope Pius XI.

In the early 1930s Richard Kahn, Keynes's protégé from Cambridge, England, was invited to my parents' home for Saturday lunch. He had a letter of introduction from one of my father's friends. I have two recollections of his visit: In observance of the religious prohibition against riding on the Sabbath, Kahn walked from his hotel on 42nd Street near the East River to my parents' home adjacent to Columbia University. Second, he asked me about new trends in the Economics Department at Columbia. I waxed enthusiastic about V. G. Simkhovitch's work on "Approaches to History," which despite my clear-cut presentation, left Kahn totally at sea. The discoverer of "the multiplier" could not believe that a budding economist would be concerned, as I was, with improved formulations of the relations of values to reality. Of course, not all or even most graduate economics students at Columbia shared my enthusiasm.

When I was awarded a Cutting Traveling Fellowship, I requested and received permission not to spend the year in Europe. I proposed instead to study the seasonal stabilization of employment with which certain U.S. corporations had experimented in the 1920s. With my doctorate in hand, I wanted to gain some first-hand knowledge of the structure and operations of the economy. During our many Sunday hikes in Westchester, a close family friend, Harry Friedman, later president of General American Investors, had provided perspectives on the economy that I could not fit into my academic framework. Through my teacher Leo Wolman, who had become chairman of the Labor Advisory Committee of the National Recovery Administration, and others, I obtained letters of introduction to the chief executive officer or other senior officials of many of the premier U.S. corporations including Kodak, General Electric, U.S. Steel, Westinghouse, Goodyear, General Motors, Sears, International Harvester, Procter & Gamble, Standard Oil of New Jersey (Humble), Metro-Goldwyn Mayer, Del Monte, Long-Bell, and Cudahy.

I spent ten months in the field, traveling through forty states. It soon became clear to me that my research subject, seasonal stabilization, was overshadowed by the events of the Great Depression; I shifted my focus to explore why the business community and the nation as a whole had developed such an optimistic view of the economy during the 1920s. The New Era got its name from the belief that the economy would no longer be subject to recessions and depressions. Furthermore, I looked for reasons why the depression, which had arrived late in 1929, brought the economy close to chaos and collapse in late 1932 and early 1933.

I was appalled during these years to see more and more New Yorkers foraging for food in garbage cans, to read about conservative farmers in the Midwest threatening to hang sheriffs who sought to foreclose on their neighbors' farms, and to hear my teacher H. Parker Willis forecast that if New York City banks closed, farmers would no longer send their produce into the city. This conjured up the possibility that the population might be put on food rations. My confusion was heightened by the fact that when various students asked Wesley Mitchell, the acknowledged authority on business cycles, for his recommended solutions to the crisis, he sidestepped the question by stating that his research was still under way. But I sensed that he did not favor heroic measures. He implied by his temporizing that the business cycle would sooner or later reverse itself; that was the core of his analytic schema. But by mid-1932 J. M. Clark held a different opinion. He considered it possible, even likely, that the downward trends would continue to feed on themselves until the whole structure collapsed. He therefore favored an interventionist policy.

It took me the greater part of four years to sort out and bring some order to my views of what had happened to the U.S. economy during the New Era, the Great Depression, and the New Deal. In 1938, I finally handed over my manuscript for *The Illusion of Economic Stability* (1939) to Ordway Tead, my editor at Harper's. The story that I had woven together placed primary attention on the role of expectations; I traced how an elastic banking system reinforced expectations in both the expansionary and contracting phases of the cycle and emphasized the key role that a major technological development, such as the automobile, played in stimulating the investment boom of the 1920s and the negative impact that followed the inevitable slowing in the rate of growth.

It is difficult for most of today's economists, whose education postdates the Keynesian revolution of 1936, to imagine the world before the new macroeconomics came and conquered. I recall a discussion in Washington in the fall of 1933 with a senior staffer from the U.S. Treasury who brought along Benjamin V. Cohen. Cohen, a high Roosevelt aide, was enthusiastic about the New Deal's innovative programs and turned aside my concerns about the government's spending policies with the comment that John Maynard Keynes had recently explained once again to the president's men why such spending was no cause for alarm.

But I remained skeptical and when a young physician finally began to put some savings aside and asked me what he should buy, I suggested that because he enjoyed Jensen's silver, he buy some nice pieces. He followed my advice; I have often reflected that he probably got more pleasure from the silver than he would have from some appreciated stock certificates had he been lucky enough to invest in the right company.

I was clearly upset about the danger of inflation. I asked my friend Harry Friedman, the investment banker, to invest my Cutting Fellowship funds in the stock market because I was worried that the dollar might undergo rapid depreciation during the year when I was traveling. I recall his scribbled reply: "You are sufficiently recently out of school not to realize that logic governs neither the actions of men nor the gyrations of the stock market. However, I am buying some Endicott Johnson shares for you."

The better students who came to the Graduate Department of Economics at Columbia in the early and mid-1930s, especially those from the stronger undergraduate and graduate departments such as those at Harvard, Yale, Princeton, Pennsylvania, and Chicago found the department at Columbia strange. There was no party line; the students had no firm theoretical base; the department made no effort to provide an integrated curriculum. Mitchell's primary energies were invested in the National Bureau of Economic Research, and Clark was so shy that students hesitated to start a conversation with him because he might lapse into total silence for half an hour.

In 1932–1933, a group of us brought about the first change in the curriculum: We persuaded Mitchell, Clark, and Angell to offer a seminar on economic theory. In the mid-1930s, when I had begun to teach as an assistant in the School of Business, I was instrumental in establishing several further reforms, largely through persuading its dean, Roswell C. McCrea, who also served as chairman of the Economics Department, to do the following: to reduce the number of subjects on which doctoral candidates were examined from seven to six, to invite Milton Friedman to give a course on "Neoclassical Economics," to have Wesley Mitchell substitute for his lectures on "Current Types of Economic Theory" a new seminar on "Economic Theory and Economic Change," in which I would serve as his assistant. Furthermore, McCrea obtained the consent of the Committee on Instruction in the School of Business for me to offer a new course on "Economics and Group Behavior," which was cross-listed in the Department of Economics' offerings. This was probably the first course in what later became known as "human resources."

Against Mitchell's advice, I also offered a course based on the great books in economics—from Adam Smith's *Wealth of Nations* to John Maynard Keynes' *General Theory*. Mitchell considered that teaching the history of thought was wrong for a young researcher, but I knew that the doctoral students in both the department and the Business School needed help in preparing for the examination in theory, because I served as the principal examiner. Mitchell or Clark would come only on special request.

Taking a lead from students of Frank Knight who had edited his essays, *The Ethics of Competition* (1935), Moses Abramovitz and I asked Clark's permission to prepare a comparable volume of his essays, *Preface to Social Economics* (1935). Abramovitz had obtained a teaching position at Harvard; therefore, the negotiations with Clark fell to me. After some initial strained sessions characterized by Clark's long silences, the ice finally broke and thereafter our discussions about the selection of his essays became a pleasant task.

When I looked up John Maurice Clark in *Who's Who*, I found an entry for John Bates Clark, J. M.'s father. I was sure this was an error and that he was dead, because he had retired from the department around the time of the first world war. But inquiry disclosed that he was alive and well and would soon celebrate his eighty-fifth birthday, an occasion that our graduate student group decided to celebrate. It was a pleasant evening and many of J. B.'s former students returned to the campus to do him honor. My most vivid recollection of the evening was of J. B.'s wife turning to her dinner partner, a graduate student, and inquiring what had happened to that bright young Scandinavian who had been her husband's pupil at Carleton College. It turned out that she was referring to Thorstein Veblen, who when he died in 1929, was over seventy. J. M. Clark had written his obituary for the *American Economic Review*.

My first meeting with Milton Friedman is still sharply etched in my memory. After my field research in 1933–1934, I returned to the campus in the fall of 1934 with a year's grant from the Columbia University Council for Research in the Social Sciences to write up my findings. This effort eventually became *The Illusion of Economic Stability* (1939). I sought out the interesting new arrivals, and my friends arranged that I have lunch with Milton. I told some stories about union-management troubles in Detroit that I had heard during my visit with General Motors; Milton interjected some far-out comments that led me to believe that he had a wry sense of humor. But the third time around I realized that he was not trying to be funny; he was dead earnest. I knew at that moment that any serious discussion between Milton and me was at an end unless I wanted to enter into a debate, a style of conversation I have always avoided.

Many years later, when Milton was visiting professor at Columbia, his wife, Rose, and he came to a small dinner party at our home. The other guests were the Potofkys and the Piores. Jack Potofsky was the head of the Amalgamated Clothing Workers of America; Nora Piore had been a union organizer during the early New Deal days. Her husband, Emanuel, was vice president of research for IBM and a key player in national science policy.

I still recall snippets of the conversation that evening. Milton insisted that Barry Goldwater, despite his overwhelming defeat, had been the preferred candidate; that Milton's widowed mother had been able to help support her family because of the absence of unions and a minimum wage; and that most of the New Deal legislation had been a bad mistake. It is worth recalling that during the 1964 campaign, Senator Goldwater had to create some distance from Friedman, who was his adviser, because Friedman recommended that Social Security be scrapped.

During the New Deal days, I commented to my college teacher and life-long friend T. C. Blaisdell, who at the time was working for the National Resources Planning Board, that Paul Samuelson, who was going to spend the summer on the staff of the board, was exceptionally gifted but that he would probably never make a contribution comparable to that of J. M. Clark (under whom Blaisdell had written his dissertation). I had run into Samuelson during periodic visits to Harvard, and I had reviewed for the *Saturday Review of Literature* (March 1939), *An Economic Program for American Democracy*, which the best and the brightest of the Keynesians in Cambridge, Mass. had written and published in 1937. These Keynesians had accepted Professor Alvin Hansen's stagnation theory, which stipulated that the United States had run out of opportunities. I was not persuaded; I considered the long depression a reaction to the earlier speculation at home and abroad and to the mismanagement of policy that followed the collapse of the stock market and the economy. Although my good friend Moses Abramovitz had been a participant in the discussions leading to the drafting of the *Economic Program*, at the end he refused to sign.

Another vignette of the times: Charles Kindleberger and Henry Villard were members of the seminar in which I assisted Mitchell. I recall the day when these returnees from Cambridge, England, tried to push Mitchell into a corner about the nature of economics and about who could legitimately be called an economist. In their light, only macro-theorists could claim the title of economist. Mitchell, a long-suffering teacher, finally got annoyed with the two of them and stated in an unaccustomed loud voice that he believed that any serious researcher who studied any economic issue of his own choosing was an economist. He emphasized the words "serious researcher."

Mitchell also believed that his former pupil and closest collaborator, Arthur F. Burns, might be too deliberate. He knew that Arthur and I were friends and he suggested on occasion that I seek to persuade Arthur to work a little more quickly. When Mitchell made this request, he knew that I was unlikely to follow through and that even if I did, Arthur would continue to move at his own deliberate pace.

When Mitchell asked me about possible topics for our seminar on Economic Theory and Economic Change, I suggested "Economics and Psychology," knowing of his earlier interest in the subject (*The Backward Art of Spending Money*, 1937) and because of my own interest in finding a way to develop a more realistic behavioral model for economics. The simplistic assumptions of rationality and optimizing behavior that lay beneath mainline economic theory did not seem to me to be congruent with the malaise of the U.S. and other developed economies.

My interest in the psychological foundations of economics was of long standing. While I was at Heidelberg, I read the work of Sigmund Freud with care. I had long conversations with my favorite cousin, Sol W. Ginsburg, a psychiatrist and psychoanalyst who had a deep concern for the reality factors in the lives of his patients. Sol had encouraged me to attend Karen Horney's lectures at the New School for Social Research, which later were published as *The Neurotic Personality of Our Time* (1937), an exciting course made more exciting by the fact that Erich Fromm and Ruth Benedict were fellow students.

Mitchell liked the suggestion and for a year we both worked with a select group of students, but we made limited progress. At the end of the year, Mitchell, who had been trying to shift my interest from history and theory to empirical research, urged me to develop my own psychological assumptions. He promised to help me get funding for empirical research; because of his efforts, the Columbia Council on Research in Social Sciences gave me my first grant in 1939 to undertake studies of the Welsh coal miners, the long-term unemployed in New York City, and to begin explorations into labor leadership—all of which resulted in books some years later.

In the mid-1930s, a group of younger economists from Columbia, Yale, and Harvard met for a weekend of talking, walking, and drinking at the Connecticut home of John DeWitt Norton. The only senior who joined us was Joseph Schumpeter, who was the luminary on the Harvard campus where, among other activities, he was advocating the greater use of mathematics in economics.

I recall a walk with Schumpeter in which I sought his advice. I told him that a summer neighbor of our family in Maine was Marston Morse, then head of the Harvard mathematics department and later a member of the Institute of Advanced Studies at Princeton. I was reasonably sure that if I needed tutoring in mathematics Morse would be willing to help me. Under the circumstances, what did Schumpeter advise me to do? He surprised me by suggesting that I wait and see whether the greater use of mathematics in economics would in fact pay off. If it did, he said, I could then brush up on my math. I am still waiting. On a related issue, Schumpeter proved to be less relaxed. I had sent him a reprint of my review of Thorstein Veblen's essays, *What Veblen Taught* (Mitchell, ed., 1936), which he speedily acknowledged with a postcard stating, "A great sociologist, but *not* a great economist."

Morse, who ran into some of the economists at Dunster House at Harvard, asked me what he should read to become acquainted with the work of the "mathematical economists." I called his attention to some of the bright young men who were publishing and then suggested that he look at the mathematical appendix of Alfred Marshall's *Principles of Economics* (1890). Some weeks later he told me that the contemporary contributors did not impress him, but that it was clear that Marshall had real mathematical talent.

During World War II, Morse served as a senior consultant to the army's chief of ordinance. My office in the Pentagon was near his, and we ran into each other from time to time. Still unimpressed with the new breed of mathematical economists, he insisted that the excitement about "operations research" was also misplaced. He emphasized that when complex issues concerning ballistics had to be solved, the generals had to seek help from the mathematicians.

Harold Hotelling, who came from Stanford to Columbia in 1931, according to his own appraisal, as well as that of many of his students and colleagues, was a genius. But he often lacked judgment. For example, I called on Alexander Sachs in the fall of 1933 when he was serving as the head of the Planning Division of the National Recovery Administration. When he heard that I came from Columbia, he pulled out a piece of paper on which there was an esoteric equation. He said that Hotelling, who had come to his office earlier that morning, told him that if government would put his equation into practice the economy would soon be back to full employment!

At one of my monthly lunches with J. M. Clark I asked what he thought of the ever-larger number of articles in the economic journals that made heavy use of mathematics. He said he was often intrigued by them until he got to the end when he discovered that time and again, the solution was nonsensical. As one of the "five wise men" who wrote a United Nations report on economic growth, Clark warned in 1949 of the inflationary bias in the Keynesian approach, a warning that the world ignored, for which it later paid a big price.

As I look back on my Columbia education, this is how I sum it up. I had to learn the rudiments of neoclassical theory on my own, and I never became skilled in using it. Abramovitz has told me on more than one occasion that my lack of "proper" grounding meant that I did not have to invest so much effort in unlearning this limited theory. My view of a dynamic economy was fashioned before the appearance of Keynes's *General Theory*, a system of analysis that never became second nature to me, as it did to most of my slightly younger colleagues. And heeding Schumpeter's advice, I never went back to brush up and improve my mathematical skills. I learned two important lessons from my mentors. Wesley C. Mitchell turned me into an empirical researcher and taught me by example the importance of a life-long commitment to a chosen area. And John M. Clark taught me the importance of seeking to use and adapt extant theories so that they could illuminate new problems more effectively and provide better guides to public policy. These lessons have stood me in good stead while I have watched my colleagues develop sophisticated models that have become an end in themselves. I was happy to belong to an older generation that did not shy away from being called institutionalists and that carried the name with honor.

Looking back with the advantage of five decades of hindsight, the evolution of my approach to economics appears to have moved through the following stages. As the son of my father, I took it for granted that societal development had to be appraised from a historical vantage, an orientation that was reinforced by my Heidelberg experience. Further, my knowledge of the tortured history of the Jewish minority among both Christians and Arabs over two millenia had impressed upon me the power of the irrational in the lives and experiences of peoples and nations. I balked at accepting the basic premise of rationality, the cornerstone of neoclassical economics. My early infatuation with Freudian psychology reinforced my bias against rationality as an explanatory principle.

The devastating depression of 1930–1933, which coincided with my years of graduate study, undermined the authority of the inherited tradition, which, it must be recalled, was not held in high esteem by my mentors. But the sad plight of the U.S. and world economies called out for attention and remedial action, a challenge to which I wanted to respond.

It was Mitchell who showed me how. He encouraged and helped me to turn away from theory and to use, as best I could, empirical research to explore the determinants of economic behavior among different groups of the population—from Welsh coal miners to U.S. labor leaders.

Dissatisfied with the theories and trends of mainline economics, skeptical of the economists' assumptions about human behavior, convinced that ours was clearly not the best of all possible worlds, I had to strike out on my own to seek answers to questions that I considered to be important for understanding and policy. The fact that I had strong support from Mitchell and my other mentors provided the reassurance I needed to make the attempt.

# 3

# Sources of Skepticism

My underlying skepticism about the potential and relevance of economic theory to account for the changing contours of the U.S. economy was reinforced by the gap between the established doctrines of neoclassical economics and the deepening depression of 1930–1933. Theory held that the movements of prices would bring demand and supply into equilibrium, with the result that there could not long be significant underutilization of plant and people. But as one year followed the next during the 1930s, it became clear that the market and the price system were not working as theory had postulated and that empty factories and unemployed workers were increasingly characteristic of the U.S. economy as well as of the principal European economies.

## History Versus Theory

My earlier experiences helped me to avoid easy acceptance of the doctrine of the self-equilibrating market. As an eleven year old, I had been exposed to the early stages of the German inflation. My stay in Heidelberg in 1928–1929 and my later travels through Western Europe had proven to me that there were no easy answers to account for the differences in the economic well-being between these countries, such as Holland and Italy, or even between different sections of the same country, such as the standard of living in Palermo and Naples compared to Milan and Venice.

My studies in Heidelberg also proved that it was impossible to understand the development of modern Germany from the time of Napoleon to the Young Plan (a modification in German reparation payments) of the late 1920s solely, or even primarily, in terms of unfettered capitalism in which the market called the tune. Many powerful non-economic forces had played a role in the transformation of the large number of independent Germanic kingdoms and principalities into the unified country that in 1871 became modern Germany. Philosophy, ideology, religion, the military, the universities, the many varieties of workers' movements, from nonsocialist to international socialist, all had contributed to the transformation that brought Germany by 1914 into a leadership position in European and world affairs.

It had also been clear to me in 1928–1929 that the difficulties that the German economy was then encountering in clearing up the residue from the inflation that had wrecked the middle class in 1923, in struggling to meet the onerous reparations payments, which Keynes had earlier warned could not be made without lasting damage to both the defeated and the victors, in expanding jobs for the new entrants into the labor force—paled in the face of political challenges that threatened its social fabric. Extreme groups on the right and the left were battling in the streets. A decade after Germany's defeat in World War I, its leaders were still trying to identify those responsible. There was no basis for lasting cooperation between the bureaucratized Social Democrats and the Catholic Center party. A rebirth of nationalism and militarism was in the offing.

Two personal anecdotes provide a perspective into the soul of Weimar Germany on the eve of Hitler's successful drive for power. My landlady, the widow of a German officer, forbade her maid to shop at the nearby grocer because he was a Catholic; she insisted that the maid walk three additional blocks to patronize the Protestant greengrocer. And when Marshal Erich Ludendorff came to Heidelberg to lecture on behalf of an ultrarightist organization, the business elite in the area was out in force to do him honor for his military leadership during the war, however skeptical they may have been about his current political involvement.

Peter Drucker's book entitled *The End of Economic Man* (1939) provides important insights into the success of the Nazis. His hypothesis was that the business elite decided to support Hitler to escape from a worsening economic crisis. This issue has recently resurfaced in the acrimonious debates over the contemporary research efforts of a young Princeton scholar, David Abraham. His work has been impugned by a senior Yale historian, whose scathing critiques have embroiled an ever-widening circle of scholars and academic departments.

Whether or not the original Drucker view about the valuable support that Hitler received from the business establishment, recently endorsed by Abraham, can be substantiated, I have always believed that the widespread unemployment of the young German intellectuals was a potent contributor to Hitler's eventual victory. As the depression of the early 1930s eliminated the prospect for more and more young people to find jobs and start their careers, intellectuals as well as others joined the party. Many who did not join became tolerant of the revolutionary doctrines that Hitler put before the German electorate. Hitler's victory demonstrated that a fragile government could not survive a high level of unemployment. The acceptance of Keynes' doctrines in the latter 1930s in the United States and in other countries was probably hastened by statesmen and the public that sought an alternative to rearmament as the solution for high-level unemployment.

There is broad agreement among the schools of developmental psychology that basic patterns of thinking and behavior are determined relatively early in life and if reinforced, are likely to become firmly established. I grew up in a household where my father, a master scholar in postbiblical literature and the Talmud, law and legend alike, was an intellectual skeptic to his last breath, often revising and discarding his earlier theories even after they had won broad acceptance. My mother, a committed activist, had little respect for the originators of ideas and the writers of books, my father alone excepted. I recall her opening gambit at a dinner party. She asked the dean of the School of Business and chairman of Columbia's Department of Economics what he did. He replied that he was an economist. "Oh," she said, "another faker like my son!"

My earliest research efforts in the arena of economic history and the history of economic doctrines reinforced my skeptical orientation. My first published work, *Studies in the Economics of the Bible* (1932), addressed a subject that the great Max Weber had called "indigestible," the biblical laws of the Sabbatical and Jubilee years during which slaves were manumitted, loans forgiven, the land lay fallow, debts were cancelled, and the ownership of the land returned to the seller.

Although my father shared Weber's belief that the subject should be left alone, he helped me as I sought to make sense about laws that appeared to be at variance with the survival needs of an agricultural population. I finally concluded that the manumission of Hebrew slaves probably took place and did not jeopardize the economy of ancient Israel. At most, only a few ultraorthodox groups during the Second Commonwealth followed the biblical injunction of letting their lands lie fallow every seventh year. With regard to the cancellation of debts and the return of the land to the seller as stipulated by the laws of the Jubilee Year, the most reasonable explanation appeared to be that the code was the utopian ideal of a prophet and never became the law of the people. I have always been uneasy about whether I distinguished clearly and correctly among religious precept, legal code, and economic behavior.

## The Limits of Theory

I learned more from my background readings and reflections about the life and work of Adam Smith and the development of economics as a discipline (*The House of Adam Smith*, 1934). My more important findings and conclusions included the following: Smith's advocacy of a market economy was not a disembodied intellectual effort, but represented his carefully crafted alternative model to the entrenched mercantilism of his day, which he viewed as both inefficient and inequitable. My careful reading of *The Wealth of Nations* revealed that Smith was highly critical of the master merchants and manufacturers and that he surely was not an ideologue leading a campaign for enlarging their scope of action, which as he repeatedly pointed out, resulted in socially undesirable outcomes for the mass of farmers and laborers.

My studies revealed that ideology and theory were potent elements in the increasingly severe political struggles in Great Britain that accompanied the first stage of industrialization, which occurred after Smith's death in 1791. Largely ignored in his lifetime, Smith's opus became the fountainhead for those who advocated the speedy establishment of the competitive market as the new organizing principle for the British economy.

The retelling of the Smith story helped me to see more clearly the following dynamic interactions: The resort to theory construction as a way in which engaged economists sought to influence public policy; the inevitability that the new model would be bounded by past and present realities; the rapid rate of change characteristic of modern industrial societies; and the opportunities, dangers, and outright misapplications of older theories to the new realities. This means, then, that the relations among the economists' preferences, the structure of their models, the economies that their works describe, and the ideological and political values that come to be attached to accepted doctrines need to be carefully sorted out and kept in purview. My reconstruction of Adam Smith and the theories that derived from his work resulted in my being inoculated for life against any simple view that economic theory is a disembodied intellectual effort without roots in economic reality or political conflicts.

My skepticism about economic theorizing was heightened by a brief encounter with a case illustration of applied Marxist analysis. One of my Columbia professors explained to his class that the reason Britain did not intervene on behalf of the South during the Civil War when Britain's imports of cotton dried up was her increasing dependence on wheat from northern states to feed its population, a theory propounded by Louis Bernard Schmidt (1923). Here was a pat case in support of Marx's economic interpretation of history, so pat in fact that it aroused my suspicions, particularly because of the speed with which it had been accepted by historians.

A careful review of the data that the professor had used to support his theory disclosed that they were not nearly as supportive of the importance of northern wheat to Great Britain as he had suggested. But that was only the first weak link in his interpretation. I asked whether the British ministers knew about the role that northern wheat was ostensibly playing to ensure adequate food imports and to keep the price of bread within reasonable limits. Unless the men who were responsible for British policy knew and appreciated this linkage between our northern exports and essential food supplies for the British public, the argument would fail, no matter what the data suggested. It turned out that there was not a scintilla of evidence that either Lord Palmerston or any other influential official knew about the linkage between northern wheat and British neutrality.

The most interesting aspect of this reevaluation, at the time and even now more than half a century later, was the haste with which the new thesis had been accepted by most U.S. historians. The infatuation among intellectuals on both sides of the Atlantic with Marxist theory and interpretations during the distressed 1930s created a background conducive to the speedy adoption of this and many other plausible, but not necessarily correct, theories.

## The Depression and the New Deal

The New Deal parries and thrusts in all directions in its efforts to stimulate the weakened U.S. economy also added to my underlying skepticism. Roosevelt had made a major shift in his budget position between his 1932 campaign and the early years of his first administration. During the campaign he promised to cut federal outlays below the level set by Herbert Hoover, but once in the White House he forgot this commitment and moved to much enlarged federal outlays.

In the early months of his presidency, Roosevelt was intrigued by the theories of two Cornell professors of agriculture, George F. Warren and Frank A. Pearson, who advocated tying the value of the dollar to the changing prices of hogs. But despite his interest in this esoteric theory, Roosevelt was also willing to listen to the advice of an eastern establishment banking specialist on leave from Harvard University, who was helping the secretary of treasury find a path out of the current morass. And then the president, having dispatched Raymond Moley, one of his trusted Columbia brain trusters to London to represent the United States at a critical international economic conference, rejected the joint declaration on monetary policy calling for exchange stabilization and an ultimate return to the gold standard. To complete the tale of the confusion in the banking-financial-trade arenas we must recall the influence of the Keynesians in convincing Roosevelt to increase federal spending to whatever level was necessary to fuel the economy.

The price and wage arrangements of the National Recovery Act were put together in a haphazard way and the effort was collapsing under its own weight even before the Supreme Court in the kosher-chicken case (*Schechter Poultry Corporation v. U.S.*, 1935) wrote finis to this brave new departure.

I did not follow closely the equally ambitious departures that the Roosevelt administration undertook to revive U.S. agriculture. Although I had recognized the havoc wrought by the depression on the economic well-being of most farm families and farm communities and their need for succor and support, I had many reservations about the federal government's attempt to force an increase in farm prices by encouraging farmers to cut back their plantings and harvests. I recognized the need for governmental action, but was skeptical of the policy goals of the Agricultural Adjustment Act.

The New Deal directed many efforts toward providing work and income to millions of unemployed in the United States. The unwillingness of the prior administration to relieve the growing destitution of millions of adults and children seemed to me to have been a policy of stupidity with a strong seasoning of immorality and political brinkmanship. The public could be pushed, I felt certain, only so far before it would take the law into its own hands, as some desperate farmers had done in 1932 by warning off sheriffs from foreclosure sales by bringing hanging ropes along to the threatened event. It seemed to me at the time, and subsequently, that the massive New Deal programs to put people to work were basically sound because useful output was produced and the programs did not interfere with the recovery of the private sector.

But it was also clear, particularly after the sudden and severe recession of 1937–1938, that Roosevelt and his advisers were political improvisers who used whatever economic theories were at hand and who had no more than a passing commitment to any of them. When the seven years between 1933 and 1940 are assessed as a whole, the best mark we can give the New Deal is in the B-range. The economic decline was arrested, the economy expanded, many structural reforms were put in place, but the New Deal had only mediocre success in reemploying the millions of former and new workers who needed and wanted jobs.

During the year that I spent in the field (1933–1934), I focused on how large corporations adjusted to a depression that they did not anticipate. What I learned added further to my skepticism about the ability of extant economic theories to capture the realities of a rapidly changing economy.

Here are a few of the "unexpected" results that I uncovered as I sought to reconcile what I had been taught about the economy and what I found in the field. If, as my teacher Wesley Mitchell had demonstrated, business cycles were characteristic of our modern industrial economy, how could one explain the 1920s sobriquet the "New Era," which spoke to the elimination of such periodic fluctuations? A reassessment of Mitchell's and his collaborators' studies suggested that they had placed disproportionate emphasis on monetary and price movements, with lesser attention to physical output and employment. A focus on real changes in output indicated that the U.S. economy had been substantially free of a serious depression since 1893, if one put to one side the readjustment after World War I. Hence, the exuding optimism of the 1920s was in substantial consonance with the nation's experience.

The reconstruction of the New Era demonstrates the validity of Thorstein Veblen's earlier insight (*The Theory of Business Enterprise*, 1904) that businessmen are highly responsive to group psychology; if a buoyant mood becomes established, they follow in its tracks; and as long as the credit system can accommodate them, the optimism can feed on itself and for a time, justify itself. In recent years the "theory of rational expectations" has made a great impression on the professoriat. According to the theory, economic agents will act rationally, on the basis of past information, to discount efforts by government to alter the cycle by manipulating monetary and fiscal policy, thereby largely nullifying such efforts. But I was impressed by the irrational factors that led businessmen, as well as economists and politicians, in the New Era to misread the present and the future. The term *misread* can be a misnomer, given that the market is governed in no small measure by expectations to which the wily businessman will seek to adjust, avoiding if possible, the wrong side of the turning point. I recall the chief executive officer of Goodyear telling me that in 1921 and again in 1929, his company opened new plants just as business turned downward.

On a visit in 1933 to the headquarters of General Electric, I had back-to-back discussions with two senior executives: The first executive was desperately looking for copper and the second was still using up excess inventories left over since 1929!

In a visit to U.S. Steel in Pittsburgh, I heard the vice president for industrial relations (he was retired shortly thereafter) boast that he had recently electrified the fences surrounding the major plants to keep "the damn union people out." In fact, my visit with the local organizing head took place on a mountain top; he got into my car to decrease the probability that we would be attacked.

On a visit to Tennessee Coal and Iron, the principal U.S. Steel subsidiary in Birmingham, Alabama, I learned that a corporate directive dated late 1929 to economize in the use of stationery was not acted on until late 1932!

Another interesting conundrum was illustrated by members of the staff at Procter & Gamble. They explained that their company and Lever Brothers had battled during the depression, but the outcome was a draw: One had used price cuts; the other had spent more on advertising. Each was unable to gain market share. This tale seemed to fit in with the new "monopolistic competition" theory of Edward Chamberlin of Harvard (*Economics of Monopolistic Competition*, 1933). But at Sears Roebuck, Donald Nelson, the vice president for merchandizing, later the War Production Board chief, related a cautionary tale. Sears had decided to experiment with rounding prices from $.49 to $.50, $.98 to $1.00, $1.49 to $1.50. It conducted a controlled experiment by making the changes in some of its catalogues and not in others. When the results were analyzed, headquarters discovered that the price changes on some items resulted in a large increase in demand, in others, no change, and in still others, a striking decline. Because the staff could not account for the declines and the company had come out even, it decided to stay with conventional pricing practices. As I suggested in a note to the *American Economic Review* (June 1936), assumptions about the rational behavior of consumers are easier to make than to prove.

During my visit to General Motors, I learned that the company had recently started a consumer-research unit to ferret out consumer preferences through market research techniques and to use the information to help guide the design engineers in making model changes. This seemed an eminently sensible approach but hardly congruent with competitive theory holding that producers and consumers deal with each other at arm's length via the impersonal price structure.

My visit to General Motors in November 1933 occurred at a time when the union organization of the automotive work force was getting under way. I was startled by what I heard from senior executives: All tactics short of murder were being employed to thwart the union's drive. Those who have read *We Never Called Him Henry* (Bennett, 1951) can reconstruct the ugliness of that period and will have a better appreciation of why even a half-century later, Detroit is not likely to cast aside easily what is left of the adversarial approach that has dominated labor relations in the industry for so many years.

At International Harvester I learned of a pricing experiment that the company had undertaken at the low point of the depression in late 1932. It offered some standard items below marginal costs, but sales did not increase. I doubt if the International Harvester executives knew Keynes's views that only a substantial and sustained increase in total spending would help to turn the economy around and enable large and small employers to increase their sales. In any case, they did sense the need for new macroeconomic policies.

No one had a clearer perception of the new dependency of even the largest corporations on governmental policy than General Robert E. Wood, the chief executive officer of Sears Roebuck. During the weeks I spent at Sears, I heard Wood state his broad approval of the efforts of Washington to help the recovery of the economy, particularly efforts to help farmers get back on their feet. Wood recognized that Sears commanded a more-or-less fixed percentage of whatever money farmers had to spend on consumer goods and therefore any efforts by Washington to increase their income could only be good for Sears. I suggested that the government's agricultural support policies might add to farmers' incomes at the expense of urban consumers. Wood dismissed this out of hand. He reiterated the idea that more money for farmers meant more money for Sears. Wood was simply more outspoken than most business leaders, many of whom had decided that Washington was their best hope for survival.

Early in my field investigations, I called on Justice Louis Brandeis. He asked me to return at the end of the year and report to him on what I found. In my report to him I suggested that his fear of the power of the large corporation, a fear that my teachers also had instilled in me, was exaggerated. I had found repeated evidence that the premier U.S. industrial corporations were inefficient and made a large number of poor decisions affecting investments, products, and markets. It seemed to me that left to their own devices, they would eventually go under. Justice Brandeis said that I might be right but that he was worried about how many small businesses the large corporations would harm and destroy before they themselves finally failed.

The project that Moses Abramovitz and I undertook in 1934–1935 to publish a collection of John M. Clark's essays led me to read again with care his considerable corpus of work. The exercise further deepened my skepticism. Clark was a mainline economist who was adept at turning neoclassical economics on its head. He demonstrated repeatedly that if one inverted some of the most hallowed of neoclassical propositions, such as the downward sloping demand curve, the inversion was likely to be more congruent with reality (*Preface to Social Economics*, 1935).

Clark's influence went beyond market economics. In *Alternative to Serfdom* (1948), he took on F. A. Hayek, who had earlier written *The Road to Serfdom* (1944). Clark demonstrated that any sensible discussion of the marketplace must always be set within the larger framework of the community and the nation. The specialization of labor facilitated by the market requires a legal infrastructure, among others, that only government can provide.

Many of my experiences in the world of ideas and the world of affairs since the outbreak of World War II have added to my skepticism about the ability of inherited economic doctrines to provide a useful model for understanding dynamic, developed, as well as more stable, less-developed economies. These experiences heightened my skepticism about the ability of established theory to be a major instrument for the reformulation of economic policy.

The academic community with its commitment to Marshallian economics was poorly prepared to understand and respond to the unraveling of the U.S. economy that set in with the stock market collapse of 1929. The market had reached new highs when small investors had taken their savings out of banks and bought stocks in the summer of 1929 on tips from their barbers and cabdrivers. Most academic economists were inarticulate during the deepening depression. This was further proof to me that the discipline could contribute little to policy. Moreover, I found little intellectual sustenance in the many justifications advanced by Roosevelt and his advisers in support of the numerous departures that characterized the New Deal. I was willing to applaud the energy and determination of the new administration to shore up the economy, but I found little to cheer about in terms of their economic judgments.

My extended exposure to corporate America in 1933–1934 had convinced me that many of the basic assumptions of entrepreneurial behavior that served as the foundation for studying the economics of the firm were remote from the thinking and behavior that I encountered among the leaders of U.S. industry. I could not square the decisionmaking in the prosperous 1920s or the depressed 1930s with the textbook models of the competitive market.

Finally, I knew that the dominant approaches of economics were awry because, with the rare exception of J. M. Clark, most theorists did not know how to set the economy within the larger societal framework; they did not leave room for major forces other than the automatic pursuit of profits, which clearly was a limited principle on which to construct a pertinent analytic structure. The Marxists had a larger system at their command, but a born skeptic could not be persuaded that Communist party discipline based on the leadership of Joseph Stalin was the road to the future.

By the late 1930s, I felt that the search for a general theory of economic development was doomed to fail. The most that one could hope for from economics was to sharpen and deepen the ways in which researchers approached certain problems. Economics was "a way of thinking," not more, but not less.

## PART TWO

# Economics Triumphant

In the four chapters that follow I review the rehabilitation of mainline economics after its nadir during the Great Depression. President Roosevelt's New Deal and the world war that followed resulted in an increase in the demand for economists to work in the federal government. There they acquired growing influence as analysts and policy advisers. John Maynard Keynes's *General Theory* (1936) provided the intellectual underpinnings for macroeconomic policy emphasizing that through deficit spending governments could stimulate a sluggish economy. The new national income accounting provided governments with additional techniques to help guide their interventionist policies. From 1943 to 1974, the U.S. economy performed remarkably well, although inflationary troubles first started to appear in 1965.

The thirteen U.S. Nobel laureates whose contributions are reviewed pursued their inquiries primarily during this period of the economy's high performance. The review demonstrates that most of the problems that they explored and the answers that they developed were embedded more in the internal dynamics of theory construction than in the external realities of the rapidly changing economy. The temporal coincidence of the flowering of economics and the growth of the advanced economies fueled the public's admiration for economists, and those accolades further contributed to the overevaluation of economics.

# 4

# The Institutionalization
# of Economics

### The Heyday of Economists

Although the first and greatest of the economists, Adam Smith, was for many years a professor of logic and moral philosophy, he retired from academic life before he was fifty to accept a short tutorship that assured him economic independence for the rest of his life. After a decade of concentrated writing, he accepted an appointment as commissioner of customs. He spent his last decade in this position and died at the age of sixty-seven. Two of his most important successors, David Ricardo and John Stuart Mill, had no academic base or roots. Ricardo made his fortune as a banker and later served as member of Parliament; Mill pursued a varied career, initially with the East Indian Company in a white-collar position that allowed him ample time to write. The great critic of mainline economics, Karl Marx, lived for most of his life upon the bounty of his devoted disciple, Friedrich Engels, although he supplemented his stipend with irregular earnings from journalism.

By the end of the nineteenth century, economics had been captured by academia, in both Great Britain and the United States, and even earlier on the continent. Alfred Marshall, who came to dominate economics in the Anglo-American world, was named professor at Cambridge University in 1885.

When I finished my doctoral studies at Columbia in 1933, the annual crop of new economists in the United States totaled around 150, more than half of whom were graduates of the small number of Ivy League institutions plus a few large universities in the Midwest and West.

At the end of the worst depression in the nation's history, as President Hoover left the White House, there were only a few well-known economists in the federal service: Louis Bean and Mordecai Ezekiel in the Department of Agriculture; Herbert Feis in the State Department; and E. A. Goldweiser at the Federal Reserve Board.

The situation was no different in the private sector. Alexander Sachs was the Lehman Brothers's house economist before going to Washington in 1933 to serve as the director of planning for the National Recovery Administration. Gossip at the time was that Sachs would not be missed because most of the Lehman partners never consulted him. At the annual meeting of the American Economic Association in 1936, when John Maurice Clark spoke at the presidential dinner, the attendance numbered about 150.

One of the lasting reforms that must be credited to the New Deal was the tremendous change in the quantity and quality of trained personnel—particularly lawyers and economists—who joined the federal bureaucracy. Despite this transformation, however, the War Department in 1941 had only one economist, Aaron Director, among its senior staff. When General Bretton B. Somervell, the newly appointed chief of the services of supply, asked Director to prepare an inventory of scarce metals that the United States had on hand, Director informed the general that that was not an assignment for an economist. The War Department suddenly found itself without an economist, and it took no early action to correct this lack.

The explosive growth in the number and proportion of college and graduate degree recipients in the post–World War II era makes it difficult to compare the number of economists in the decades prior to and after the war. To complicate matters, recent decades have seen large increases in the number of MBAs, as well as of graduates who have majored in statistics, operations research, and management science. Even if we strictly define an economist as one who has been awarded a doctorate in economics, the annual increase from 1933 to the present is on the order of tenfold.

Prior to the federal government's increased demand for economists that was generated by the many programs initiated by the New Deal, college teaching was the principal area of employment for the professionally trained economist. A few found their way into business, but among the twenty or so large corporations that I visited in 1933–1934, I recall only one corporate economist, at Procter & Gamble. There may have been others, but most companies had no such designated position. The New Deal opened up the first large-scale alternative employment opportunities for economists, and the war agencies expanded the demand not only in Washington but also in the many regional, state, and metropolitan agencies that became involved in materiel allocation and price and wage regulations.

At the war's end, most large U.S. corporations, poised to expand both at home and abroad, had learned about the advantages of strong staffs through exposure to and participation in the armed forces or in agencies involved in the civilian war effort. They eagerly recruited MBAs and also added economists to their expanding staffs.

Another significant development occurred in the early 1930s. In 1930–1931, Simon Kuznets had made sufficient progress in his research on national income accounting in response to the request of the Department of Commerce to help it conceptualize and systematize its collection and publication of such accounts. One of Kuznets's students at the University of Pennsylvania, Robert R. Nathan, who later played a key role as head of the Planning Division of the War Production Board, joined the Department of Commerce to carry out this assignment.

The combination of the national income accounts and the new Keynesian macroequations in 1936 provided a powerful new forecasting tool for economic and business analysts in every sector of society—government, business, communications, academe. Even before the invention of the computer, the demand for economists capable of using the new national income accounts for forecasting increased. Many different types of employers—individual corporations, trade associations, various levels of governments, specialized institutions such as the Federal Reserve banks—sought to hire these analysts. Much later, the market expanded still further as more powerful and less costly computers facilitated more detailed forecasts. Because economists often differed in their forecasts, sometimes by a significant degree, demand was further stimulated by large employers who felt more secure if they had a range of forecasts at their disposal.

Other developments contributed to the enlargement and proliferation of the market for economists in the post–World War II era. One was the direct outcome of the need to find better answers to pressing military and naval problems. Linear programming began to engage the interest of economists, statisticians, and operations researchers who with the cessation of hostilities, recognized that this new methodology, although still in an early stage of development, could be improved and applied to a wide range of production and inventory problems.

The return to peace and accelerated political and military actions led to rapid decolonization and set the stage for a blossoming of a new field dubbed "development economics." The developed nations individually, and through international bodies, made sizable sums available to various developing nations to speed modernization. Many new positions for economists opened up at the donor level and in the field. Some U.S. universities that became involved in the developing world had at any one time several hundred specialists, including many economists, on field assignments in the less developed countries.

The United States emerged from World War II convinced of the value of research and development, a lesson it had learned well because of the successful outcome of the Manhattan Project. As a result, Congress allocated substantial funds to the Department of Defense and also to various established and new civilian agencies for research programs, some of which provided new employment opportunities for economists.

There was also considerable expansion in the staffs of established and new research institutions. The newly created National Science Foundation initiated support for economics and economists in 1960; the Ford Foundation had earlier made considerable funding available to economists, particularly in connection with its projects in the developing world. In 1962, the U.S. Department of Labor initiated an external support program for research and development in "manpower economics," which by the late 1970s had leveraged about one-quarter of a billion dollars of federal funds. The Department of Health, Education and Welfare (HEW) also financed two large demonstration projects, one on the influence of income transfers on labor force participation, the other, on health insurance. In addition, for many years HEW funded the Poverty Institute at the University of Wisconsin. The institute has had a large staff of economists and other social scientists.

The foregoing is a selected account of some of the institutional and financial developments that affected economics and economists in the post–World War II period. Even such an abbreviated account helps to identify the altered environment for economists. From the New Deal of 1933 to the end of the Great Society programs in 1969, economists were definitely "in."

Although many explanations have so far been adduced for the growing popularity of economics and economists, the most important factor is still to be identified. The public, including many in leadership positions, had concluded that economists had played a useful role in helping to extricate the United States from the devastating depression of the early 1930s; that they had performed well in many different sectors of the war effort; and that most importantly, their new theories and techniques, grounded in Keynesian macroeconomics, had contributed to a remarkable postwar boom in the United States as well as in Western Europe, Japan, and in certain third world countries. Many believed the economists who said they knew how to fine-tune the economy; their record, at least until the end of the 1960s, seemed to substantiate their claims.

## Disillusion with Economics

During the past fifteen years, there has been a major change in public opinion about the relevance and utility of economics both as a system of thought and as a guide to policy. The Keynesian approach, which informed government policy in most of the developed world in the early postwar decades, was found deficient once inflation ignited in the United States in the second half of the 1960s. And after the first oil crisis in 1973, the countries of Western Europe discovered that they could no longer operate their economies with a 2 to 3 percent unemployment rate. In the eight years between 1974 and 1982, the U.S. economy experienced three recessions; the last resulted in the most severe reductions in income and employment during the entire post–World War II era.

The European economic record during the past decade has also been unimpressive. Great Britain has had almost no expansion of jobs and has seen its unemployment rate rise to above 13 percent, where it has remained. West Germany, which had earlier commanded respect and admiration because of its economic miracle, also experienced hard times when it was unable to generate new jobs and had an unemployment rate approaching 10 percent. The performance of the French economy has been somewhat worse than West Germany's. Sweden, which had been viewed as the exemplar of the welfare state, with low unemployment, a high standard of living, and a narrowing gap between rich and poor, stumbled badly. It managed to keep its unemployment rate relatively low, but its growth rate declined precipitously, and this upset its balance of payments and forced a slowdown of its earlier programs aimed at establishing greater equity. Its expectational system of more for everybody proved to be out of phase with the new reality.

As these untoward events unfolded, the consensus among economists disintegrated. Without alternatives, committed Keynesians maintained their allegiance as long as possible. I recall Arthur F. Burns, then Chairman of the Federal Reserve Board, remarking in 1975 that the only suggestion he could elicit from his colleagues at the Brookings Institution was that the country should spend its way out of the recession.

Paul McCracken, former chairman of the Council of Economic Advisers for President Richard Nixon, headed a study group for the OECD in 1975–1976 that concluded, after months of deliberation, that the recession could be controlled with proper policies and that the West European countries could look forward to a renewal of their long-term expansion.

The United States was forced off the gold standard in 1971; thereafter, foreign exchange rates were at the mercy of the market with occasional interventions by the central banks to contain speculative movements. Many economists had looked forward to the dismantling of fixed exchange rates, but as time went on, it became increasingly clear that flexible exchange rates also brought problems. A minority of economists who believed that the market adjustment process was creating undue instability in international financial and trade movements advocated a return to the gold standard. This proposal did not commend itself to most economists who considered it impractical, if not impossible. Others put forward proposals for a major international effort aimed at creating a reserve currency that could be drawn upon if and when the dollar could no longer meet the demands made on it. Because the U.S. government did not wish to diminish any more than necessary the role of the dollar in international finance, this suggestion received only half-hearted support.

The explosive growth of the Eurodollar market and the post-1973 recycling of the oil revenues of the OPEC countries demonstrated the flexibility of the international banking system. However, this remarkable flexibility carried a high price: It greatly reduced the effectiveness with which national governments could use monetary and fiscal policy to direct their economies. In recent years, the proliferation of many new forms of money subsequent to the introduction of the new computer technology and deregulation has further reduced the ability of the Federal Reserve system to discipline the money market and through it, the economy.

There has long been a hard core of anti-Keynesians, led by Milton Friedman, who have argued that the supply of money is the only element that central banks should consider in their efforts to assure economic growth. When inflation started to heat up after 1965, the monetarists took to the offensive. As the "fine-tuners" lost their touch, the monetarists gained a significant number of converts. But most economists, despite their growing confusion and loss of direction, were unwilling to accept the resurrected doctrine that made every aspect of the economy revolve around changes in the supply of money. The antimonetarists insisted that velocity, the quality of credit, interest rates, and money substitutes had to be considered. The repeated failure of the monetarists to have their forecasts substantiated by events reduced their influence to a point where the presidential campaign of 1980 turned out to be a contest between discredited Keynesianism and supply-side, or as some dubbed it, "voodoo" economics.

Presidential candidate Ronald Reagan promised to accomplish the following: balance the budget by the end of his first administration; shrink the federal government; strengthen the armed forces; and cut taxes. The only way to achieve these objectives would be through the successful operation of the Laffer Curve, which postulated that lower taxes would lead to greater investment and higher income and thus to greater tax revenue. The outcome, however, turned out to be quite different. The armed forces received major increases in appropriations; instead of evaporating, the federal deficit rose to an all-time high as the Federal Reserve Board held a tight rein on money to check inflation; the public sector as a percentage of gross national product, instead of declining, increased; the anticipated expansion of investment, which was delayed until 1983, resulted in tax revenues that were far below what they might have been without the tax reduction program of 1981.

In the 1984 campaign, President Reagan took credit for the strong revival of the economy and promised that if reelected, he would not increase taxes. Walter Mondale sought to frighten the public about the large deficits in the hope that it would support a candidate who favored a tax increase. It is difficult to conceive of a more tangled web: The ostensibly hard-money, conservative Republicans enjoying the fruits of a Keynesian defense boom; and the Democrats, the traditional friend of the poor, advocating a tax increase. Most voters apparently decided that in the welter of claims and counterclaims, it made sense to support the incumbent who took credit for the radical drop in inflation and the strong recovery in income and employment.

One conclusion is inescapable: Economists of differing persuasions had difficulty in developing convincing rationales in support of, or in opposition to, the administration's policies. And it was equally difficult to find a coherent thread that tied together the several planks of the Democratic platform. These difficulties were the measure of the economists' decline.

Some may contend that the foregoing argument is exaggerated and that most of the profession continues to see the world from the same vantage point. They can point first to consensus among economists who strongly favor deregulation, a process begun under President Jimmy Carter and that has continued under President Reagan. This is a valid formulation: Most economists favored deregulation of the airlines, trucking, and banking—to take the most striking examples.

Second, the profession continues to favor the country's pursuing a free-trade policy, even though some are unaware of how far Washington has moved through the mechanism of voluntary trade agreements to limit exports to this country.

On the issue of industrial policy, the profession broadly agrees that any new tripartite structures involving cooperation among business, labor, and government to establish national goals and policies would not work.

However, the striking rise in the unemployment rate from under 4 percent in the late 1960s to just under 10 percent in 1982, with a decrease to only around 7 percent in 1986, has elicited more analysis than new policy directions. Many academic economists, but by no means all, accept that there has been a substantial rise in the natural, noninflationary rate of unemployment from its earlier level of 3 to 4 percent in the 1960s to around 7 percent today. Proponents have developed two theories to account for the rise. The first cites the large increase in the number of young people and women in the labor force, groups with known higher turnover rates. The second cites the elongation of the job search process that has come to characterize the unemployed. With income transfer supports available, proponents argue that there is less pressure on the unemployed to take the first job they locate. They can and do extend their period of search, and this tends to raise the unemployment rate. These economists believe that labor markets, like other markets, tend to clear in the short run and that these new theories go far to account for the substantial rise in the natural unemployment rate.

Other economists believe that labor markets do not clear, surely not in the short run. In their view, the high level of unemployment in the 1980s reflects first the consequences of a public policy that has aimed to reduce inflation and to keep it down. This policy has forced the economy to run slack and has resulted in an elevated level of unemployment. We can see how elevated by inspecting the targets contained in the Full Employment and Balanced Economic Growth Act of 1978. The targets for 1984 were 3 percent for adult and 4 percent for total unemployment. The actual rates were 6.5 and 7.5, respectively.

With the notable exception of the late Arthur Okun, who early recognized the necessity of developing new approaches to contain both unemployment and inflation and who spent his last years attempting to find ways of meeting this crucial challenge (*Prices and Quantities: A Macroeconomic Analysis*, 1981), many economists, perplexed and baffled, have turned their attention to more tractable issues.

The frustration and avoidance of the issue of unconscionably high levels of unemployment have characterized not only U.S. but also European economists. Only in early 1985 was a new organization put together in Great Britain that cuts across party lines and includes the business community, trade unions, and academe and addresses the nation's appallingly high unemployment rate.

The volatility of the world's economy since the early 1970s has tested economists in other troubled areas as well. Consider their role in assessing the energy problem that President Carter considered to be a top national priority in 1977. The academic experts, as well as the energy economists, seriously misjudged both the staying power of OPEC and the future trends in demand. A few academic experts had prophesied an early collapse of OPEC, arguing with analogies of the difficulties of prior international cartels. Their prophecy of doom was off by a decade. And their miscalculations were matched by others who overestimated the staying power of OPEC. In contrast, most of the petroleum industry's economists vastly overestimated the level of future demand. One conclusion is unequivocal: Unable to forecast the trend of future demand, economists could not provide their national governments with reliable policy guidance.

Economists deserve a better mark when it comes to a related national issue that surfaced at about the same time—the protection of the environment. Experts, as well as the public, held a variety of strong positions, but professional economists were able to contribute significantly to the development of methodologies that could make first and second approximations of the relative costs and benefits, over the short and longer term, of different societal interventions. Although the answers that the economists proffered depended heavily on their assumptions about present and future costs and benefits, this limitation notwithstanding, they were able to provide an analytic framework that could assist in the search for improved policy.

One of the most trenchant criticisms leveled at economists is their resort to the neutralizing power of "other things being equal." This has enabled them to disregard dynamic factors such as changes in population, technology, and tastes. An unfriendly critic might say that the studied neglect of these potent factors assures that economic theorizing cannot be pertinent either for understanding current events or for pointing future directions.

## The Post–World War II Era

There is no gainsaying the fact that the post–World War II era has seen striking changes in demography, technology, and tastes in both the developed and developing world. These changes have had a profound influence on the shaping and reshaping of national economies and the international economy. Let us review each of the three dynamic factors in the U.S. economy. On the demographic front, the current and persistent problem of excessively high unemployment among minorities and minority youth is closely tied to the doubling of the national birthrate immediately after the war; the relocation of millions of blacks from southern farms to northern urban ghettos; and reductions in morbidity and mortality. Demographic changes have also altered radically the participation rates in the labor market of both men and women. Over half of all women are currently at work, compared to one-third in the late 1940s; most men retire before the age of sixty-five and only one in seven continues to work, part- or full-time thereafter; and substantial population increases have taken place in the South and West speeding the growth of these regional economies. We do not contend, of course, that economists have been oblivious to these changes or that they consider them trivial, but there is much that their macromodels fail to record, such as the economic and social consequences for large numbers of minority youth, adult black men, and black female heads of households, especially those in large urban areas who are unable to obtain and hold jobs.

Technological changes, broadly defined for our purposes, that include research and development also receive less attention than their due. As noted earlier, one of the important legacies of World War II was the recognition by Congress and the public that large public as well as private outlays for research and development could contribute significantly to speeding economic growth and well-being. In recent decades, economists have made important contributions to assessing the factors that have accelerated the growth of different economies and that account for changing trends in productivity, although they are baffled by the recent decline in U.S. productivity. But for the most part only a small number have explored the role of technology in the growth and decline of important industries and even fewer have addressed the policy issues of the appropriate partnership among the multiple sectors—government, nonprofit, and for-profit—in establishing and maintaining an optimal environment for speeding the growth of a high-tech economy.

With regard to changes in taste, which in mainline economics play a critical role in shifting the demand curve, economists have hidden behind the easy dodge that *de gustibus non disputandum est.* Most economists are willing to start their analysis with whatever distribution of tastes exists in a population. But the incontrovertible fact is that influencing tastes is a major strategy of all businesses, either changing them so that consumers are encouraged to buy specific products or reinforcing them so that consumers do not shift to a different product. In recent decades, there has been an accelerated diffusion of tastes from the most advanced developed economy, that of the United States, to the other developed and developing economies, but the processes of diffusion and the consequences have not been carefully assessed.

Except for a time early in the first Reagan administration when there was a serious threat to eliminate all National Science Foundation support for basic research in the social sciences, including economics, it is difficult to identify any occasion when the leadership of the economics profession spoke out about federal policy for research and development expenditure, in contrast to the leadership of the physical sciences and the biomedical community, which continually pressures the principal government agencies to increase the size and direction of research funding. Whereas most economists acknowledge the role of basic research in propelling the economy, few have given the field the attention it warrants.

As we shall see in a later chapter, post–World War II economics has focused attention on the role of human capital, but for the most part this interest has centered on improving and refining the analysis of established problems in the labor market such as the causes of wage differentials, race and sex discrimination, lifetime earnings profiles, the comparative earnings of union and nonunion employees, and the relative contributions of education, on-the-job training, and improvements in health. It suffices to point out here that only a few economists have been concerned with the large societal issues of whether the nation can adequately educate and train the increasing number of professional and technical personnel it currently needs or could profitably employ in the future. And even fewer economists have been concerned with the range of related policies that might speed the pace of economic development.

As noted above, the post–World War II era was characterized by important changes in the role of women in paid employment, changes that I once characterized as the most "revolutionary" event of the twentieth century, of greater importance than the rise of communism or the development of nuclear power. Many economists, as well as other social scientists, have studied one or another facet of this revolution; the human capital school has centered its attention on the forces that influence women to remain at home to rear their children or to seek employment out of the home, part-time or full-time.

The second-order consequences of this revolution are the growth of female-headed households and the disproportionate number of children, particularly minority children, who are being reared in families mired in poverty. One need not be a sophisticated student of human development to appreciate that the combination of one parent, low income, minority status, usually reinforced by poor housing, poor schooling, and poor neighborhood environment, virtually ensures poor socialization and poor labor market skills that foreshadow a life of deprivation and frustration.

Over a decade ago, a group of colleagues from the Conservation of Human Resources Project held a series of discussions with with George Low, at that time the deputy director of NASA and later president of Rensselaer Polytechnic, that resulted in a book *The Economic Impact of Large Public Programs* (1976). Defense, nuclear power, and space have played major roles in stimulating the level and direction of federal spending for research and development over the past decades and these in turn have affected major areas such as the airplane, communications, electronics, and computer industries and public utilities. These large expenditures also made an impact on the training of specialized personnel and on the welfare and well-being of many communities, particularly in the South and West. Large federal spending also has negative effects when major military bases are closed; when large numbers of engineering and technical personnel are laid off, as happened in 1970–1971; and when key research talent is deflected from the profit-making sector of the economy.

These brief comments make a single point. Economists, concerned as most of them are with perfecting their understanding of the competitive market, have paid little attention to this critical arena of federal spending that has had and doubtlessly will continue to have a major influence on the performance of the U.S. economy and the welfare of our society. The Europeans may exaggerate when they claim that the recovery under Reagan is only a spurt of "defense Keynesianism," but this interpretation cannot be ignored when we assess our recent economic recovery.

I shall now call attention to a limited number of themes that were identified earlier as major factors in the transformation of the economics profession and in the work of economists in the half century since the advent of the New Deal.

There was an explosive growth in the number of professionally trained economists who acquired doctorates. The number of college and graduate students who have had general economics and allied training in statistics and operations research has enlarged the pool of competent analysts by an order of magnitude. This striking increase in supply was clearly a response to the associated increases in the demand by government, business, and major nonprofit organizations.

Nonacademic economists work for the most part on employers' specific problems, from estimating future demand in the industry and in the firm to developing criteria for a government agency charged with regulatory responsibilities. Other economists make their living from forecasting.

The principal activities of the academically based economist are teaching, research, and in some cases, consulting. Up to the end of the 1960s, the dominant doctrine was Keynesianism, with a hubris that grew out of the conviction that economists had learned how to fine-tune the economy and thereby assure its continued growth. But with double-digit inflation and several recessions, two of which were severe, following in short order in the mid-1970s and early 1980s, Keynesianism was deserted by many, and the exponents of the competitive market, with the University of Chicago School in the lead, took command.

My friend Moses Abramovitz of Stanford University has asked, "How can this radical shift be explained?" I have no ready, surely no complete, answer, but I have pointed out in this chapter that economists are more comfortable with the problems that they can solve with traditional techniques rather than with the problems, possibly of greater moment, that cannot be analyzed with the same degree of "scientific" discipline.

I have noted that a host of major issues, from the level of funding for basic research to the expanded role of women in the labor force, to the impact of defense, all of which have major influence on the economy as well as on our political and social development, have engaged the attention of only occasional investigators. Mainline economists prefer to stay with conventional problems, conventional in the sense that they are focused on the competitive market, analyzable with the techniques of microeconomics, and presumably value-free even if often distant from policy.

This is not a satisfactory answer to Professor Abramovitz's question about the reasons for the economists' flight from Keynesianism back to the neoclassical model of the competitive economy with its associated belief that the less government the better. Let us try again. The first point is that even in the heyday of Keynesianism, most economists continued to use neoclassical price theory. After all, that was the recognized strength of Paul Samuelson's famous textbook (*Economics*, 1967): It linked, if it did not integrate, Marshall and Keynes. Therefore, it is probably an exaggeration to see the reemergence of the neoclassical approach as a major discontinuity with the intellectual environment of the 1950s and 1960s.

A second line of explanation would call attention to the advances made in applying mathematics and advanced statistical concepts and techniques to economic problems. This effort, which has commanded the best energies of the best minds entering the profession, inevitably led to a renewed focus on the neoclassical and general equilibrium paradigms. Mathematical modeling in economics is best carried out within a system of analysis that permits strong assumptions, that can deal with a few variables at a time, that requires little empirical data, and where the quality of the scholarly exercise is judged more by the elegance of transformational processes than by the relevance and utility of the results.

I suggested many years ago that one of the reasons for the continued survival and strength of the neoclassical model has been its use in the classroom. It is a powerful pedagogical tool that enables faculty to differentiate easily between the more talented and the less talented students, talent being defined as the skillful manipulation of the model. In the absence of attractive alternatives, applying mathematical concepts and techniques to the neoclassical model has much going for it.

If this explanation has merit, we can identify an important institutional reinforcement. Because talent and competence in economic analysis have increasingly come to be associated with mathematical skill, it did not take long, particularly in the period of rapid expansion in higher education when newly minted doctors of philosophy received tenure within two or three years after they had obtained their degrees, for the new breed of economists to assume critical positions in making faculty appointments, in editing journals, in membership on research grant committees.

Finally, the disenchantment with the Great Society programs, a reaction that shifted the center of U.S. politics to the right, did not leave economists untouched. Many economists moved quietly and without fanfare toward the right—as did so many others.

The solution to the puzzle points to the following: The growing dominance of the neoclassical approach reflects its resilience during the period of the Keynesian revolution, its ability to accommodate the new mathematical techniques, the capture of leadership positions by the new breed of mathematical economists, and the political conservatism inherent in a competitive market model, a position that fits the temper of the times.

There is yet another way to extract the core of this chapter's argument by shifting attention from the ways in which economists are trained and work, with emphasis on their macro- and micro-model-building, to the challenges they face in pursuing policy analyses for which they are poorly prepared intellectually and for which they are poorly positioned when it comes to making a career for themselves. All of the emphasis in their undergraduate and graduate instruction is on refinements within the discipline that emphasize the nuances in the construction of theories and in the sophistication of methodologies. Graduate students are discouraged from pursuing courses outside their discipline—the "soft" social sciences such as history, political science, sociology, and anthropology are looked down upon by their teachers and their peers who insist that there is little point in young economists deflecting their energies.

But even if some young economists were more broadly trained and acquired a deeper understanding of the forces that propel a modern economy as it seeks a better balance among such conflicting goals as economic growth, defense, and the pursuit of equity, they would be hard pressed to find jobs and pursue careers where such integrative skills, talents, and judgments had scope and were rewarded. Academe reserves its major rewards for the innovator on the cutting edge of theory; the senior officials in large corporations, industrial or financial, look to their economic staffs for technical support; and the federal bureaucracy has need for an array of experts in various fields from regulation to foreign trade. Economists, like other professionals, are surely influenced by the availability of jobs and career prospects. During the New Deal and the Great Society they were drawn to the expanding opportunities that had a strong reformist orientation inside and outside of government. More recently, the money flows have been in the opposite direction, in support of conservative positions and policies, and many economists have responded accordingly.

Only a very few economists are lucky enough to be able to carve out a career that enables them to pursue policy research focused on assessing the strengths and weaknesses of current institutions and to point out actions that could result in their improved performance. Keynes once suggested that if economists were lucky, they would become as useful as dentists, but that day still appears to be far off.

# 5

## We Are All Keynesians

The institutionalization of economics went hand in hand with a major transformation in established economic doctrine. It is indeed questionable whether in the absence of the breakthrough that came to be designated as the "Keynesian revolution," economists would have experienced the popularity that came to be attached to their discipline.

To set the stage and to appreciate better the post–World War II interactions between theory and policy, a few summary observations of the earlier relationships between theory and policy may prove illuminating. Throughout the nineteenth century and particularly during its second half when the United States was laying the groundwork for its emergence as the leading industrial nation, the dominant economic doctrine was initially classical and later neoclassical, preoccupied with competitive markets and free trade as the principal spurs to economic growth and prosperity.

But these strongly held views and commitments did not impede the U.S. Congress from passing successive tariff acts erecting barriers to slow the flow into the United States of foreign goods that competed with locally produced outputs. Members of Congress saw no contradiction between their beliefs and their policies: When the two were discordant, clearly, the latter took precedence.

When it came to industrial organization, the matter was less clear-cut. As the country took large steps toward industrialization, Adam Smith's entrepreneur—the owner-manager—was left behind. In the entrepreneur's place, large combinations and trusts increasingly came to dominate the industrial landscape. In 1890, Congress passed the Sherman Antitrust Act in the hope that the competitive market could be protected from the multiple perversions that the new giants were introducing, including price fixing, dividing the market among themselves, pursuing practices to drive out small competitors, and many other untoward actions that made a mockery of the doctrine "let the best man" win. Although Louis Brandeis early in the century wrote a small book entitled *The Curse of Bigness* (1965), neither the law nor the reformers were able to do more than break up an occasional monopoly. The trend toward bigness followed its own dynamic.

Academic economics, however, paid little attention to this ineluctable trend. Most of the major universities had a course or two devoted to combinations and trusts, but the dominant theory that they taught and continued to develop was anchored in the paradigm of the competitive market.

The only significant departure from neoclassical economics in the period between World War I and World War II was the development of "empirical economics" under the leadership of Wesley C. Mitchell at Columbia University and the National Bureau of Economic Research. Mitchell's teaching and research centered around the business cycle. But Columbia's Economics Department under Mitchell was off the beaten track. The neoclassical approach continued at center stage in most institutions long after the evidence had accumulated that it was unable to explain what was happening to the U.S. economy and that it had little to offer in pointing new directions.

In 1936 John Maynard Keynes published *The General Theory of Employment, Interest, and Money* (1936), which provided the first significant alternative to the ensconced theory. By the end of World War II sufficient time had passed to enable the new theory to have captured most of the citadels of learning as well as to have won the allegiance of most of the younger economists employed by government and business. When the war began to wind down in Europe the winter of 1944–1945, a group of economists then working in various federal agencies in Washington, D.C., spent an evening discussing the domestic outlook after the armistice. The overwhelming opinion among the senior analysts anticipated a rapid and large increase in unemployment after the armed forces demobilized most of the 12 million service personnel then on active duty. I do not recall a single participant suggesting that *The General Theory,* or any other theory, could point the way for the U.S. economy to avoid returning to the high level of unemployment that characterized the late 1930s when the rate never dipped below 10 percent. The group knew about the efforts of Paul Hoffman and his collaborators on the Committee for Economic Development who were carrying the message to the hinterland that employers should speed their planning to convert to peacetime operations, but they gave this campaign small prospects of success.

When Germany surrendered on May 7, 1945, Congress began to address some of the many challenges that confronted the country. Among the subjects on its agenda was the Full Employment Bill of 1945, which spelled out a new role for the federal government in assuring that the nation would not again be victimized by high unemployment. The legislators could not agree as to the appropriate role for the federal government and they were unable to mark up a bill. However, they were impressed by the striking drop in unemployment that had accompanied the war effort. In 1944, the unemployment rate had declined to as low as 1.2 percent. Here was proof that a country did not have to sit by and passively accept a persistently high rate of unemployment. Strong demand, albeit demand initiated by government, could obviate such a danger.

In the following year, Congress again considered the appropriate role for the federal government in the stabilization of the economy. The legislators eventually passed a compromise bill entitled the Employment Act of 1946 (not the Full Employment Act), which stipulated that "It is the continuing policy and responsibility of the Federal Government to use all practical means . . . [so that] there will be afforded useful employment opportunities . . . for those able, willing and seeking to work and to promote maximum employment, production and purchasing power." The act provided for the establishment of a Council of Economic Advisers in the Executive Office of the President and required that the president prepare and submit to the Congress an annual *Economic Report*.

Because the U.S. economy made the transition from war to peace with remarkable agility, the government was not called upon to undertake new actions to meet its new responsibilities. By 1950, the country was again at war, this time in Korea. The Truman administration resorted to formal and informal resource allocation, price-fixing, and higher taxes to meet the economic challenges brought by the war. When the Eisenhower administration took over in 1953 and succeeded in bringing the war to an end, it moved quickly to reduce taxes in the conviction that such action would stimulate the economy, which, in fact, occurred.

Aside from reducing taxes, the new administration eschewed improvisation. The economy made progress under its own momentum. It was not until the second Eisenhower administration that the economy faltered, first in 1957, and again in 1959–1960. With the Employment Act of 1946 on the books, the Eisenhower administration concluded that it was no longer essential that the federal government submit a balanced budget every year. In a year when the economy was slack, as in 1959, it could tolerate an unbalanced budget. However, the president added, it should limit its departure from sound financing to a single year.

Eisenhower's conservative secretary of treasury, George Humphrey, led a major struggle in and out of the administration to keep the federal government on the straight and narrow path of sound fiscal and budgetary policy. He repeatedly warned that if the government failed to act responsibly it would bring on a depression that would "curl one's hair."

## The New Economics

The first major engagement of the new economics on the national political arena followed John F. Kennedy's hairbreadth victory over Richard Nixon in 1960. For the first time, the Council of Economic Advisers, both members and staff, was composed of committed Keynesians. With Chairman Walter Heller in the lead, the council started to educate both the president and the public that it made no sense for the country to accept a steadily rising rate of unemployment. After each recession since 1957 the level of unemployment had moved to a new high.

By inclination a conservative and acutely aware of his paper-thin victory, the president listened but was not convinced. It was not until his address at Yale University in June 1962, when the economy's feeble expansion appeared to falter, that Kennedy became converted. He moved into the Keynesian camp by challenging the doctrine that government deficits are always a prelude to inflation. During that summer, Kennedy announced his support for a major tax reduction to stimulate the economy.

Despite strong lobbying efforts on the part of the council and other supporters of the tax reduction program, Congress moved circumspectly and did not pass the bill in 1963. It took the unsettled mood in and out of Congress that followed the president's assassination and the determination and drive of President Lyndon B. Johnson to get the tax reduction bill passed in 1964. Most of the nation's economists favored the bill. John Kenneth Galbraith opposed it on the basis that we needed more public spending for improved social programs, not more spending by consumers on nonessentials and luxuries. I opposed it on different grounds: I considered it unwise to provide Congress with a rationale for reducing taxes since I questioned whether Congress would learn the other half of the new lesson—that when the economy strengthened, Congress would have to raise taxes. Further, the indicators in 1964 suggested that the economy was on an upward slope, and I saw no particular reason for Congress to accelerate the advance.

Let's be clear: Except for the outlays legislated during the New Deal to provide jobs and incomes for large numbers of unemployed, underemployed, and poverty-stricken citizens who were victimized by the Great Depression and its aftermath, most of which efforts predated the publication of Keynes's *General Theory*, the tax reduction early in the first Eisenhower administration and the deficit budget that he forwarded to Congress late in his second administration, Keynesianism had played little role in the formulation of U.S. economic policy—until the major tax reduction act of 1964.

In its early years, Kennedy's Council of Economic Advisers had to fight a guerrilla action with a minority of economists in and out of the federal government who questioned that enlarged government spending was the way to stimulate the economy and lower unemployment. The "structuralists," as they were known, argued that many of the unemployed would not be reabsorbed by the rise in total demand because they lacked skills or had other characteristics (residence in depressed areas) that would interfere with their obtaining jobs. In 1962, Congress responded to this structuralist argument by passing the Manpower Development and Training Act (MDTA), followed by a modest appropriation. The conflict between the macroeconomists and the structuralists ended with a clear victory for the former. But the new MDTA program revealed that there were hundreds of thousands, possibly millions of individuals on the periphery of the labor force, who had little prospect of regular jobs with opportunities for advancement unless they could obtain remedial education, skill training, and other forms of employment assistance, including antidiscrimination moves.

In 1964–1965 the macroeconomists and the structuralists again confronted each other. The president had established the Commission on Automation, with broad representation from business, labor, and academe, to determine whether recent technological changes were a threat to the job security of American workers. Robert Solow, a prominent economics professor from MIT and a staff member of the council in 1961–1962, took the lead in persuading his more skeptical colleagues such as Walter Reuther that even if automation led to some workers' losing their jobs, with proper macroeconomic policies in effect, these workers would be quickly reabsorbed and the total demand for labor would expand.

In 1965, Arthur Burns and I traveled to Detroit on behalf of Columbia University to speak to an alumni group. I recall Burns's concern with the most recent price data, which he read as a warning that inflation might be in the wings. Concern about inflation had been high on the agenda of most macroeconomists, both conservative Republicans and liberal Democrats. In the last years of Eisenhower's second administration, Richard Nixon served as chairman of an inflationary watch group, of which Allen Wallis, a true Chicago School adherent, was the director.

In developing their full employment budget analysis and their expansionary economic goals for the Kennedy administration, the Council of Economic Advisers determined that unemployment could be reduced to 4 percent without engendering a price rise. The council believed that structural improvements in the labor market might eventually justify a 3 percent goal.

In advising President Johnson on his 1966 budget, the council recommended a tax increase, superimposed on an expanding economy, to prevent increased spending for Vietnam from leading to steep price increases. The president, determined to protect his Great Society programs from hostile actions by congressional appropriation committees, turned a deaf ear to the council's recommendation. It is not possible to charge the Keynesians with having neglected the inflation threat. From the end of the Korean War in 1953 to 1966, concern with inflation had dominated macroeconomic policy. The emphasis that Eisenhower placed on price stability helped to create a climate in which expectations about inflation were low or nonexistent. This climate provided some leeway for the Kennedy administration to open the throttle for a more expansive policy after mid-1962 with relatively little risk. But the Kennedy advisers proceeded cautiously by favoring wage and price guideposts to moderate the actions of oligopolistic industries and strong trade unions to raise prices and wages in order to gain special rewards for themselves. In the absence of such controls the advisers feared that reinforcing price and wage advances could ignite inflation. In 1963, President Kennedy took on the powerful steel industry and forced a rollback of what appeared to him to be unjustified price increases. Low inflationary expectations, excess capacity, and government guideposts all contributed to keeping price advances between 1962 and 1965 to about 1 percent per annum.

Although the Kennedy administration gave priority to accelerating economic growth and to reducing unemployment, it recognized as one of its major responsibilities protecting the dollar, which had come to support the post–World War II expansion of international trade and finance. Dollars had long been convertible for gold at $35 an ounce. Both President Kennedy and President Johnson gave repeated assurances to other nations that the United States, cognizant of its leadership role, would maintain this rate. A shift to flexible exchange rates, or to devaluation, was ruled out. To underscore its determination, the United States first resorted in the mid-1960s to a voluntary slowdown of the export of capital abroad and when this approach failed, it established mandatory controls in 1968 to protect its pledge to maintain the integrity of the dollar.

Mandatory control over the export of capital was only one of several dramatic events that pointed to the growing volatility of the U.S. economy. The combination of steadily declining unemployment together with an acceleration in prices undermined the administration's guideposts. From a level of about a 1 percent annual increase in the consumer price index in the first four years of the 1960s, the middle three years, 1964–1966, saw the index rise to just under 2 percent and the last four years averaged 4.6 percent, or about a fivefold acceleration over the early years of the decade.

Comparable acceleration occurred in wages and earnings. Average weekly earnings in current dollars in the dominant private nonagricultural sector of the economy stood at slightly over $80 in 1960 and just under $120 in 1970, a rise of 50 percent within a single decade.

Although the Johnson administration asked Congress for a tax increase in 1967, it was not until 1968 that the difficult negotiations between the White House and Capitol Hill were completed, and by the time the new taxes took effect, the wage-price spiral had accelerated. Constraining an expansionary macropolicy proved more difficult than initiating such a policy.

After the longest sustained period of economic expansion in the country's history—106 months—the economy turned downward in December 1969, but consumer prices continued to advance at a rapid clip, 5.9 percent in 1970 and 4.3 percent in 1971. Wages also continued their upward drift. The recession of 1969-1970 was shallow and brief, but in August 1971 President Nixon faced a crisis because of the continuing demands by foreigners who sought to convert their dollars into gold. In 1960, the United States had just under $18 billion in gold stock in its reserves; by 1965 the figure was below $14 billion, and by 1970 it stood close to $11 billion, a decline of just under 40 percent in a single decade. The promises of his predecessors notwithstanding, President Nixon had little option but to put an end to the right of currency holders to convert their dollars into gold. A by-product of this decision to end convertibility of the dollar was the elimination of the fixed system of foreign exchange rates among the major trading nations. Henceforth, flexible exchange rates, determined by the market and influenced on rare occasions by the interventions of the central banks, would govern the international movements of goods and money.

Against the advice of his secretary of the treasury, George Shultz, President Nixon, disturbed by evidence of the continuing inflation, opted for price and wage controls, an approach supported by the chairman of the Federal Reserve Board, Arthur Burns, who had earlier been Nixon's counselor in the White House. Disagreements among the president's advisers were matched by disagreements among experts outside of government about whether price and wage controls were indicated and whether, if introduced, they could meet the challenge of halting the inflationary spiral.

Only a year and two months separated the institution of controls from the next presidential election, and the administration, which had deliberately avoided establishing a large bureaucracy to oversee the controls, moved within the year to dismantle most of the controls. Price and wage advances moderated during the period when controls were in place, but the administration's primary objective was not achieved.

The inflationary spiral was not broken. Nixon won a landslide victory over his opponent, Senator George McGovern and a badly split Democratic party. Most people, including many economists, have forgotten that 1972 and 1973 saw the highest rates of growth experienced by the U.S. economy in the decade and a half ending then, just under 6 percent for each of the two years. This high growth rate coincided with expansions in most other developed economies. These expansions engendered a scramble for raw materials that put additional pressure on the price structure even before the first oil crisis of 1973.

A concatenation of unfavorable events quickly followed. The long post–World War II recovery and reconstruction boom in Western Europe began to run out of steam. In 1974, the United States experienced the onset of the most severe recession in the post–World War II era. Despite the recession, during which the U.S. economy suffered a two-year decline in the GNP, consumer prices increased 11 percent in 1974 and over 9 percent in 1975. Fuel, oil, and coal prices to the consumer increased in 1974 by over 57 percent!

The pileup of difficulties on the economic front, both domestic and international, was made worse by the ignominious resignation of President Nixon in August 1974. Because the Democrats were in control of both houses of Congress, it was difficult for President Ford, a conservative Republican, to provide strong leadership. In retrospect, we can see more clearly what was barely discernible at the time, namely, that the dominant Keynesian approach, which had been the helm of most developed economies for the previous quarter century, could no longer set the course.

With OPEC suddenly raising the price of oil three- or fourfold, inflation accelerated. In turn, most developed countries found it necessary to tighten their monetary and fiscal policies even at the cost of increasing unemployment. The international economic outlook definitely underwent a change, and not for the better.

The Japanese were able to meet the challenge. Many of the developing countries did not lose their expansionary momentum, and the international banking system responded well by recycling the new wealth of the OPEC nations. But the long post–World War II boom had come to an end, an event that had been foreshadowed when the United States in August 1971 was forced to close the gold window.

With the possible exception of Japan, the developed economies were under increasing pressure in the mid-1970s, and their prospects did not appreciably improve during the ensuing quinquennium. Growth lagged, unemployment increased, prices continued to rise—a combination that came to be known as "stagflation." When President Carter took office in 1977, he decided that he had to "reflate" the economy because unemployment, although down from 8.3 percent in 1975, was still above the 7 percent level, much more than the country was willing to accept. The consumer price index continued to advance and increased over 11 percent in 1979 when OPEC precipitated the second oil crisis. In 1980, the consumer price index climbed another 13.5 percent. Although the Federal Reserve Board had belatedly begun to shift course and to tighten credit, the price index in 1981 registered still another advance of over 10 percent.

The deflationary actions of the Federal Reserve Board resulted in two back-to-back recessions in the United States, a mild one in 1980 and a more severe one in 1981–1982. During the second recession, unemployment approached the 10 percent level, averaging 9.5 percent in both 1982 and in 1983.

In the presidential election of 1980, the incumbent Jimmy Carter had difficulty in presenting a coherent approach to the electorate because he was clearly implicated in the preceding inflationary outburst and the decline in business activity. His challenger, Ronald Reagan, attacked inflation, big government, big public spending, wasteful social programs, high taxes, and large federal deficits and promised if elected to reverse these untoward trends. He also stressed that the United States had to enlarge its outlays for defense in order to protect its interests better in a world threatened by an aggressive USSR.

## The Reagan Approach

The Democrats had had their chance and had muffed it; the electorate decided that it had not only little to lose if it changed parties, but that it might possibly come out ahead. Reagan, true to his word, introduced new legislation with a threefold focus: a tax reduction, a reduction in outlays for civilian programs, and an increase in defense spending. Congress went along and gave the president most of what he requested.

The recession of 1981–1982 was much more severe than the recession of 1974–1975, which had been the most severe in the post–World War II era up to that point. But costs aside, the recession finally accomplished the objective of breaking the inflationary spiral. The consumer price index, which had advanced 10 percent in 1981, slowed to 3.2 percent in 1983. The softening in the prices of oil and other raw materials unquestionably contributed to the marked improvement in consumer prices, but most of the credit goes to Paul Volcker and his colleagues on the Federal Reserve Board.

The core of Reagan's economic policy was in concept and commitment anti-Keynesian: He had promised to eliminate the federal deficit by the end of his first administration. He hoped to accomplish this through reduced federal expenditures and higher private investments, which he anticipated would be stimulated by lower taxes. But when the next presidential campaign rolled around in November 1984, the record of accomplishments fell far short of the promises that candidate Reagan had made in 1980.

True, several accomplishments were clearly visible. The back of the remaining inflation had been broken; the economy, disregarding the costs of the severe recession of 1981–1982, had definitely improved; unemployment was down and employment was up; taxes had been reduced; nominal interest rates had dropped; and the budget for the armed services had been substantially increased.

If U.S. elections are fought and won largely on economic issues, as the political scientists insist, then it is clear that the U.S. electorate by a wide majority decided that the president had fulfilled enough of his promises to justify a second term. But many economists, possibly even a majority, were uneasy, if not downright critical, of the policies pursued by the Reagan administration.

They were unable to figure out how supply-side theories (summarized by the Laffer Curve) could be given credit for any of the short-term achievements. And when it came to the longer term, they were distinctly uneasy. The dollar had greatly appreciated, creating a major hurdle for U.S. export industries; the real rate of interest had not declined, which was a barrier to new investment; the federal deficits were rising, not declining, and were not likely to be brought under control; for the first time since World War I, the United States had become a debtor nation; bank failures were rising; the Third World debt problem had not been resolved; and after three years of recovery, unemployment remained above 7 percent.

No one can predict the future shape of the U.S. and world economies. It will be revealed only with the passage of time and from the vantage of a retrospective evaluation. But as Paul Volcker has pointed out, a recession is due before the end of the second Reagan administration unless the United States is to exceed its previous record of the 106 months of sustained expansion. Whether the recession will be precipitated by events overseas or set off by domestic events that will in turn precipitate troubles in the economies of the developed and developing world remains to be seen. Even more important will be the length and depth of the downturn when it comes. But such an untoward development may not occur in 1987 or possibly even later.

## Alternative Theories

In this chapter I must still consider the alternative theories that economists developed as guides to understanding and policy once the Keynesian approach was found wanting. At least a decade has passed since Keynesianism fell from favor. I shall inspect briefly the more important alternatives that have been advanced.

Even in its heyday, Keynesian theory failed to command the support of the entire economics profession. A few economists remained unconvinced by Keynes' theory that the rigidity of wages in a depression made it impossible for the labor market to clear, which in turn led to the underutilization of both industrial capacity and the labor force. Moreover, economists questioned that the cure for such chronic underutilization of resources rested with expansive monetary and fiscal policy whereby governments would compensate for the shortfall in private investment.

Prominent among the anti-Keynesians were the "monetarists," who held that fluctuations in the money supply were the cause of, not the cure for, business fluctuations. They resurrected the "quantity theory of money," a foundation stone of neoclassical economics, which in the 1920s and 1930s had been elaborated into a policy instrument by Irving Fisher of Yale and Henry Simons of Chicago. Oversimplified, monetarists believe that once the central bank—in the United States, the Federal Reserve System—begins to stimulate a sluggish economy by expanding the monetary base, it will sooner or later, when prices rise and keep rising, be forced to reverse its earlier expansionary actions. As a consequence of those actions, the economy will go into decline.

The monetarists see only one way out of this dilemma: The central bank, they hold, should adhere to a fixed rule of expanding the money supply by 3 or 4 percent a year so that there will always be sufficient means of payment to accommodate the long-term growth of the economy. They argue that any other approach is doomed to failure. To make their point, the monetarists argue that increases in the money supply at best can have only short-term and nonsustainable effects on physical output and employment.

Many Keynesians acknowledge that there is some truth in the formulation of the monetarists, but they look in vain for the empirical evidence that fluctuations in the money supply alone can explain everything that occurs in modern, complex, international economies in which the category of money itself is being continuously transformed and expanded.

A second effort to fashion a more valid explanation of economic development to replace the inadequate Keynesian approach focused on a reassessment of the behavior of the labor market. It should be recalled that full employment, as defined by the Council of Economic Advisers at the beginning of the 1960s, was set at 4 percent as an interim goal, with a long-term goal of 3 percent. During the decade of 1975–1985, the annual recorded rate fluctuated between 5.8 (in 1979) and 9.7 percent (in 1982). Conservative economists, reflecting on this growing discrepancy between the earlier goal and the more recent experience, have come up with some ingenious explanations. These include the ideas that the two sets of figures are not comparable, or the unemployed "prefer" not to work, or the higher unemployment rate reflects structural shifts that cannot be avoided.

Women and youth represent a much larger fraction of the labor force in 1960–1970 than in earlier decades and because they habitually have a looser connection to the job market (high turnover), it is not surprising that the unemployment figures experienced an upward tilt. Some significant fraction of the additional unemployment, surely 1.5 percentage points, can be accounted for by this compositional shift.

A second interpretation aimed at minimizing the steep rises in recorded unemployment in recent years relates to one or another variant of "search theory." Economists know that unemployed workers do not accept the first job they locate. By searching longer (which tends to keep the unemployment rate up), they may locate a more desirable job, one that pays better, or one that has other desirable qualities. Some analysts such as Martin Feldstein, the former chairman of the Council of Economic Advisers (1982–1985), have called attention to the combined influence of transfer payments (unemployment insurance) and the tax rate on two-income families, both of which reduce the net monetary cost of remaining unemployed, especially if one subtracts work expenditures such as the costs of travel and eating out.

Another interpretation of the much higher unemployment rate in recent years is traced by some analysts to the structural changes under way in the U.S. and world economies. It is inevitable in their view that the rapid decline of many of our smokestack industries be accompanied by the disemployment of large numbers of workers, many of whom will not quickly, and some of whom will never, be reemployed.

The difficulty with the foregoing theories is not that they are necessarily wrong but that they are too fragile to provide a valid explanation for the phenomenon at hand, which points to a 40 to 50 percent rise in the unemployment rate in the past decade.

In 1958, the British economist, A. W. Phillips, published a seminal article on the relationship of changes in unemployment to changes in money wages in the United Kingdom during the preceding century. It fitted well into the intellectual climate of the day: It supported the Keynesian doctrine by demonstrating that unemployment and inflation were inversely related. The more an economy is stimulated by an increase in money and prices, the lower the rate of unemployment. It is not often that economic formulations can be checked by recourse to a century of reliable data, but that is what Phillips did. Small wonder that he got such an enthusiastic hearing and gained such widespread acceptance. It should, however, come as no great surprise to learn that once the Keynesian approach came under attack, the Phillips curve, as it had been dubbed, was looked at anew; critics who reworked the data concluded "that we can firmly reject the notion of a Phillips curve. . . . At least in the long run, it is untrue that more inflation leads to a lower unemployment rate" (Barro, 1984).

One more major effort has been made in recent years to fill the intellectual void created by the demonstrated weaknesses of the Keynesian approach. Although the doctrine of "rational expectations" was first unveiled by John Muth (1961), it was not until the mid-1970s, after Keynesianism came under heavy attack, that Robert Lucas (1975) of Chicago applied the new doctrine to economic fluctuations. Taking off from the increasingly accepted postulate that economic actors must make their decisions with only imperfect knowledge, Lucas argued that they do the best they can with the data and information that are available to them or that they can obtain at an affordable price within real time.

In the context of macroeconomics, the school of rational expectations argues that active interventions by the Federal Reserve System, in the form of either increasing or decreasing the money supply, will be discounted by informed traders and consequently, will not have any significant impact on their trading decisions.

As with so much of economic theorizing, there is a kernel of truth in this formulation: People seek to use such information as is available to them to inform their present judgments and future actions. But this simple statement does not support the claim that in the United States, business cycles can be modeled according to the theory of rational expectations. It is further afield to contend that traders on the basis of their study of the past will be able to discount the future actions of the monetary authority. It is still more speculative to argue that because of such discounting on the part of traders, all forms of governmental intervention will inevitably fail.

This brief excursus leads directly to a conclusion that many economists have been working assiduously and ingeniously to fill the intellectual and policy vacuums created when Keynesian theory could no longer provide a satisfactory interpretation of events in the developed economies and certainly could no longer point directions for policymakers. But conscientious efforts are not the equivalent of useful results. By no stretch of the imagination does monetarism, the "natural" rate of unemployment, or rational expectations fill the gap.

Where does that leave macroeconomics as a system of thought and as a guide to action? I have intimated before that as an economist educated before *The General Theory* was published, I never fully mastered the corpus or accepted its sweeping policy prescriptions. Moreover, whereas most economists in positions of influence in the United States during the post–World War II era were Keynesians, it does not follow that the generally good performance of the U.S. economy up to the mid-1970s can be ascribed to the influence of Keynesian doctrines on macropolicy. One can merely claim that the two were congruent, or to put it another way, Keynesianism did not provide wrong signals.

The intense discussions and disagreements during the past decade in both academe and the political arena speak to the loss of intellectual security and political consensus that had earlier accompanied the broad public and professional acceptance of the Keynesian synthesis. Clearly no alternative system has as yet been fashioned, much less succeeded in gaining acceptance. The skeptical economist can enjoy the formulation that is more widespread in Europe than at home: The Reagan expansion of post-1983 is Keynesianism reincarnate, based largely on burgeoning defense expenditures.

# 6

# The Economics of the
# American Nobel Laureates

A book entitled *The Skeptical Economist* must make clear to the reader the nature of and reasons for the writer's skepticism. The obligation is that much more compelling once the writer acknowledges that he does not pretend to work on the cutting edge of the problems of economic theory that have engaged the attention and energies of the leading students of the discipline. The sources of my skepticism are centered around the following: the subjects that engage the leaders of the profession; the boundaries within which they circumscribe their inquiries; and the gaps that exist between their analytic efforts and the policy problems facing the society to which they belong.

A related question that warrants attention: Why a chapter on "The Economics of the American Nobel Laureates"? The answer, if not self-evident, is at least close at hand. If one is engaged in assessing the relationships between theory and policy in a social science, such as economics, then it behooves a participant observer to single out for critical assessment not the contributors whom he admires or disapproves of based on a congruence or difference in ideas, politics, or style but rather to select for close inspection the work of major contributors, the more so if a prior selection of such contributors has been made and commands broad acceptance.

In 1968, the Central Bank of Sweden as part of its Tercentenary celebration established a prize in "Economic Science" to be awarded on the same principles and rules as the original Nobel prizes established in 1901. The Nobel prizes are awarded to those who have made "the most important discovery or invention" in the fields of physics, chemistry, physiology, and medicine during the year. According to a recent article by Assar Lindbeck (1985), who has been a member of the Prize Committee in Economics since its establishment in 1968, there was uncertainty among some natural scientists who were members of the academy about whether a social science such as economics would be scientific enough to warrant a prize given on an equal footing with prizes in the hard sciences, such as physics and chemistry. To reduce the inevitable bias in any selection process, I have singled out the American Nobel laureates in economics as representative of the best of contemporary economic thought in this country and if the Swedish Academy has done its work well, in the world. The requirement to be included within the American prizewinners is that the selectee be a U.S. citizen at the time of the award.

In the period from 1969 to 1985 inclusive, there were a total of twenty-three awards in economics, of which U.S. citizens received thirteen. Five of this group were born and educated in whole or in part abroad: Simon Kuznets, Wassily Leontief, Tjalling Koopmans, Gerard Debreu, and Franco Modigliani.

In preparing this chapter, I read the addresses that the recipients delivered in Stockholm on the occasion of the award ceremony. At that event each prizewinner is asked to summarize and elaborate on the facet of his work that the Swedish Academy singled out as the basis for awarding the prize. I deemed it best to circumscribe this chapter by focusing attention on the Stockholm lectures. The ideas put forward in these thirteen presentations exceed my ability to deal with them comprehensively. At best, I can identify some of the highlights.

In each instance I shall explore the same group of questions: What is significant about the problem that the author selected? What is significant about the manner in which he approached it? What policy implications flow from his analysis? To provide some structure to the chapter, I shall follow, with modification, the principles employed by Professor Lindbeck in his article cited above. It is not easy to categorize and group investigators who, having won a Nobel prize, have made significant advances that help differentiate them from their colleagues, even from other Nobel laureates. But even a loose categorization schema is likely to be better than none. Accordingly, I use a fourfold category scheme: (1) General Theory—Paul Samuelson, Kenneth Arrow, Gerard Debreu; (2) Methodology—Wassily Leontieff, Tjalling Koopmans, Herbert Simon, Lawrence Klein; (3) Money and Finance—Milton Friedman, James Tobin, Franco Modigliani; and (4) History and Policy—Simon Kuznets, George Stigler, Theodore Schultz.

## General Theory

With regard to the first group, the titles of their talks are revealing: Samuelson, "Maximum Principles in Analytical Economics"; Arrow,

"General Economic Equilibrium: Purpose, Analytic Techniques, Collective Choice"; Debreu, "Economic Theory in the Mathematical Mode."

It is not clear why the explosive growth in the use of mathematics in economic analysis occurred in the post–World War II era when the first breakthroughs can be traced to the early 1800s; Léon Walras expounded his general equilibrium theory in a mathematical format as early as 1874. Perhaps the simplest explanation for the delay is in the shift in the problems that engaged the economic theorists who set the style for the profession. Alfred Marshall, whose work dominated Anglo-Saxon economics from 1890 to 1936, considered mathematics a useful shortcut, but he did not give it a place on center stage.

Simple geometric and algebraic manipulations had been used by economists for years to explain the behavior of producers and consumers and particularly to demonstrate how demand and supply under varying conditions tend to equilibrate in selected markets or in the economy as a whole. Significant advances in mathematical formulations were also stimulated by developments in modern statistics and the new Keynesian macroeconomics with its basic equations. As noted earlier, World War II precipitated new strategic and operational problems that could best be approached by the use of sophisticated statistical/mathematical models. It might be difficult to prove the following contention, but as a participant-observer, I think that the combination of the malfunctioning of the U.S. economy in the 1930s, the new opportunities for employment of economists after the victory of President Roosevelt, and the constrained job market in the natural sciences (including mathematics) attracted a new strand of mathematically talented young scholars into economics. Whatever the explanation, economic analysis was captured by the mathematical economists after 1945 and Samuelson, Arrow, and Debreu have been among the major contributors.

The prize citations give us an understanding of the nature of these Nobel laureates' contributions: Paul Samuelson, "for the scientific work through which he has developed static and dynamic economic theory and actively contributed to raising the level of analysis in economic science"; Kenneth Arrow (who divided the prize with John R. Hicks of Great Britain), "for their promising contributions to general economic equilibrium theory and welfare theory"; and Gerard Debreu, for having "incorporated new analytic methods into economic theory and for his vigorous reformulation of the theory of general equilibrium."

Some common elements are discernible in these prize citations: Each of the laureates has helped to improve the existing theory by introducing new ways of formulating critical questions and by providing new tools to analyze them. This brings me back to my catena: What questions did they single out? How did they improve the answers? What policy significance flows from their work?

It is not generally known among noneconomists and it is often overlooked by members of the profession that for most of its history, economics has continued to accept Adam Smith's basic formulation that rests on two complementary assumptions: Each buyer and seller in the market is interested in improving his position by engaging in haggling and bargaining; and because of the operation of the price system, demand and supply in the long term will tend toward equilibrium without human intervention. The "unseen hand" can be relied upon to accomplish the daily task of coordinating millions and billions of transactions.

In his 1970 Nobel Prize address, Samuelson said: "What is it that the scientist finds useful in being able to relate a formative description of behavior to the solution of the maximizing problem? That is what a good deal of my own early work was about (p. 250). . . . With the assistance of mathematics I can see a property of ninety-nine dimensional surfaces hidden from the naked eye" (p. 253). He went on to talk about the black magic "by which a maximum formulation permits one to make clearcut impressions about a complicated system involving a large number of variables" (p. 253). Samuelson then recalled that there are limits to the maximizing principle as he discovered when he tried to apply it to the dynamics of the accelerator-multiplier problem. In his concluding observation, he quoted Herbert J. Davenport, Thorstein Veblen's friend, who had said, "There is no reason why theoretical economics should be a monopoly of the reactionaries" (p. 261).

Even on the basis of these highly selected excerpts, we can get a little perspective on the direction of Samuelson's work. As a scientist, he undertook to strengthen the corpus of economic theorizing by making use of an array of sophisticated mathematical tools that enabled him, in addition to correcting earlier errors, to draw new inferences about both static and dynamic problems. He emphasized that "the fanciest of our economic tools are being utilized in enterprises both public and private" (p. 249), and as his closing comment noted above reveals, the new and improved theory can be useful to those who seek to make the economy not only more efficient but also more equitable.

Kenneth Arrow, who won the Nobel prize in 1972, two years after Samuelson, had centered his early work on strengthening the theory of "General Economic Equilibrium," which, he explained in the opening remarks of his Stockholm lecture, used as its point of departure Adam Smith's explanation as to why a balance tends to exist between "the amounts of goods and services that some individuals want to supply and the amounts that other, different individuals, want to sell" (p. 253). Arrow presented, almost as asides, a number of challenging observations.

"Most laymen have no appreciation of the system's strength; they are unwilling to treat it as any considerable departure from normal conditions. . . . Yet, there is no reason to believe that the same forces that work in peace-time would not produce a working system in time of war. . . . The coherence of individual economic decisions is remarkable. It is truly amazing that the lessons of both theory and over a century of history are still so misunderstood."

Arrow then addressed "the Hicks-Samuelson Model of General Equilibrium" and distinguished between its relevance for the study of efficiency and its relevance for distributive justice. He pointed out that the theory is incomplete or inconsistent with prevailing economic doctrines (p. 258). Among Arrow's comments were the following: It is not clear that the system of equations defining general equilibrium has a solution at all, and in a fixed-coefficient technology, there may not be a unique profit-maximizing position for any set of prices. The argument that the marginal rate of substitution must equal the price ratio for each individual breaks down if some consumers make no use of a range of commodities. Demand and supply are not necessarily equal when a distinction has been drawn between scarce goods and free goods. There is a tendency in general equilibrium theory to shift from a local to a global analysis, and Arrow argued that equilibrium prices can be achieved only on the basis of a global viewpoint.

Some of Arrow's most important contributions were made when he extended the theory of general equilibrium to take explicit account of "uncertainty," which he believed provides as much of a normative ideal as an empirical description and leads to different criteria for social policy. Arrow then completed the loop and reminded the reader that if "we want to rely on the virtues of the market but also to achieve a more just distribution, the theory suggests the strategy of changing the initial distribution [of supplies]" (p. 269). He ended by developing a theory of social choices but found that his four required conditions are contradictory.

Arrow went a long way to make the general theory of equilibrium more sophisticated; in the process, he corrected several errors and identified important ways in which the theory could be extended. Most importantly, he clarified many of the open issues to which Abram Bergson had earlier called attention in distinguishing between Pareto-efficiency and social welfare.

In 1983, Gerard Debreu, a French mathematician who had moved as a young man to the Department of Economics at the University of California in Berkeley, received the Nobel Prize for his "rigorous reformulation of the theory of general equilibrium." Debreu and Arrow had been collaborators since the early 1950s, but Debreu's work was directed primarily to developing the mathematical formulations of the theory and not to its policy extensions.

Debreu explained his preoccupation with strengthening the mathematical underpinnings of general equilibrium as follows:

> Axiomatization, by insisting on mathematical rigor, has repeatedly led economists to a deeper understanding of the problems they were studying, and to the use of mathematical techniques that fitted those problems better. It has established secure bases from which explorations could start in new directions. It has freed researchers from the necessity of questioning the work of their predecessors in every detail. Rigor undoubtedly fulfills an intellectual need of many contemporary economic theorists who, therefore, seek it for its own sake, but it is also an attribute of a theory that is an effective thinking tool. Two other attributes of an effective theory are simplicity and generality. . . . Simplicity makes a theory usable by a great number of research workers. Generality makes it applicable to a broad [range] of problems.

Debreu concluded that axiomatization makes available to practitioners "the superbly efficient language of mathematics."

At this point, I am more concerned with the contributions of these three U.S. laureates to economic theory than with assessing their contributions to economic policy. Most contemporary economists rely on general economic equilibrium as their preferred theory; therefore, the clarification, simplification, and extension of that theory must be viewed as a significant advance because the theory provided the discipline with a powerful engine of analysis. Moreover, the adaptability of the theory to mathematical formulations can also be viewed as an advance for the reason stressed by Debreu, namely, that mathematics is such a "superbly efficient language."

What remains open, however, are the questions of whether the specific and concrete uses to which the improved theory has been put have led to important innovations in how decisionmakers think about and, more importantly, are able to solve problems high on their agendas. The answer to this challenge is equivocal. Economists differ markedly in the weights they give to the subjects that they place on their agendas, and furthermore, they differ in their assessments of what constitutes a significant advance. In recent decades, the United States has resorted twice to price controls to slow inflation; it has recognized the importance of protecting the environment (in efforts ranging from interdicting the use of dangerous chemicals to protecting the coastline); it has altered its policies governing the pricing of oil and natural gas; and it has sought a middle way between encouraging free trade among developed and developing nations and shielding many domestic industries from intense foreign competition.

The contributions of the three Nobel laureates added to the power of the extant theories used to assess prices and markets. But it is no downgrading of their achievements to suggest that as of now, their accomplishments are to be found more in the realm of improving the models that economists employ rather than in the contributions that their improved models have been able to make to policy.

## Methodology

My second grouping, under the heading of "Methodology," has four contributors—Wassily Leontief, Tjalling Koopmans, Herbert Simon, and Lawrence Klein—which is the order in which they were awarded the Nobel Prize between 1973 and 1981. But it will probably simplify the analysis and add an element of continuity to the argument if I consider Koopmans's work first, and Simon's last, because in many respects, Koopmans is closest to the theorists and Simon's position is the most radical of the four.

Kenneth Arrow acknowledged his indebtedness to Tjalling Koopmans in these terms: "An essential precondition of our studies was the basic work of Tjalling Koopmans (1951) on the analysis of production in terms of activity analysis. In this, he extended von Neumann's work into a systematic account of the productive structure of the economy. He saw it as a set of activities, each of which could be operated at any level but with the overall levels constrained by initial resource limitations" (p. 265).

Koopmans, in his lecture at the Nobel Prize ceremony, a prize he shared with Leonid V. Kantorovich of the USSR, started with "the productive programs of the individual plant or enterprise," which, he pointed out, was a subject long neglected by economists and considered by some, including A. C. Pigou, as falling outside the discipline. Kantorovich's work of 1939 did not become known in the West until the late 1950s or early 1960s. The general linear model was rediscovered by George Dantzig and his associates while they were working on problems for the U.S. Air Force in World War II and extended, as Koopmans pointed out, to "annual funding problems, inventory and warehousing problems, oil refining operations, electric power investments and many other problems."

Koopmans emphasized that because technology and human needs are universal, it was reasonable to start the analysis with what he called a "pre-institutional theory of the allocation of resources, which postulates allocation efficiency." Koopmans then complicated the analysis by calling attention to the nonlinearities that flow from increasing returns to scale and that bring with them "different problems of institutional frameworks conducive to best allocation" (p. 265). In the second part of his presentation, Koopmans discussed models that allow for technological change and alterations in population size that affect the complex relationships between this generation's consumption level and that of future generations. His final paragraph made clear his perception of the role of the economist qua economist as distinct from his role as citizen: "The economist as such does not advocate criteria of optimality. He may invent them. He will discuss their pros and cons, sometimes before but preferably after trying out their implications. . . . But the ultimate choice is made, usually only implicitly and not always consistently, by the procedures of decisionmaking inherent in the institutions, laws, and customs of society."

Although Koopmans initially in his Nobel Prize address focused on a relatively narrow question in exploring the concepts of optimality within the enterprise, he expanded his reach to explore the uses of these concepts to alternative aggregate growth paths for an entire economy and concluded with a still more ambitious formulation about how this methodology might be used for "development programming."

Wassily Leontief called his Stockholm address, "Structure of the World Economy: Outline of a Single Input-Output Formulation." His opening sentence defined his approach. "The world economy, like the economy of a single country, can be visualized as a system of interdependent processes. Each process, be it the manufacture of steel, the education of youth, or the running of a family household, generates certain output and absorbs a specific combination of inputs. Direct interdependence between two processes arises whenever the output of one becomes an input of the other."

The case that Leontief explored involves a United Nations study of the "Impact of Prospective Environmental Issues and Policies on the International Development Strategy," with an eye on the contours of the world economy in the year 2000 and with separate calculations for the developed and less developed countries under varying assumptions of pollution controls.

Leontief called attention to three sets of constraints: a technological relationship between the level of output and the required quantities of various inputs; the total (physical) amounts of outputs and inputs of each type of good having to be in balance; and a schema developing the interdependence of the prices of all goods and services and the values-added paid out per unit of output by each industry.

The physical subsystem has nine equations with fifteen variables; the prices-values-added system, eight equations with fourteen variables. To arrive at a unique solution, Leontief pointed out that one must fix the values of twelve variables on the basis of outside information. He further pointed out that "the most important but also the most demanding step . . . is the determination of values of hundreds or even thousands of structural coefficients" (p. 830).

Leontief ended his presentation by stressing that his input-output approach does not permit the investigator "to draw any special or general conclusions before he or someone else completes the always difficult and seldom glamorous task of ascertaining the necessary facts" (p. 833).

Input-output analysis represents a significant new approach to the systematic study of industries, national economies, and even the world economy. Moreover, data rather than speculations become the controlling element. But the difficulties and costliness of the data collection and data manipulation are so high that the system remains more a promise than a reality. There are additional difficulties that derive from the fact that a considerable number of the technical coefficients do not remain stable and that the steep rise and decline of various indicators add further complications to the computational task. But Leontief's ambitious input-output schema is a powerful corrective to the dominant model-building exercises characteristic of so many contemporary economists who believe that they can capture the essence of economic activity by resorting to a few strong assumptions, a handful of facts, and sophisticated mathematical transformations. Leontief reminded them that if they are serious about what they are doing, they have no option but to address and solve the data question. Unless and until they do, they cannot and should not be taken seriously.

Lawrence Klein's Nobel Prize lecture in 1980 carried the title: "Some Economic Scenarios for the 1980s." As the long-time director of Project LINK, a multination system of econometric forecasting with its base at the Wharton School, Klein drew on two models—the Wharton model for the U.S. economy and a world model. At the time of his Stockholm lecture, the LINK project involved seventeen OECD industrial countries, eight socialist, and four regional models of developing countries. Klein's analysis proceeded within the framework of a general equilibrium system, but unlike the studies of the other Nobel laureates that we have so far reviewed, Klein worked with masses of real data drawn from the recent past (1945–1970), which he analyzed for trends that provide a point of departure for his baseline projection for the 1980s. His principal finding for the U.S. economy was a retardation in its rate of growth from 4 percent up to 1970 to approximately 3 percent since that time. In addition to slower growth, Klein read the data as pointing to more inflation, higher interest costs, an elevated rate of unemployment, and balance of payment problems. Klein put heavy weight on the rise in the price of energy and on lower productivity growth, the causes of which he said remain obscure.

Klein explained that his trend projections for 1990 are predicated on introducing as much business cycle control as possible for the initial two to three years and then putting the major emphasis on recent medium-term trend paths. His solution is constrained by the following: equality between the real growth rate and the real interest rate; a stable savings ratio; a stable wage share of GNP; a stable velocity ratio; and tolerable deficits, internal and external. The model contains about 1,000 or more interrelated equations.

In his search for a set of economic policies that can provide a balanced solution, Klein called attention to the following dimensions of his model: Fiscal and monetary policies are appropriately constrained so that public expenditures as a percentage of GNP are continued on trend and taxes are kept high enough to generate an essential domestic budget balance. In his analysis of the "Base Case of the World Economy," Klein's results paralleled those for the U.S. economy; this reflected his belief that "most parts of the world are experiencing the same kinds of economic pressures and converging towards a similar response and outcome" (p. 281).

Klein identified eight major world disturbances from the Korean War to the Iranian Revolution during the 1950s, 1960s, and 1970s. In modeling the world economy for 1990, he structured his approach into two parts. He developed his base case on linear projections and then superimposed disturbances on it (p. 289). He anticipated a shortfall of oil by mid-decade that could lead to a 50–100 percent increase in its price (p. 290). He warned that the world could also face a record insufficiency of food. And he warned of the possibility of simultaneous debt defaults.

Klein ended his presentation with a basically optimistic scenario. He pointed out, however, that it would not be easy to return to a 4 percent growth rate even if there were a significant shift of the U.S. economy from a consumption to a savings and investment orientation.

If one of the central objectives of economic analysis is a deeper understanding of economic reality and if another, more ambitious, objective is to improve short- and mid-term forecasts, the Wharton model and Project LINK represent a major advance. The key components are imaginative modeling, good programming, recourse to powerful computers, and the active and sustained participation of many collaborating economists in a large number of nations. However, the econometric forecasts are found seriously wanting when the 1985 experience is juxtaposed with the 1980 projections: Oil has dropped in price and food surpluses are common. However, we can reach a more favorable view of this effort if we compare LINK with the difficulties experienced by the National Bureau of Economic Research when it sought in the

1930s (before the development of econometrics and the computer) to analyze the congruencies between business cycle movements in the United States and a few large European countries.

Many economists, in the United States as well as abroad, are not aware that in 1978 the Nobel Prize for economic science went to a professionally educated psychologist, Herbert Simon of Carnegie-Mellon "for his pioneering research into the decision-making process within economic organizations." Simon has been one of the most creative minds on the American academic scene. His contributions span a range of subjects and disciplines, from his early important work, *Administrative Behavior* (1947), to his continuing work in the field of artificial intelligence.

Simon has made significant contributions to decision theory; it is this work that won him the Nobel Prize. Lindbeck, in his article to which we referred earlier, noted in passing that the Swedish Academy has been disinclined to honor investigators whose primary thrust has been the critical demolition of the work of others. In spite of this observation, it is difficult to read Simon's address on "Rational Decision-Making in Business Organizations" as anything other than a broadside indictment of major trends in neoclassical economics that continues to postulate that economic agents are rational and pursue a maximizing approach in all their decisions.

Simon presented a strong case to support his thesis that these assumptions are contrary to the ways human beings behave and that the results that obtain from these strong assumptions are bad theorizing and lead to worse policy. There were three critical elements in Simon's reformulation of the theory of decisionmaking in the firm. The first held that decisionmakers "satisfice," they do not maximize. Decisionmakers "satisfice" because they lack the information and knowledge to calculate all the alternatives they need to reach a maximizing answer. The fact is that they must operate under what Simon called "bounded rationality." Further, Simon emphasized that even with modern computers, it is not cost-efficient to undertake all of the calculations that would be required for the decisionmaker to make a choice that would maximize his gains.

Reworded, Simon's thesis held that "replacing the classical theory by a model of bounded rationality begins to emerge when we examine situations involving decision-making under uncertainty and imperfect competition" (p. 497). Simon ascribed importance to the process of decisionmaking and called attention to the problem of "subgoal" identification, the resolution of which hinges in large measure on the "knowledge, experience and organizational environment of the decisionmaker," which in turn, will be influenced by "self-interest and power drives" (p. 500).

Simon speculated about why the neoclassical revival, rather than an alternative approach directed to improving decision theory, occurred after 1960. He offered a series of speculations, one of which suggested that economists become "satisficers" when it comes to their own theories; "the flowering of mathematical economics and econometrics . . . have absorbed their energies and postponed encounters with the inelegancies of the real world" (p. 504); they have failed to allocate their resources appropriately among neoclassical theory, macroeconometrics, and descriptive decision theory. In his conclusion, he called attention to the most potent of all reasons: "You cannot beat something with nothing" (p. 509). "Once a theory is well entrenched, it will survive many assaults of improved evidence." It will prefer to hold on to "contrary-to-fact assumptions" rather than risk, I would add, the collapse of the elaborate superstructure.

Despite his intellectual stature, Simon's impact on mainline economic analysis has been marginal. Moreover, it is likely to remain marginal until the profession finally decides that the behavior of the firm can no longer be postulated but must be studied. As long as economists use the model of Adam Smith's entrepreneur in explaining the decisions that General Motors has or has not taken during the past decade, Simon will continue to be an outsider.

Are there any generalizations that can be drawn about the work of the four Nobel laureates whose contributions I have grouped under the heading of methodology? There appear to be several. Each prizewinner has been concerned with the development of a new approach that would bring economic analysis closer to the real world, even if the problems he addressed vary widely from the best use of inputs within a firm to developing an econometric forecasting model for the world's economy. A second point is that each developed his methodological approach to utilize the computational capacity of the computer. Another similarity is that each relied on theory to inform his approach while perfecting new methods that would facilitate the collection and assimilation of large bodies of statistical data.

One further observation bears on the amount of detailed knowledge of the specific economic environment that each approach requires: from the firm's resources and modes of production in the case of linear programming to the broad institutional influences that shape the decisionmaking of a large corporation. Without detailed knowledge and understanding of the factors and processes that are involved, solutions would not be possible. These four economists have moved a substantial distance from the traditional paradigm that relied on the manipulation of a few strong assumptions such as utility maximization and market competition.

## Money and Finance

I now come to the work of three contributors whose principal efforts have been focused on gaining a deeper understanding of the role of money and finance in the operations of modern economies: Milton Friedman, James Tobin, and Franco Modigliani. Milton Friedman, Nobel Prize laureate in 1976, is a product of the Graduate Department of Economics at Chicago in the early 1930s. At that time, the department was populated by many stars, including Jacob Viner, Frank H. Knight, Henry Schultz, Lloyd Mints, and Henry Simons, all of whom Friedman singled out in the published version of his Nobel address. Friedman was also influenced by Arthur F. Burns, who taught him during his undergraduate years at Rutgers, and Harold Hotelling, Wesley C. Mitchell, and John M. Clark, with whom he studied at Columbia in 1933–1934. After various research assignments on the East Coast, a one-year teaching post at the University of Minnesota in 1945, and an earlier year at Wisconsin, Friedman joined the Chicago University faculty in 1946, where he remained until his retirement from active teaching, though not from lecturing and writing, in 1977.

Friedman began his Nobel lecture with a reaffirmation of his view first developed in the early 1950s that there are no fundamental differences between the social and the natural sciences. "In both, there is no 'certain' substantive knowledge; only tentative hypotheses that can never be 'proved,' but can only fail to be rejected, hypotheses in which we may have more or less confidence. . . . In both, experiment is sometimes possible. . . . Positive scientific knowledge that enables us to predict the consequences of a possible course of action is clearly a prerequisite for normative judgment."

Friedman told how his teacher Wesley C. Mitchell explained to him that scholars have every incentive to pursue a "value-free" science. Otherwise, Mitchell had said, they will not know whether the course of action they recommend will in fact promote the objective they recommend. I had pressed Mitchell hard on several occasions during the Great Depression to formulate some preferred policy alternatives, based on his lifetime of study of "business cycles." He repeatedly refused, saying that he did not know enough. There is an unbridgeable canyon between Mitchell's and Friedman's views and behavior with respect to value-free social science. Friedman has supported a host of political initiatives, from recommending the scrapping of Social Security to favoring a constitutional amendment to force Congress to submit balanced budgets.

Friedman selected for his Nobel lecture "Inflation and Unemployment" as a case study, in his words, of the "positive scientific character of economics." He demonstrated how new data and new analyses have contributed to changing economists' views about the relationship of the two and undermined the prior belief of the profession in the fixed relationship between them.

Friedman put forward the hypothesis of a natural rate of unemployment, in which the important variables are not the nominal changes in prices and wages, but the real forces that underlie the long-term movements of the economy. Once the "unanticipated" consequences of inflation are taken into account, as they will be, unemployment will settle at its natural rate and any attempt by policymakers to affect its level will lead to excessive inflation or deflation (p. 249). Friedman suggested that it is wrong to assume that a high level of recorded unemployment is evidence of inefficient use of resources. "This view is seriously in error," he said (p. 249), because a low rate may be forcing workers to be employed for more hours than they wish or it may reflect a highly static, rigid economy with a fixed place for everybody.

Next, Friedman explored the existence of a positively shaped Phillips curve and suggested that this is what happened in six out of seven industrialized countries in the two quinquennia 1966–1970 and 1970–1975.

Further on, Friedman presented what he called "A tentative hypothesis" which held "that the rate of unemployment will be largely independent of the average rate of inflation" (p. 254), once the changes in the inflation rate are fully anticipated. He acknowledged, however, that transitional periods may be measured in quinquennia or decades, not years.

Friedman concluded that "the present situation cannot last." It will either "degenerate into hyperinflation . . . adjust to a situation of chronic inflation . . . or governments will adopt policies that will produce a low rate of inflation." In Friedman's view, he has told "a perfectly standard story of how scientific theories are revised."

Whereas many of the Nobel laureates have held consulting positions with the U.S. government or with international agencies, James Tobin was the only one among the thirteen American prizewinners who held a senior policy position, serving as an original member of Kennedy's Council of Economic Advisers (1961–1963).

In his introductory autobiographical notes Tobin reported that he was attracted to economics for two reasons—a taste and talent for theoretical reasoning and quantitative analysis and the hope that "improved understanding could better the lot of mankind." Tobin studied at Harvard in what he called the golden age—the middle and late 1930s. After war service, he returned to Harvard to teach, and in 1950 he moved to Yale, where he has been ever since.

Tobin entitled his Nobel lecture "Money and Finance in the Macro-Economic Process," the subject area that has commanded most of his research interests and energies. This is suggested by the citation of the Swedish Academy that accompanied his award: "for his analysis of financial markets and their relations to expenditure decisions, employment, production and prices."

At the outset, Tobin reminded us that "Theoretical macro-economic models of one kind of another are very influential. They guide the architects of econometric forecasting models. They shape the thinking of policy makers. They color the views of journalists, managers, teachers, housewives, politicians and voters" (p. 312).

While Tobin held that the major conclusions of the Keynes-Hicks apparatus remain intact he added some important features including more precision regarding time—the model is one step in a dynamic sequence, not a repetitive equilibrium into which the economy settles. He believed that it is necessary to track stocks of investment and capital as well as savings and wealth. Furthermore, the traditional aggregation of all nonmonetary assets into a single asset with a common interest rate is not justified. As many categories as are appropriate for the purpose at hand should be introduced. He stipulated that the transactions that affect changes in the money stock be analyzed because they alter the wealth and portfolio positions of economic agents. Walras' Law requires that demand functions be explicitly specified for the whole range of assets.

At the beginning and at the end of his lecture, Tobin called attention to important theoretical and practical issues that he would not address. He noted that he had no answer for why "paper that makes no intrinsic contribution to utility or technology is held at all and has positive value in exchange for goods and services" (p. 314). But he did not believe that the answer to this "deep question" is prerequisite to pragmatic monetary theory. Finally, he noted that he had focused on "the ways fiscal and monetary policies alter macroeconomic outcomes in the short and the long run" but he had left to others the optimal design of such policies (p. 342).

In discussing "macro economics and full general equilibrium," Tobin noted that he is taking off from Kenneth Arrow's Nobel lecture, "Were there a full set of simultaneously cleared markets for all commodities, including commodities for future and contingent delivery, there would be no macroeconomic problems, no need for money, and no room for fiscal and monetary stabilization" (p. 315). Tobin noted Arrow's demonstration that the general equilibrium paradigm cannot assure that collective or public goods will be supplied in optimal amounts. Instead of hiding behind the concept of "market failures," as most traditionalists do, to explain alien phenomena, Tobin, following Keynes, believed that the core issue relates to the "virtual absence of future markets . . . other than money itself" (p. 315). And he continued, "In short the financial and capital markets are at their best highly imperfect coordinators of saving and investment. This failure of coordination is a fundamental source of macro-economic instability and of the opportunity for macro-economic policies of stabilization" (p. 316).

The heart of Tobin's presentation was directed to "A Multi-Asset Model of the Delineation of Output and Prices in the Short-Run," based on a four asset discrimination: equities, government bonds, base money, and foreign currency assets. The sum of the four supply flows is total savings. Tobin then demonstrated that "asset demand functions cannot be expected to be stable in the face of significant variations in the economic environment" (p. 328). Tobin saw the innovative aspect of his approach to be the "integration of saving and portfolio decisions." Conventional models seek equilibrium solutions "independent of flows of new savings." But his new model is superior in that it introduces continuous or discrete time so that the analysis is dynamic in that "flows alter stocks which in turn condition subsequent flows" (p. 331).

In the concluding section of the paper he considered possible extensions and elaborations of the model. Tobin reminded us that "financial policies are not neutral in the long run any more than in the short run" and that "in the background is the competition between capital and public debt for allocation of limited wealth. . . . Macro-economic market failures make it possible that government financial interventions can improve welfare, but they by no means guarantee that actual policies will do so" (p. 342).

The 1985 winner of the Nobel Prize in Economics, Franco Modigliani, was the fifth foreign-born U.S. citizen among the thirteen winners, having arrived in this country in 1939, a refugee from fascist Italy. He took his doctorate at the New School for Social Research where he worked with Jacob Marshak, an earlier refugee who had come to the United States via Germany and for whom Modigliani has the most profound intellectual and personal regard. After a number of short-term appointments at various institutions in the East and Midwest, Modigliani in 1962 joined the faculty at MIT, which has been his permanent home.

The title of his Stockholm lecture, "Life Cycle, Individual Thrift and the Wealth of Nations," dealt with a theme that has been central to his work for more than three decades. Modigliani began by reminding his audience that Keynes, in his repudiation of traditional economics, challenged the deeply held view that thrift via capital accumulation and greater productivity was the source of economic progress and wealth creation. Keynes, postulating that savings were a function of income, warned that the drive to save would result in an insufficiency of consumption and could bring on a depression that could keep an economy mired in an underemployed state because of the tendency to "oversave."

After noting the major empirical studies by Kuznets and others that undermined the Keynesian approach to savings, Modigliani reviewed the original formulation of his Life Cycle Hypothesis (LCH), which he had developed initially with his student Richard Brumberg in the early 1950s and later expanded and reconstructed in 1979. The core of the theory is that the consumer will choose to consume at a reasonably stable rate that will depend on the present value of his labor income plus bequests and "not at all on income accruing currently" (p. 6).

In summarizing the key implications of his revised 1978 theory, Modigliani called attention to the following: The savings rate of a country is entirely independent of its per capita income; different national savings rates are consistent with an identical individual (life-cycle) behavior; the savings rate with identical individual behavior will be higher in countries with the higher long-run growth rate; the wealth-income ratio is a decreasing function of the growth rate; an economy can accumulate a very substantial stock of wealth relative to income, even if no wealth is passed on by bequests; the main parameter that controls the saving rate is the prevailing length of retirement (pp. 8–9).

The heart of Modigliani's presentation was taken up with a systematic review and assessment of the successive contributions to both the theory and the empirical studies of the LCH. He focused particular attention on the role of bequests and the bequest motive (pp. 17ff). He concluded that bequeathed wealth in the United States accounts for no more than 20 to 25 percent of the total. He emphasized that the bequest motive "is important only when one reaches the top 20 percent of the distribution of resources" (p. 27). That means "that something like 4/5 of households tend to behave broadly in accordance with the *basic* LCH" (p. 28).

Modigliani concluded with a few summary policy implications. With respect to short-run stabilization policy, he noted that monetary policy can affect aggregate demand not only via investment but "also through the market value of assets and consumption. Attempts at restraining or stimulating demand through transitory income taxes or rebates can be expected to have small effects on consumption."

Long-run propositions: "Expenditures financed by deficit tend to be paid by future generations; that financed by taxes is paid by the current generation." Modigliani noted that the crowding-out effect may be moderated by inflows of foreign capital, by the debt leading to productive government investment, and by the existence of slack in the economy. He concluded that LCH suggests that "a good case can be made for a so-called cyclical balanced budget" (p. 30). Keynes may have been seriously wrong in his analysis of savings—and that is the burden of the contribution of the LCH—but in the end, Modigliani did not differ from Keynes in his policy prescription.

## History and Policy

For reasons more of convenience than of logic or analytic clarity, the three remaining American Nobel Laureates—Simon Kuznets, George Stigler, and Theodore Schultz—have been grouped under the rubric "History and Policy." Another justification for grouping them together is on the principle of exclusion: None of them fits more appropriately under any of the other headings of theory, methodology, or money and finance.

Simon Kuznets won the Nobel Prize in 1971, three years after it was established and a year after it had first been awarded to an American, Paul Samuelson. He had been a student of Wesley C. Mitchell at Columbia University and later, as a member of the National Bureau of Economic Research, he had spearheaded some of the bureau's most important studies on seasonal, cyclical, and secular trends, work that was crucial to Mitchell's continuing investigations into the business cycle. But Kuznets was too independent a researcher and too interested in developing larger syntheses to continue working closely with Mitchell. Kuznets continued his affiliation with the bureau for some time, but Arthur F. Burns replaced him in the early 1930s as Mitchell's principal associate.

The citation that accompanied Kuznets' Nobel Prize provided a clue to the scale and scope of his research within one of his several fields of specialization—economic growth. "For his empirically founded interpretation of economic growth which has led to new and deepened insight into the economic and social structure and process of development." The title of his Stockholm address was "Modern Economic Growth: Findings and Reflections." In his opening sentence, he stated, "A country's economic growth may be defined as a long-term rise in capacity to supply increasingly diverse economic goods to its population, this growing capacity based on advancing technology, and the institutional and ideological adjustments that it demands." All three components of the definition are important.

It is worth noting in connection with Kuznets' boundary setting that most economists have omitted both technology and institutional adjustment from their models because, among other reasons, they did not know how to encapsulate them. Moreover, most contributors to economic analysis have not found it necessary, feasible, or even desirable to develop their theories on the basis of a close study and ordering of the facts of economic life. These last comments supplement Lindbeck's commentary (1985, p. 45): The prize to Kuznets is also "a good example of an award for inductive rather than deductive analysis, as Kuznets' forte has been to find new facts, and interrelations—i.e. "new truths"—about the real world, with the help of common sense reasoning and with a minimum of formal models."

Kuznets identified six characteristics of economic growth during the past 200 years, predicated on the development and diffusion of technological advances, which he pointed out, affect

> barely one quarter of the world's population: High rates of growth of per capita product; the high rate of rise in productivity; a high rate of structural transformation of the economy; closely related and extremely important changes in the structures of society and its ideology; the propensity of economically developed countries to reach out to the rest of the world by means of modern transport and communication—thus making for one world; and the spread of modern economic growth, limited by the fact that modern technology has not yet effectively penetrated three quarters of the world's population.

Kuznets' subsummary divided the foregoing six propositions into two that relate to aggregate rates, two to structural transformation, and two to international spread.

In developing "some implications" from the above, Kuznets first took note of the limitation of the national income accounting systems that fail to include many costs (pollution) and benefits (greater longevity). He then pointed out that growth leads to shifts in the relative position of different groups in a society and that a key determinant of long-term growth is the flexibility of the society to moderate such conflicts through the sovereign state. Kuznets emphasized the fact that a powerful new technology will bring about surprises and unexpected results that can be recognized only in retrospect.

Kuznets concluded his presentation with some remarks about the less developed countries. He emphasized that growth "demands a stable, but flexible, political and social framework" (p. 254), but stated that most less developed countries do not have such a framework. He went on to suggest that modern technology with its emphasis on labor-saving devices, and Western institutions with their emphasis on financial responsibility and the pursuit of economic interest "may not be suited to the more traditional life patterns of the agricultural communities that dominate in many less developed countries." Kuznets saw his work as linked directly to Adam Smith whose *Wealth of Nations*, he pointed out, could have been called "The Economic Growth of Nations."

George Stigler is the most recent of the three Chicago recipients of the Nobel Prize in Economics (1982). Like Kuznets, he has a strong historical orientation, even though his interest in history has more to do with the intellectual development of economics as a discipline rather than with the evolution of modern economic societies.

The citation stated that he had been awarded the prize "for his seminal studies of industrial structure, functioning of markets, and causes and effects of public regulation." His Nobel lecture, "The Process and Progress of Economics," was primarily a contribution to "the sociology of knowledge" that used the development and refinement of economic theory as a case in point. Specifically, Stigler dealt with two facets of his own work in which he made fruitful contributions to economic analysis—information theory and regulation. Because the heart of his presentation dealt with economics as a science and economists as scientists, we shall focus on these two elements.

Here is Stigler's definition: "A science consists of interacting practitioners" (p. 253). A prescientific stage in economics such as mercantilism is characterized by the absence of such practitioners and hence the absence of cumulative progress; progress becomes for Stigler the hallmark of a science. Economics as a science dates from the publication of Smith's *Wealth of Nations* in 1776. According to this definition, philosophy, history, even theology would qualify as a science; the term would then become a synonym for any discipline.

Stigler then defined economics as an empirical science, the central task of which is to "provide general understanding of the real world, and ultimately all of its theories and techniques must be instrumental to that task" (p. 256). "If the problems of economic life changed frequently and radically, and lacked a large measure of continuity in their essential nature, there could not be a science of economics. . . . The change of problems and methods would also undermine the training of economists" (p. 257).

According to Stigler, "the most fundamental of these central problems is the theory of value," which must explain how the comparative values of different goods and services are established. Until that problem is solved, "it is not possible to analyse for scientific purposes what will be produced and in what quantities, how the resources will be employed . . . and how the resources will be valued" (p. 257).

But Stigler knew that "an empirical science has a second, and vastly more important, interest in and responsiveness to, contemporary problems: its received theory will at times be incapable of dealing with these problems" (p. 257).

Stigler presented a series of interesting observations about the behavior of any group of scientists, including economists: They are hostile to new theories because the new threatens their capital with obsolescence; they are averse to risk and few will make the sizable investment of fashioning new theories rather than relying on the existing corpus; and finally, "it takes a theory to beat a theory."

With genuine modesty, Stigler explained that his major contributions to the theory of information and to the economics of regulation benefited from the fact that he did not have to combat well-entrenched theories. He simply had to make use of "that principal tool of economic analysis, the theory of utility-maximizing behavior. Once the economist can identify the costs and returns from various actions, this theory allows him to make predictions of behavior that have been reasonably successful" (p. 263). The key word was *reasonably*. Herbert Simon, as we noted earlier, would surely dissent.

Stigler concluded his address with this pungent statement: "Still, learning more about how this search for new knowledge proceeds is itself a worthy search for new knowledge, and we shall not abandon it." It is indeed fortunate for economics that one of its leading practitioners has had a deep and continuing interest in the cumulative growth of economic knowledge. What remains problematic is whether "each epoch in economic life would require its own theory," and as Stigler added, in that case, "short epochs would get short-lived theories" (p. 257). But that is exactly the conclusion that John M. Clark reached in the late 1950s. He told me at one of our monthly lunches that he had concluded that the best of economic theories in our fast-changing world could not expect to survive more than one decade.

Theodore W. Schultz, the third of the Chicago laureates, shared the Nobel Prize in 1979 with Sir Arthur Lewis, who though a member of the Princeton faculty, was a British citizen and therefore is not included in this review. The citation read: "For their promising research into economic development with particular consideration of the problems of developing countries." Unlike his colleagues Stigler and Friedman, Schultz did not study at Chicago but took his degree at Wisconsin and spent the early years of his academic career at Iowa State College in Ames, which in the decade of the Great Depression, had a talented group of economists and statisticans on its faculty. He moved to Chicago in 1943.

His Stockholm lecture is called "The Economics of Being Poor." Its contents are a succinct presentation of what Schultz had learned from his intensive and extensive studies of agricultural economies throughout the world, with particular insights that he obtained by applying the concepts of human capital to the lives and prospects of farm populations, particularly in the less-developed nations. Schultz set forth a series of strong propositions, the cullings of a lifetime of field research and tough thinking. Most of the people in the world are poor and most of them are farmers. They have to spend half of their income on food. Economists are wrong when they assume that poor people are not interested in improving their lot or that they would be incapable of taking advantage of opportunities to do so.

Furthermore, economists have overrated the importance of tillable land and do not give appropriate weight to improvements in human capital as long-term factors that affect agricultural progress and the welfare of farmers. Many things have changed since Ricardo and Malthus first formulated their theories of rent and population, and continued reliance on their approaches has blocked understanding of current-day problems and prospects for the future.

Schultz's main recommendation was to improve the human agent via investments in population quality, specifically child care, home and work experience, the acquisition of information and skills through schooling, and specific investment in health (p. 245). The resources to make these investments would have to come largely from alterations in the ways in which farm families live (fewer children) and from their increased productivity. But Schultz noted, economic incentives are distorted to the disadvantage of most farmers because governments want to keep food prices low for their burgeoning urban populations. And these same governments believe that industrialization is the key to economic development.

Despite repeated egregious errors of economic policy by most third world governments, the human capital stock is improving as a result of large educational outlays, improvements in health, and the diffusion of agricultural research, spearheaded by international bodies but reinforced by local efforts. Schultz ended by quoting Alfred Marshall, "Knowledge is the most powerful engine of production; it enables us to subdue Nature and satisfy our wants." Schultz was surely right in maintaining that the improvement in human capital and advances in knowledge hold most of the answer to rural poverty. And it would be difficult to contest his view that governmental economic policies are frequently disadvantageous to the farm population. But two critical issues remain: How can weak governments encourage rates of change that may exceed their capacity to shape and direct? (See Kuznets earlier.) And second, is it correct, as Schultz suggested, that the rise in the numbers of the population is not a serious threat to improving its quality? Weak governments and slow progress in family planning efforts are likely to impede, in the short and middle term, significant improvements in the stock of human capital.

## Overview

It should be recalled that I undertook this summary of the lectures delivered at Stockholm by the thirteen American Nobel Laureates in Economics between 1970 and 1985 to obtain an overview of the state of contemporary economic analysis as exemplified by the work of its leading contributors. A few tentative generalizations can be extracted from this review.

At one level the Nobel laureates, with the possible exceptions of Simon Kuznets and Herbert Simon, appear to be engaged in the same task or tasks—to improve, refine, and extend the major corpus of economic analysis, both neoclassical and general equilibrium.

At another level, we can distinguish among them on several fronts: Their methodological approaches have varied from almost exclusive preoccupation with the mathematical underpinnings of the theory (Gerard Debreu) to the econometric approach of Lawrence Klein.

Using their views of Keynes's synthesis as another criterion, we can identify those for whom Keynes's macroeconomic structure served as the foundation for their work (Tobin, Klein, and Modigliani); those who believed that Keynes's emphasis on monetary and fiscal policy were at best time-conditioned, at worst, misleading and erroneous (Friedman); those whose approaches were only tangentially affected by Keynes's work (Koopmans and Leontief).

Another interesting axis along which the work of the laureates can be considered is their closeness or distance from issues of policy. The three Nobel laureates from Chicago—Friedman, Stigler, and Schultz—were willing, even eager, to extend their analysis to the policy arena. All insisted that by intervening in the operations of markets, "government" usually succeeds in making matters worse. Arrow, Kuznets, Tobin, and Modigliani had a more open view: they recognized important institutional factors that prevent markets from either performing with optimal efficiency or assuring distributive justice. Consequently, they envisioned various roles for governmental intervention, while acknowledging the possibility that many interventions may turn out badly.

As suggested above, Simon Kuznets and Herbert Simon did not fit into any of these categories. Kuznets, while using important economic categories such as capital, savings, and productivity, worked on a much larger canvas that allowed him to consider the interactions among major systems—economic, technological, demographic, political, and even ideological—to explain long-term economic growth. Simon, by noting the importance of bounded rationality in a world of uncertainty, subgoal optimization, and the costs of information gathering and computing, has launched a major attack on mainline economic theorizing. As Stigler pointed out, it is not easy for new ideas to make headway against entrenched opinions and these difficulties are multiplied when they threaten the capital investment of the establishment. But it is well to remember that sooner or later contemporary theories will have to prove themselves in the marketplace of ideas or face major write-downs in their values.

# 7

# Changing Times, Changing Theories

It was pointed out in Chapter 5 that there was no clear concordance between the dominant economic theory of the day and the transformations of the U.S. economy during the long sweep of industrialization following the Civil War. In Chapter 6, I set out the highlights of the contributions that the thirteen U.S. Nobel Laureates have made to economic theory and analysis during the period that the prize had been awarded.

In the present chapter I shall look more closely at the duality between the work of the Nobel laureates and the changing times that must serve as a point of reference for assessing the relevance of the methods, theories, and policy recommendations that the prizewinners advanced.

The majority of the laureates, eight of thirteen, began or completed their graduate studies in economics in the 1920s or early 1930s. Only five—James Tobin, Franco Modigliani, Kenneth Arrow, Lawrence Klein, and Gerard Debreu—belong to the younger generation, that is, students who were trained largely in the 1940s. In light of this distribution, there are good reasons to start an account of "Changing Times" with the 1920s, a decade that played a formative role in shaping the experiences of the older prizewinners.

## The New Era

In the early 1920s, the U.S. economy was still characterized by a large agricultural sector: 30 percent of the population earned its livelihood from farming. At the same time, the United States was the most advanced industrial nation in the world as it was in the forefront of large-scale manufacturing, best exemplified by Henry Ford's assembly line. Although we boasted of a superior railroad system that linked East and West and North and South, it took four days to travel from New York City to San Francisco. Sixty years after the end of the Civil War, the South was still on the periphery, not in the mainstream, of the nation's economy. The vast majority of U.S. blacks, most of whom barely eked out an existence, lived on the deteriorating cotton farms in the Southeast. Southern white farmers and millhands were only slightly better off.

The country had a large urban population, circa 51 percent. But the move to suburbia had just begun with the much enlarged sales of automobiles to the more affluent members of the middle class. In 1928, a leading member of the Columbia Economics Department, E.R.A. Seligman, completed a major investigation financed by General Motors in which he put his professional sign of approval on consumers' buying cars on credit!

Only a small number of married women, and a still smaller number of married women with children, were employed away from home. For the most part, working wives were drawn from among black and immigrant groups and from lower-income white females who lived in mill villages.

In 1929, the last year of the booming 1920s, the total GNP amounted to $103 billion and the population totaled 122 million. The per capita income, therefore, amounted to $850 in 1929 dollars.

A few additional characteristics of the New Era economy are worth noting. Trade unions were relatively few; their greatest concentration was in transportation, construction, printing, and selected manufacturing sectors in the North such as men's and women's clothing. The trade unions were not represented in the heartland of U.S. industry (steel, rubber, automobiles, farm machinery, chemicals).

Only a minority of the population had graduated from high school, and fewer than one in twenty of the younger age group were college graduates.

At the end of World War I, the United States was transformed from a debtor to a creditor nation, and during the booming 1920s, U.S. banks made many soft loans to developing countries that helped to stimulate and sustain the long period of U.S. prosperity but sped and deepened the depression once the loans turned sour.

U.S. agriculture had expanded during World War I and during the immediate postwar boom, but it was caught in the vise of the price collapse of 1920–1921 from which it never recovered. Despite the opposition of the Republican party, which dominated the national political scene throughout the 1920s, to any extension of the federal government's intervention in the economy, Congress took an initial step to assist farmers in 1926, a policy from which it has not been able to extricate itself to this day.

There are two ways to view economic changes. The first emphasizes the elements of continuity. The other focuses attention on the new. Since the 1920s, dramatic changes have occurred in the size of the population, the productivity of the economy, and the labor force participation of women. The agricultural sector, which today provides employment for no more than 3 percent of the labor force, has declined substantially, urbanization has increased, and radical changes in communications and transportation have occurred.

## The Internationalization
## of the U.S. Economy

The last provides a bridge to the second principal arena of change. The U.S. economy has been transformed from one with a local and regional basis to a national and international economy, and most recently to one with world linkages. We noted earlier the continued isolation of the South from the rest of the nation, as late as the New Era and one might add as late as the Great Depression. It was not until World War II with the spur of defense dollars, and later with the widespread introduction of air-conditioning, that the South was effectively integrated into the national economy.

The economic integration process was speeded by the outmigration of millions of poorly educated, unskilled blacks; the belated recognition of the quality of the South's water resources (for the expanding chemical industry); the lure of its antiunion tradition; and an ample supply of low-cost labor.

Although the United States could boast in the 1920s of having the largest national market of any developed country, only a relatively few large corporations such as General Electric, Dupont, Sears Roebuck, International Harvester, Kodak, the Bell System, and the automotive, steel, chemical, and rubber companies had learned to exploit the economics of mass production and were truly national enterprises.

The dust-bowl migration in the early 1930s from the south-central states to the West Coast was a prelude to the much larger migration that followed the nation's entrance into World War II. The latter migration moved easterners and midwesterners in unparalleled numbers into training camps in the South and into the burgeoning defense jobs that opened up in the aerospace industries, located for the most part in the South and West. Many of the newcomers liked what they found in these new places and relocated there after the war.

This large relocation of the population was aided by the presence of the automobile in all classes and regions, and it was further stimulated by advances in air travel. The substantial and sustained increase in per capita and family income in the late 1940s and in the 1950s and 1960s sped the development of the national market. Many large and even medium-sized companies integrated their production and distribution more closely by providing credit directly or indirectly to customers purchasing expensive items (television sets, refrigerators, and other household appliances) and by national advertising making their brand names known throughout the continental United States.

The end of the war also found the United States in a new leadership role in international affairs. Through substantial relief and rehabilitation grants and loans, the United States assisted its allies, as well as its recent enemies, to survive in the immediate postwar years when their economies were in ruin. And later, the United States provided critical assistance (e.g., the Marshall Plan) to help these countries rebuild and modernize their economies. The United States also took the lead in putting the Bretton Woods agreement into effect in 1944. These provided a solid foundation for a rapid expansion in international finance and trade that functioned effectively for over a quarter of a century, that is, until 1971 when President Nixon took the United States off the gold standard.

A growing number of large U.S. corporations, because of the new leadership of the United States in world affairs and because they were reinforced by the realization that as Europe and Japan revived, they would provide attractive business opportunities, shed their provincialism and increased their presence abroad. They did this initially by increasing their exports and later by opening overseas manufacturing branches to avoid being locked out of the newly organized Common Market.

But we should not overestimate the increased participation of U.S. corporations in the international economy. Most successful U.S. corporations remained primarily domestically focused and underestimated the growing competitive strength of both the recovering German and Japanese economies, as well as the strength of the newcomers including Brazil and the Pacific Basin countries. Many major U.S. corporations, not only in consumer electronics, which the Japanese entered strongly in the late 1960s, but also in such basic industries as steel, rubber, farm implements, and automobiles suddenly found that they were outmatched in their own domestic marketplace in both price and quality. The most dramatic case was the successful invasion by the Japanese of the U.S. automobile market, an invasion from which the "Big Three" are still reeling.

There is mounting evidence that the foregoing is only prelude to what is still to come. More and more sectors of the U.S. economy are being restructured as more and more U.S. corporations begin to operate as a "world company" in a world economy. Many U.S. corporations are reassessing, with an eye to global specialization, every facet of their activities, from where they acquire their basic resources to the locations where they concentrate on selling and servicing their products. Offshore manufacturing in the Pacific Basin, twin plants along the Mexican border, overnight reliance by New York headquarters on computer services as far away as South Korea are signposts of the future.

## The Revolution in Money and Finance

The Federal Reserve Act, passed a year before the outbreak of World War I to avoid crises in liquidity, was put to the test when the inflated wartime prices collapsed in 1919 and early 1920. However, many companies succumbed, and others, even companies as large as Sears Roebuck, were on the brink. As a consequence, many large corporations during the New Era decided to become less dependent on the banks for operating capital. Instead, they went to the stock market to raise additional equity. The banks in turn, looking to their options, became heavily involved in the real estate and stock market speculation of the late 1920s. And some floated bonds for overseas borrowers whose credit worthiness was soon found wanting.

The deflationary forces unleashed by the collapse of the New Era would have found many banks exposed regardless of the behavior of the Federal Reserve System, but those who have studied the period believe that its policy of tight money added to the devastation. This much is clear: By early 1933, a major reconstruction of the U.S. banking system had to be undertaken forthwith. Thousands of banks had closed, never again to reopen; many were merged into larger institutions; many depositors had been wiped out and others had lost significant proportions of their savings. To help restore trust in the banking system, the federal government found it necessary to establish a new insurance system for bank depositors. Congress also passed new legislation that circumscribed the arenas within which different types of banking and other types of financial institutions were permitted to conduct business.

The banks played a leading role in the financing of World War II; the Federal Reserve System became an increasingly important institution in the postwar era when the United States was thrust into the leadership role in the international financial markets by the Bretton Woods agreement and by subsequent events. For many decades, banking reforms dating from the era of the New Deal appeared to be working well. The country was free of bank failures.

There was often no consensus, however, among key leadership groups—the administration, Congress, business, labor, the academics—about how well the Federal Reserve was performing its central bank functions. Some groups wanted the system to reduce interest rates in the hope and belief that construction and other interest-sensitive industries could expand more rapidly, whereas others pressed for a more constrained policy, warning that the continuance of easy money would lead to a boom and a price rise that would shortly thereafter precipitate a recession.

During the 1960s, the stock market entered a long boom that more or less paralleled the expansion in business activity that lasted 106 months. One concomitant of the strong stock market was the favorable environment it provided for the major explosion in mergers and acquisitions, the first such boom since early in the century.

Several of the nation's largest banks, recognizing the leadership role of the United States and the dollar in the international financial markets after World War II, moved to develop their overseas business, and a few, particularly Citicorp, were highly successful. When the dollar came under pressure in the early 1970s, U.S. banks with their European counterparts were able to establish and expand a major supplementary system, known as the "Eurodollar" market, based on the overseas dollar deposits of large U.S. corporations. Later, a Eurodollar bond market followed. Despite these new developments, which were paralleled by the growing presence of foreign banks in the United States, the banking system had remained substantially unaltered since the early days of the New Deal. It was a highly regulated sector in which bankers made a good living most of the time because of the spread between the rates they paid depositors and the rates they were able to charge customers.

During the past decade, and particularly the last quinquennium, the structure of banking is being fundamentally transformed. The combination of rapidly advancing computer technology and deregulation, together with the large corporations' playing a more active role in managing their own finances, has initiated a revolution that is still under way. The outlines of that transformation are clearly discernible: a proliferation of new types of money; a world money market that operates twenty-four hours a day; a decline in conventional commercial banking; a rush into investment banking; an explosive demand by large corporations for a host of new services from their bankers predicated on computer interactions; and the breakdown of preexisting barriers between banking and other financial service firms. In the face of these and still other radical innovations, the task of central bankers to help keep their economies on an even keel by exercising directional influence over monetary policy becomes that much more problematic.

## Human Resources

A fourth major transformation of the U.S. economy during past decades has been the growing importance of its human resources. Until World War I, when great numbers of immigrants streamed into this country (over a million a year at peak), it was not uncommon for labor contractors to be on the New York City piers to ask young men to roll up their sleeves so that they could judge their job readiness. If they passed the test, they were handed an address and told to report next day for work. The recruiters had no interest in whether the newcomers were literate or even if they could understand English. New York City had large numbers of multilingual foremen. In the intervening decades the economy tilted away from muscle power in favor of brain power, and by the mid-1980s, it has moved to the replacement of unskilled labor by robots.

Part of the explanation for this shift can be found in the decline in the agricultural work force, which in earlier decades had employed large numbers of unlettered and unskilled workers. Today, a prosperous farm is likely to be managed by a college graduate, assisted by a wife who is also a college graduate, who together have several hundred thousand dollars of farm machinery at their disposal and who resort to a computer to help them decide what and when to plant, when to harvest, and when to sell.

Much the same "upgrading" of human resources has occurred in manufacturing and even more so in the service sector. The latter, accounting for about 70 percent of GNP and even more of employment, now dominates the U.S. economy. To meet these new demands for better-educated and better-trained staff, we greatly expanded investments in education. Five of every six young people now graduate from high school, in contrast to the fewer than one in two as recently as World War II. The proportion of college graduates is now close to one in four of the age group, up from one in seventeen at the time of World War II.

This expansion of the formal educational system has been paralleled by substantial corporate investments in the training and retraining of managers and other members of the work force. The economy has shifted from an emphasis on people working long and hard to their working smarter.

As I have noted, during the past several generations there has been a striking increase in the labor force participation of women, particularly married women. Today, more than half of all women with children under six are in the labor force. The labor force participation rates of men and women aged sixteen to sixty-four in the U.S. population is 68 percent—an all-time high.

In addition to the 7 percent or so of GNP that the country currently invests in all levels of formal education, there are several additional percentage points that reflect the outlays of business, mostly for specialized training. During World War II the federal government for the first time became a large-scale investor in research and development, of which the development of the atomic bomb was the most successful outcome. In the postwar decades, both the federal government and business have expanded their investments in research and development. In 1985, they totaled over $100 billion or about 2.5 percent of GNP.

It has only recently dawned on employers, trade unions, and the members of the work force that the classic system of hierarchical organization and strict lines of authority and control from the top down are inappropriate and dysfunctional for individuals who have developed critical acumen and have acquired wide-ranging competences. Largely as a response to the fears and admiration engendered by highly successful Japanese corporations, U.S. companies are belatedly inspecting their established organizational patterns and worker supervision. As a result, many companies are slowly but surely introducing modifications. The changes are aimed at ensuring the more effective use of the human resources at the disposal of management and also at increasing the satisfaction of the work force. Taylorism—a system of narrow job specifications and tight supervision—may have been appropriate in the early era of mass production, but it is clearly an anachronism in a largely service economy dependent on an educated work force with broad access to computers.

## The Push for Equity

The long-term respect of the American public for the virtues of the competitive market did not prevent it from taking repeated economic actions as a body politic. Among the more important actions on the federal level were the passage of the personal income tax in 1913; special relief for farmers in 1926; the major initiatives of the New Deal and later of the Great Society that included work and welfare for the long-term unemployed, and unemployment insurance for the short-term unemployed; the encouragement of trade union organization aimed at improving the bargaining power of unions; Social Security for the elderly; housing subsidies for the low-income population; administrative and legislative interventions to eradicate discrimination in employment, as well as to assure minorities' access to public accommodations and to the ballot; the broadening of Social Security legislation to include the permanently disabled and the poor elderly; increased protection from injury and health hazards at the workplace; and protection of private pensions. In addition to the actions of the federal government, the states took many initiatives on their own or in association with Washington to broaden access of the poor, low-income, and middle-income families to educational, health, housing, welfare, and other critical services.

This broad array of societal interventions—the vast majority introduced during the last half century—have affected every facet of human existence from pregnancy prevention programs and prenatal care to the payment of funeral expenses and monthly subsidies to widows and children of Social Security beneficiaries. These interventions have dealt with housing, food, fuel, income support, education, health, training, savings, discrimination based on race, sex, age, and much more.

This truly explosive increase in the interventions of government on behalf of different groups in society has not escaped criticism. Since 1981, both federal and state governments have moderated somewhat the scale and scope of their efforts aimed at altering the outcomes of the market through various types of political interventions. Critics have advanced a number of arguments against the effort to increase equity among the citizenry. Because governments must raise through taxes the additional sums they require to carry out a redistribution program, the imposition of additional taxes, according to the critics, will have adverse effects on incentives and productivity to a point where total output and total employment will be reduced below what they would have been in the absence of the reforms.

Another line of criticism notes that although the ostensible beneficiaries of redistributive programs are the poor and near-poor, analysis in depth will disclose that many, in fact, are members of the middle- or even upper-income groups. Furthermore, low-income groups, the presumed beneficiaries, often lose more than they gain from such redistributive efforts because of the regressive nature of many taxes.

Other critics hold that U.S. democracy works through special interest groups, with the result that the best organized groups such as the farm bloc or an industry at bay like textiles are in a better position than others to obtain special legislation to help their members. New legislation may be enacted at a disproportionate cost to the rest of the society, including most of the nation's low-income population.

Finally, true believers in the market question the entire effort of using government to broaden equity. As they see it, liberty and freedom are supreme values that are always at risk when governmental interventions are increased. They believe that the weight of the evidence is always against the expansion of government because such expansion will inevitably diminish these most important values.

Within the present context of describing the more important changes that have occurred over the past decades in the structure and functioning of the U.S. economy, I need not enter into the debate whether or to what extent the several lines of action by government have achieved or have failed to achieve their stated goals. The one incontrovertible fact is that the many different efforts that were launched and carried out resulted in a significant restructuring of the economy.

## The Not-for-Profit Sector

The last of the six transforming phenomena that we will briefly review is the changing role of the private sector in the U.S. economy. Successive presidents from Kennedy to Reagan have insisted that the United States remains a predominantly market economy with private business accounting for about five out of every six jobs. Both the data that are used to support this judgment and the conclusion that the private sector continues to be the sole engine of economic development warrant reassessment.

As early as 1964, my colleagues Dale Hiestand and Beatrice Reubens and I addressed the shifting relations between what was conventionally subsumed under the headings of business and government (*The Pluralistic Economy*, 1965). We pointed out that since 1929, the relationship between the two had been altered in fundamental ways and that it was necessary to broaden the model of the modern economy to introduce a third critical sector—the nonprofit sector—which has come to play a major role particularly in the fields of health, higher education, philanthropy, and research.

If we combine government and nonprofit institutions into the not-for-profit sector, we find that instead of the five out of six jobs originating in the private sector, a more realistic estimate would be two in three or even three in five. As we noted in our 1964 study, it was stretching economic categories too far to count in the private sector employees engaged in producing missiles for the federal government, usually on a cost-plus contract. We believed, then and now, that federal purchases made through private contractors should be reflected on the governmental side of the ledger.

The matter is less clear when it comes to categorizing employment in industries where prices are set or controlled by government: various public utilities, oil and gas, farm products, insurance, and still others. Even if we place these large industries in the profit sector, the not-for-profit sector will still account for at least one in every three jobs and for about one in every four dollars of GNP.

This line of analysis is not the only way to assess the importance of the role of government and nonprofit institutions in the contemporary U.S. economy. If the focus is on the principal levers of economic change, heavy weight must be assigned to the leading roles of government and the universities. It is generally acknowledged that the most important industries that have helped the U.S. economy to attain its strong international position—airplanes, electronics, communications, computers, agriculture, pharmaceuticals, as well as defense and space—owe a great deal to the large flows of federal funds into both research and development and the purchases of finished goods.

Students of economic growth also agree that a key factor in the sustained growth rate of the United States between 1945 and 1965 must be ascribed in large part to gains in productivity that reflected improvements in human resources inputs, primarily the better health and higher educational levels of the population. Although profit-making enterprises certainly have invested more heavily in the training and upgrading of their work forces, the key to increased productivity are the gains in pre-employment preparation that reflect the larger expenditures of the public sector, supplemented by the large outlays of families.

There are other reasons to emphasize the growing role of the government in the performance of the U.S. economy since World War II. It was the federal government that, through its early relief and reconstruction efforts, helped Europe and Japan revive after the war and that in turn created many opportunities for U.S. multinational corporations. Although economists continue to disagree about the effectiveness of monetary and fiscal policy as stabilization devices during these recent decades, most would agree that the quarter century of low or modest price increases together with only shallow recessions helped to create a conducive environment for the long-term expansion of the economy.

In addition the diverse federal policies affecting airports, highways, the environment, oil, foreign trade, and other critical arenas such as trade unions, antitrust, taxation, and price controls, and the recent deregulation of airlines and banking have also pushed or pulled the economy in one or another direction. Even if one believes that the actions of government seldom if ever contribute to "wealth creation," the question of how to minimize the role of government in the operation of the economy must still be faced. Ours is a democracy; new roles for government usually follow the electorate. Libertarian critics argue that governmental interventions almost always detract from rather than enhance the wealth and well-being of a society. But if the majority of voters believes otherwise, its preferences cannot be ignored.

The vast expansion in the role of government in the economy from the New Deal days to the present was affirmed and reaffirmed by the electorate not once but repeatedly at all levels of government, federal, state, and local. Despite the two overwhelming victories of Ronald Reagan in the presidential elections of 1980 and 1984, his success was not seen by the voters as a broad mandate to reduce the role of government in the economy. The electorate welcomed the cut in taxes in 1981, but federal outlays in the budget for 1985–1986 as a percentage of GNP are higher, not lower, than when Reagan first entered the White House.

There is much that the foregoing series of major transformations omits such as the growth of superfirms (the GE-RCA merger); the decline in the role of trade unions; the interplay between the tax structure and business investment; the impact of the computer-communications technology on the reshaping of the U.S. economy; and still other potent developments.

My list of six subsumed such "structural" changes as the striking reduction in the size of the farm population and the striking increase in the proportion of women in the labor force; the enlargement of the market from local and regional to national and international; the transformation of banking and finance including the creation of many new forms of money; the growing importance of human resources in advanced economies; the responsiveness of most societies to the demands of their citizens for greater equity, including the need for large income transfers; and the increasing role of government in economic policy.

## The Laureates and the Real World

I shall now explore the extent to which the major themes and approaches pursued by the thirteen American Nobel laureates were informed by these six transformations and correspondingly the extent to which their analyses were able to provide policy guidance to those charged with the responsibility of keeping the U.S. economy operating close to the full utilization of its human and physical resources. Some may agree with George Stigler that such a juxtaposition is irrelevant and misleading because economics, as a science, has its own internal momentum and the primary task of the investigator is to correct, improve, and strengthen the theories and methodologies that represent the inheritance from his predecessors. I believe, however, that the true test of an economic model must finally be judged by whether it provides new and important understanding of how the economy functions and whether it can point the way to improved policy.

Only two of the laureates, Simon Kuznets and Theodore Schultz, paid attention to the major structural alterations in the labor force—the decline in the agricultural work force and the much expanded participation of women in paid employment.

It might be argued that in developing their sophisticated models and analyses, the other Nobel laureates did not consider it necessary to deal with such concrete phenomena as labor force transformations. But that changes rather than eliminates the question. What is the appropriate level of abstraction for a theory that tries—or should try—to illuminate the changing reality and help point the way to improved policy? These demographic developments were not peripheral but were the causes and concomitants of major economic and social transformations that continue to this day.

The year 1986 is the sixtieth year of large-scale governmental supports for agriculture; many farmers and farm communities are still at risk despite the $50 billion rescue program passed by Congress. And there is mounting evidence that many banking institutions, private and public, that have been extending credit to farmers are in a precarious position. If the banks are left to their own devices, their situation could lead to a financial debacle of major proportions.

The large numbers of surplus farm workers, who were displaced as farming became more technologically sophisticated, made their way into urban centers. This migration included a sizable concentration of blacks who settled in a relatively small number of Northern cities. Fortunately, a significant proportion of the migrants found jobs and were able to make a reasonable adjustment to their new metropolitan environment. But a great many, especially among the black migrants—and their children and grandchildren—have still not made a successful transition, which has resulted in great human and social loss to themselves, their urban neighbors, and the nation. Again there is no categorical imperative that commands the leaders of the economic profession to confront the maladjustment of millions of minority citizens, but the long-term economic marginality of these millions should have led the Nobel laureates to reexamine their assumptions about the ways in which labor markets clear.

The second transformation called attention to the extension of the market from local and regional to national and international. The growing importance of the international dimensions of the economy from the vantage of both analysis and policy was present in varying degrees in the work of five of the laureates. Kuznets, with his wide reach, both called attention to the differences between the developed and developing nations and pointed to factors that were spreading the diffusion of technology from the former to the latter.

Although Tjalling Koopmans had the narrowest focus, which was directed to developing a theory for the optimal allocation of resources within the firm, he found it desirable in the concluding section of his presentation to raise some issues as to how the theory might be usefully extended to deepen insight into development economics in the third world.

Lawrence Klein, in developing his econometric model to forecast the path of the economy up to the year 1990, adopted from the outset a world perspective. Many of the categories and much of the data with which he worked had a worldwide reach. He stated unequivocally that the economies of all nations were being increasingly integrated into a world economy.

Theodore Schultz was unique among the laureates in that he selected as his central theme the problem of poverty among farmers in the third world. He could have dealt with the poor at home but decided that because the poor accounted for a much larger proportion of the population in third world countries, he would focus on them.

Although Wassily Leontief's presentation was largely a methodological exercise in how to conduct and use input-output analysis, one should note that he selected a United Nations study of pollution control that had a worldwide perspective.

The extension of the market was clearly a theme of interest and concern to a significant number of the laureates. Two related questions are how comfortable did the laureates feel working within the confines of neoclassical and general equilibrium analysis and how much reliance were they willing to place on the competitive market as the preferred policy instrument.

Only Herbert Simon and Kenneth Arrow explicitly addressed the limitations of neoclassical and general equilibrium analysis, although several other of the laureates, such as James Tobin, called attention in passing to particular imperfections. In Simon's view the underlying assumptions of the neoclassical paradigm when applied to the modern corporation were seriously flawed in that the decisionmaker was in no position to figure out how to achieve a maximum outcome; and what is more, corporate managers had to act "politically" if they wanted to survive and prosper.

Arrow sharply differentiated the areas where the competitive market could assure optimal results. He argued that the model fitted the private economy but it could not be extended to the domain of public goods. In this latter instance, one could not decide, relying on competitive theory, whether or not the output produced conformed to the criteria of efficiency and equity as one could in the case of freely functioning private markets.

Simon argued that neoclassical theory had severe limitations in a world of large corporations and Arrow's reservations about general equilibrium theory were limited to the arena of public goods. Therefore, it is worth emphasizing that not one of the other laureates found it necessary to modify, much less abandon, his reliance on the dominant analytic framework, which though modified and informed could be traced back to Adam Smith's analysis of the market.

Although the laureates relied on the competitive theory as their principal instrument for analysis, only a few looked to it explicitly as a guide to policy. Arrow in a moment of enthusiasm stated that general equilibrium theory could serve as an allocation system in war as well as in peace, but aside from such euphoria, only the Chicago School (Theodore Schultz, Milton Friedman, and George Stigler) carried the torch for more competition as the preferred way of influencing the direction of public policy. Koopmans had warned specifically about such an unwarranted extension, insisting that the public in a modern democratic society would want to consider, in the shaping of policy, values that transcended the achievement of optimal efficiency in the marketplace.

The third of the six major economic transformations focused on banking, or more broadly financial institutions, or differently stated, the changing determinants of monetary and fiscal policy. I grouped some of the laureates, Friedman, Tobin, and Modigliani, as primarily concerned with issues of money and finance. The question that I must raise here is whether any of the other ten laureates paid much attention to the radical transformations in modern banking. The principal addition is Lawrence Klein, who in sketching his scenario for 1990, warned that world economic development might be derailed by a simultaneity of defaults among third world countries. The other laureates, except for the three monetary specialists and Klein, ignored the role of money and credit in the operations of the economy. The three specialists in money and finance—Friedman, Tobin, and Modigliani—differ greatly with respect to both their analyses and their policy positions. Although Friedman acknowledged that central banks could influence the short-term course of the business cycle by altering the flow of money, he concluded that such central bank "interventions" had no prospect of being useful in the long term. He reasoned that the banks would either be forced to keep increasing the supply, in which case rampant inflation would be the inevitable consequence, or else they would have to shift to a restrictive policy, which would force the economy into a recession. In the face of this unsatisfactory alternative, Friedman opted for a fixed policy in which the authorities would expand the money supply by 3 to 4 percent per annum, a rate from which they should not deviate.

Tobin put forth a quite different view and for the most part Modigliani was in his corner. For Tobin the decisions that borrowers, lenders, speculators, foreign exchange specialists, investors, and all other participants in the financial markets make to alter the composition of their portfolios are as real as the actions of other economic participants involved in the production and sale of goods and other services.

The pervasiveness of money and finance throughout all modern economies makes it critically important, from Tobin's vantage, that national and international authorities with policy leverage weigh the consequences of institutional changes so that the financial structure can bring the economy closer to a level of optimal performance.

Modigliani, in developing his life-cycle approach to spending and saving, went a fair distance to undermine some of the assumptions that Keynes had introduced: that consumption was a function of income and that modern capitalistic economies were cursed by an inherent tendency to oversaving, which was a cause of underinvestment and therefore, of recessions and depressions. The play of the variables looks quite different when one adopts Modigliani's perspective of focusing on the expenditure patterns of families that respond differently over time, namely by trying to optimize their consumption over a lifetime in the face of growing and declining income streams and changing responsibilities for children.

Both Tobin and Modigliani do not accept Friedman's policy position that the best position for the banking authorities is to follow the arbitrary rule of steady, modest increases in the money stock and forego any and all other efforts to affect the direction of the economy. Both Tobin and Modigliani see themselves as neo-Keynesians who favor an activist stance.

The fourth area of transformation called attention to the growing importance of human resources in the United States and in other developed economies. Two of the Nobel laureates, Simon Kuznets and Theodore Schultz, singled out the human resource factor in their presentations, but the others failed to refer to it or at most dealt with it only in passing. In Kuznets's view, the much enlarged investment in human resources (health, education, and training) holds the clue to the significant and over the long haul, the sustained increases in the productivity and growth of both developed and more recently, developing nations.

Schultz, together with Gary Becker and Jacob Mincer, has been one of the principal architects of what has come to be known as the "human capital" school. Taking their cue from Alfred Marshall—and one could just as easily say from Adam Smith—these Chicago economists in the late 1950s and early 1960s saw the potential of applying neoclassical analysis to human capital, making use of the apparatus that earlier economists had developed in their studies of physical capital. One of the most interesting aspects of Schultz's Nobel Prize lecture is the strong case that he made for the opportunities that developing economies can anticipate through prospective improvements in their human capital. He called attention to many such improvements that are occurring in many developing countries via advances in public health, the reduction in the number and the improvements in the "quality" of children, the positive influence of education and training, and still other innovations that are increasing the competences and potentials of their labor forces.

The fifth theme in the transformations of modern economies called attention to the greater concern with welfare and equity. Only Kuznets and Arrow dealt with the subject overtly. Kuznets, with his broad institutional view of economic growth and development and with his particular sensitivity to the roles of ideology and politics as levers for change, placed heavy weight on political pressures in democratic societies whereby the less privileged look to government to broaden their opportunities and rewards.

Arrow approached the equity issue from quite a different vantage. He argued that it was erroneous to assume that the logic of competition that performed effectively in the private market could be used as a reliable guide in the public arena. He demonstrated that there was no necessary and surely no close linkage between a market that had reached a point of Pareto optimum—no further shifts would yield a net gain— and the conditions required for distributive justice.

The other Nobel laureates who evinced an awareness of and concern for considerations of equity included the members of the Chicago School, Friedman, Schultz, and Stigler, all of whom emphasized the importance of giving the competitive market more scope so that it could broaden its influence. They warned repeatedly that interfering with the functioning of the competitive market would almost certainly have adverse effects and that the poor would be the major victims. One should note that theirs was a presumption not supported by the data, which showed that many of the poor were much better off by virtue of governments' interventions.

We are now face to face with the sixth and last of the transforming developments, the expanded role that governments have come to play in the U.S. economy and in most other developed economies since the 1930s. Most of the presentations of the Nobel laureates proceeded at such a high level of abstraction that the changing institutional environment, particularly the changing role of government, was not the center of interest to any of them. But that generalization, while true, definitely overstates the case. Paul Samuelson in his concluding remarks had a cryptic allusion to the prospect of improved economic theory's being of use to buttress a liberal policy of economic reform. It is clear that Arrow, in stressing the shortcomings of conventional theory in dealing with public goods, was concerned with the responsibilities that inevitably fall on government.

As noted earlier, Tjalling Koopmans specifically called attention to the challenge that all democratic societies face of finding a proper balance between economic and other values and goals. In recognizing the danger of simultaneous defaults by debtor nations, Lawrence Klein suggested, by implication at least, that he doubted the efficacy of governments to intervene successfully to prevent such defaults. Schultz, Friedman, and Stigler—all three from the Chicago School—argued that the growing intervention of governments would have an adverse effect on economic growth and on the economic welfare of all groups in the community, particularly the poor. But James Tobin and Franco Modigliani saw no escape from governments' playing a major role to moderate the swings of the cycle. And Kuznets, with his large view, ascribed a wide range of duties to governments in both developed and developing nations. Only Gerard Debreu and Herbert Simon avoided the issue of the changing role of government. Wassily Leontief, in selecting his theme of an input-output analysis of the control of environmental pollution, implicitly had government playing the star role.

I would be the first to acknowledge that this exercise of juxtaposing the six major transformations of the U.S. economy during the last two-thirds of this century with the themes adumbrated by the American Nobel Prize winners in their Stockholm acceptance speeches could be faulted as tendentious, possibly irrelevant, and at best, of limited value.

Most of the laureates would probably not agree with my basic premise that one critical test of the value of economic theory is whether it encompasses a reasonable picture of the reality that they are analyzing and appraising. Because that reality is changing rapidly, there is a real danger that their assumptions may be far from the truth and their findings and recommendations consequently distorted.

A second premise of mine, again possibly not acceptable to most of the laureates, is that most theories and models need to be cast on an appropriate level. I acknowledge that a highly abstract formulation can on occasion yield valuable insights to illuminate the real world and to provide guidelines to policy. But I contend that the odds are against such a serendipitous result.

The reader is free to draw conclusions about whether the only incidental attention that the Nobel laureates paid to the six major transformations that occurred in the United States during the past six decades affected the ability of their theories to advance understanding and/or action. I consider this neglect a major deficiency. In my view an economics that can inform and guide cannot be above time and place.

One final stricture: Although some of the Nobel laureates—in particular Kuznets, Arrow, and Koopmans—made room in their formulations for forces other than material accumulation as a guiding force in human behavior, most of the prizewinners proceeded as if haggling and bargaining were the beginning and end of life. I agree with Stigler that the simplifying assumptions of economics, rational behavior and the maximizing principle, permit the economist to formulate a great many propositions that are intellectually significant and that can have value for public policy. But acknowledging this agreement with Stigler surely does not imply that it is sensible, reasonable, or correct to set the framework for economic analysis so that history, institutions, and politics are disregarded or to ensure that the whole of societal experience is to be seen through the prism of these two principles. The inevitable outcome to such a restricted approach is, in my view, an economics that cannot explain what is occurring and cannot be used as a guide to future action.

# PART THREE

# Economics
# in a Lower Key

In the chapters that follow, I explain how my skepticism led me to focus my research on human resources in the belief that people, rather than physical or financial capital, were the principal source of productivity and wealth. Furthermore, I found it fruitful to move continually between the world of academe and the policy arena in order to remain alert to new areas of opportunity and to test the relevance of my emerging analyses.

Instead of pursuing the illusion that economics could be turned into a science whose hypotheses would hold if they could not be disproved by empirical data, I have preferred to develop halfway theories that were grounded in a value system and that would have to establish themselves in the political arena, the testing place of a democratic society.

# 8

## Research in Human Resources

Skepticism is a useful attitude for young researchers; it warns them not to invest their energies in intellectual pursuits that are likely to prove fruitless. But skepticism alone does not provide a constructive alternative. As I noted in Chapter 2, my mentor, Wesley C. Mitchell, urged me to undertake empirical research in the arena where economics and psychology meet because among other reasons he believed that the best prospect of strengthening the psychological foundations of economics lay there.

My other challenge in 1938 was to find a subject that would bring me close to the policy arena. I was committed to learning about "real world" problems in the hope that the findings might eventually contribute to strengthening policy. The proposal that I drew up for the Columbia University Council for Research in the Social Sciences requested funding for two related projects on "unemployment": the first, to study the coal miners of South Wales; the second, to study the long-term unemployed in New York City. I was also interested in a third project on "labor leadership," which I hoped would utilize the knowledge of a graduate student who had had extended experience as a labor organizer. Mitchell steered the project through the council, which provided initial funding in 1939 and made a supplemental grant in 1940.

### Focus on the Unemployed

The Welsh study, which I undertook in the spring and summer of 1939, was aimed at uncovering the consequences of long-term unemployment on the former coal miners as well as on their wives, children, and the communities in which they lived. Furthermore, I sought to explore why, in contrast to what economic theory suggested, the unemployed did not move to where jobs were more readily available; and I paid particular attention to the actions and nonactions of government to mitigate the worst ravages of mass unemployment. The study was entitled *Grass on the Slag Heaps: The Story of the Welsh Miners* (1942). It had a foreword by Thomas Jones, then director of the Pilgrims Trust and former long-term secretary of the British Cabinet, who had been my sponsor in the coal mining valleys.

To spend time in communities where up to 90 percent of the men had not worked for as long as ten years; where the prospect of future work, not only for the unemployed men but also for their sons and daughters, was highly problematic; where the proud institutions of chapels, trade unions, and sports associations that had once enriched the lives of the inhabitants had fallen into disarray; where the days of the week had lost meaning because one was indistinguishable from the next; and where the only break in the somber reality were the hours when heads of families gathered at the government office to collect their dole—these and other experiences have stayed with me and have significantly influenced my subsequent efforts in research and policy.

There was clearly something awry with established economic doctrines that postulated that people would move from depressed areas to locales where their prospects for jobs and income were better, such as London and the Midlands. The fact was that most of the Welsh refused to move for a complex of reasons—cultural, political, and even economic (they had accommodated to the dole). It also seemed to me that the Conservative government's budget-balancing priorities, which resulted in a minimum program of relief, were shortsighted because they undermined the self-respect, health, motivation, and skills not only of the self-reliant coal miners but also of their wives and children. One did not require the gift of prophecy to realize that if the tables were ever turned and the labor of these Welsh miners were ever again needed, they would extract a high price from employers and government. And that is what happened: The exacerbated labor-management relations in post–World War II Great Britain were fueled by the ill will that had accumulated among many sectors of the British working population during the 1930s when the establishment and the government demonstrated repeatedly their lack of interest and concern in the conditions of the unemployed and their families.

The study of the long-term unemployed in New York City was a more ambitious and structured investigation involving an interdisciplinary staff that, in addition to an economist-director, consisted of a psychiatrist, three psychiatric social workers, and a statistical consultant. The project was structured to explore whether three discrete ethnic-religious groups—Protestant Americans, Irish Catholics, and Jews (primarily of recent immigrant extraction)—differed significantly in their responses to long-term unemployment. The sample was restricted to whole families with minor children and was limited to whites. Hard as it is to believe, the number of poor black families in New York City in the late 1930s was relatively small.

A few highlights: Except for the issue of birth control, which created special problems for the Irish Catholics, we were unable to discover any significant differences among the three groups in their responses to the trauma of prolonged unemployment defined in terms of men who had not held regular jobs for the past five or more years. The sample included families on WPA (work relief) and families on Home Relief (the dole). The stresses and strains experienced by the latter were distinctly greater.

A reconstruction of the life experiences of these families demonstrated that although most of the men had earlier held jobs at the middle or lower end of the occupational and income distribution curve, they had been self-supporting and had taken pride in their ability to cope with life's problems and challenges. When they lost their jobs, they immediately looked for another; it was only after months and years of fruitless searching that they became disheartened and realized that they might never make it back into the world of paid employment, especially those who were over fifty and were no longer in the best of health.

The social workers who visited the homes of the unemployed to talk with their wives and to observe the younger children reported on the significant costs borne by each in terms of inadequate food, clothing, and recreation and the growing loss of hope. Many women recognized the deepening depression that afflicted their husbands and regretted that they could do so little to relieve it. The welfare administration's rules and regulations created tensions between adolescent children and their parents because the young peoples' modest part-time earnings were often subtracted from the family's welfare check.

At the conclusion of the field studies, the staff members made independent appraisals of the likely "reemployment" of the men in the sample, approximately 200 individuals. The psychiatrist and the social workers estimated that no more than one-third were likely ever again to obtain a regular job. I was much more optimistc, convinced that mobilization for war and war itself would create a strong demand for labor, even for the labor of these long-term unemployed. A follow-up study undertaken at the Columbia School of Social Work proved that I was right. In 1942, all but a few chronic alcoholics were back at work.

*The Unemployed* (1943) reported our findings at length. The principal lessons I extracted included the superiority of work relief over cash support; the danger of discouraging young people from working by removing all monetary incentives; the cause of unemployment being rooted in a shortfall in demand for labor, not in the inadequacies of the unemployed; the centrality of work and self-support for the integrity of the individual worker, his family, and the community. By the time our investigation was concluded, my associates and I were convinced that no society concerned about its security and survival could afford to remain passive and inert in the face of long-term unemployment. We argued that in the absence of an adequate number of private-sector jobs, it was the responsibility of government to create public-sector jobs.

## Occupational Choice

World War II interrupted our research into human resources, but on my return to the campus I restructured my interdisciplinary team: The psychiatrist and I were joined by a sociologist and clinical psychologist, and the four of us set out to explore the "process of occupational choice." The study of unemployment had led the psychiatrist and me to recognize the centrality of work in modern society. But we concluded that "work" was too big a subject for inquiry and we decided to focus on occupational choice as a first step in what we hoped would be an extended inquiry into work. The extant theories of occupational choice were inadequate. The academic literature was full of observations about occupational preferences, interests, capacities, even goals and values, but it was impossible to order and make sense out of the myriad statistical observations that investigators had gathered.

We decided to attempt the difficult but intriguing task of developing a "theory" of occupational choice. Our design focused on young men from upper-middle-class white families whose resources assured that they would have a wide range of choice. Before we finished, we broadened our design to include young women from affluent homes and a group of men from low-income families.

Our psychologist, John L. Herma, a pupil of Karl and Charlotte Bühler in Vienna and Jean Piaget in Geneva, convinced us to place our bets on a developmental model that led us to interview young males between eleven and twenty-three years of age, chosen at two-year intervals. Herma's suggestion proved useful, and we were able to demarcate the process into four periods—fantasy, exploratory, crystallization, and specification. We were able to distinguish as the individual matured the widening of the choice process as he took into account not only his interests but also his capacities and his values. The last stage in this maturational approach came when the young adult sought to find the best fit between his preferences and the external reality within which he had to make his choice. Our summary formulation emphasized that occupational choice is a *process*; that to a large extent it is *irreversible*; and that it ends in a *compromise*.

The last chapter of *Occupational Choice: An Approach to a General Theory* (1951) dealt with policy issues, specifically how parents, teachers, and counselors could use the theory to intervene more successfully— or to avoid intervening—at different stages of the choice process. Once again, we attempted to widen our understanding of key areas of human behavior where economic and psychological decisionmaking met; but at the same time we looked for ways in which the new knowledge could contribute to improved social policy.

## The Eisenhower Studies

The scale of our human resources research at Columbia University was vastly expanded in the late 1940s with the active encouragement and support of General Dwight D. Eisenhower, who had assumed the presidency of the University in 1947. It was Eisenhower's conviction that the experience of World War II, which had seen the registration of almost 20 million young Americans and the active service of about 15 million, represented a rich data base that if systematically exploited, could add significantly to the understanding of human resources and at the same time contribute to improved policies in both the private and public sectors. The Conservation of Human Resources Project, which would implement this expanded research effort, was established in 1948.

The "Eisenhower studies" resulted in the publication of five major volumes: *The Uneducated* (1953); *The Negro Potential* (1956); and the three volumes that comprised *The Ineffective Soldier: Lessons for Management and the Nation* (1959): *The Lost Divisions, Breakdown and Recovery,* and *Patterns of Performance.*

About a million young men of draftable age had been rejected for military service with the designation "mental deficiency," which on closer inspection turned out to be a misnomer. Most of them were illiterate, not mentally deficient. Several hundred thousand additional illiterates, defined as possessing less than fifth grade competence in reading, writing, and arithmetic, were inducted into the armed forces and were given initial or remedial education of up to twelve weeks to enable them to meet minimum standards for active service.

Our analysis probed the reasons for such widespread illiteracy in a nation that had long prided itself on its system of free public education. The answers pointed to the following: the prolonged discrimination against blacks in the South, including the gross underfunding of black schools; the disinclination of many isolated rural white families to send their children to school; and the ravages of the Great Depression, which resulted in serious cutbacks in all school financing.

On the positive side, the study revealed that the armed forces had been able to bring most illiterates to a minimum level of literacy in twelve weeks or less and that once at that level the vast majority had been able to perform effectively. A follow-up study of a sample of these soldiers after their return to civilian life disclosed that they were able to find and hold jobs and support themselves and their families. But the continuing declines in the agricultural work force paralleled by expansion in the industrial and service sectors warned of the declining opportunity for the illiterate and the poorly educated in the U.S. economy.

*The Negro Potential* was an analysis of both ` civilian and military macrodata to explore the waste of potential among the black minority as a result of the cumulative and continuing effects of pervasive segregation and discrimination. The manpower waste that reflected inadequate developmental opportunities (family, income, and education) resulted in the subsequent concentration of blacks in the lowest-paying jobs with few career opportunities. As late as the mid-1950s, black men were almost entirely excluded from manufacturing in the South. The chapter on "The Negro Soldier" revealed that on every index, the black serviceman had been less effective than his white counterpart during World War II. Part of the explanation was found in the limitations and handicaps with which most blacks had entered active military duty. Another part reflected the practices that the military had followed in which black soldiers were segregated, used exclusively as service troops, and were generally placed under the command of white officers.

Our analysis ended with the recognition that the occupational and job segregation that had dominated the U.S. scene throughout its history was beginning to give way and that more opportunities were opening up for qualified blacks. But the rate of black progress in the future would depend on how quickly and how well blacks could improve their educational preparation, which thereafter would primarily control their upward mobility. The hurdles were formidable because of, among other factors, the sorry state of most inner-city schools and the criteria used by the elite colleges and universities to select students.

The centerpiece of the Eisenhower studies was the three-volume work, *The Ineffective Soldier: Lessons for Management and the Nation*, published in 1959, almost a decade after our research had been launched. The rich materials formed three independent but related studies. Each explored different facets of the same theme: how the characteristics of individuals (personalities) interacted with the forces in their specific work environment and with the values of the larger society to determine the individuals' level of performance. We were able to study these interrelations between personality and performance in both civilian and military life because our data enabled us to reconstruct not only the experiences of the men while they were on active duty but also their performance prior to enlistment or induction and after their separation and return to civilian life.

In Volume 1, *The Lost Divisions,* through the analysis of the macrodata, we were able to pinpoint the slippages that characterized the personnel policies of the armed forces during World War II and that led them to reject or prematurely separate about 2.5 million young men for various kinds of ineffectiveness, the major causes of which were directly related to faulty organizational and management policies and procedures and only infrequently to shortcomings of the men themselves.

Volume 2, *Breakdown and Recovery,* presented more than seventy structured case studies of soldiers who had proved ineffective in the military and who had been discharged prior to the end of hostilities on the ground that they could no longer be usefully re-assigned. These case studies added depth to the earlier macroanalysis by pinpointing the wide range of conditions within the military that led to the re-classification of these soldiers to ineffective. Again, most of these conditions reflected failings in the personnel policies of the armed forces rather than weaknesses of the men. We were also able to demonstrate that with relatively few exceptions, once these men were back in a civilian environment, they were once again effective, capable of discharging their responsibilities as workers, fathers, and citizens.

In Volume 3, *Patterns of Performance,* we focused on a life-cycle analysis of performance. The data permitted us to distinguish among different life patterns including, for instance, those whose premilitary, military, and postmilitary performance, except for their premature separation from the service, was generally superior. At the opposite extreme were men with a life-long record of ineffectiveness. Others fell midway between the high and low performers. With detailed information about these men prior to, during, and after their military service, we were able to develop a sophisticated typology of life patterns of performance that could illuminate the dynamic interrelations among the individuals, their work settings, and the larger environment that influenced their performance. This typology in many instances could account for variations in their performance over their lifetimes.

Although we did not emphasize our differences and disagreements with established economic and psychological doctrines, our conclusions were greatly at variance with the conventional wisdom. It was clear to us that the psychiatrists on whom the armed forces had relied to exclude individuals with neuroses or to discharge them when neuroses were identified acted beyond their knowledge bases. Except at the extremes and not always then, their techniques did not enable them to predict who would or would not break down under stress. We also had difficulty in organizing and evaluating our materials in light of the simplistic assumptions, so dear to economists, that all people seek to optimize their personal goals, usually defined as maximizing their monetary gains. Our analysis had a quite different cast: It emphasized the cumulative influence of key institutions such as the family, schools, dominant value systems, the availability of jobs, the employer's organizational and management policies, and the social support systems that set the framework within which individuals must find and make their way.

## The Talented

During the early 1960s, our program of research in human resources proceeded along a new axis with a focus on the talented, both men and women. The Eisenhower studies had alerted us to the advantage of studying human resources from a longitudinal perspective; that is the approach we used in *Talent and Performance* (1964), in which we analyzed the work and careers of individuals who had won graduate fellowships at Columbia University in the immediate post–World War II era. It should be noted that initially we had included the women fellowship winners along with the men, but early responses from the women alerted us to the need to separate them for special study, which we did in *Life Styles of Educated Women* (1966) and *Educated American Women: Self-Portraits* (1966).

We found it necessary and desirable to assess each of the following dimensions of work in order to develop a broader understanding of the career development of the talented men, the focus of our first investigation: career patterns, measures of success, value orientations, work satisfaction, self-realization, life styles, and performance potential. This relatively complex analytic structure appeared to us to be necessary once we recognized the variations that were embedded in the careers of our talented group. There were marked differences among the fellowship recipients, not only in the personal assets that they brought to the work arena but even greater differences in the values and goals they sought to realize through their work and their careers. There were also variations in how they dealt with other major commitments, particularly marriage and children.

Once again, we could not fit our data into the dominant model of the economists in which all men presumably pursue their self-interest in the labor market by seeking material success and an optimal balance between work and leisure. The category schemas that we developed about the patterns of career development, work satisfactions, and goals for self-realization were considerably more elaborate and subtle and revealed the impracticality of seeking to compress men's behavior into the crude framework of neoclassical economics. To note just a few of our findings: only 3 percent of the group of 268 identified "income" as among the most gratifying aspects of their work, and only 7 percent singled it out in their listing among the "least satisfying" aspects.

Another telling illustration is the relative weight that this talented group assigned to what we described as the "nature of work" (autonomy) and "self-expression" in contrast to "rewards and concomitants" (money and psychic income). Nature of work and self-expression together were singled out by about two-thirds of the group as of overriding importance while rewards and concomitants were singled out by between an eighth and a quarter of the entire group. Here was something less than strong affirmation for the economists' rigid adherence to their income-maximizing assumptions.

The two volumes on educated women followed the general outline of the study of talented men but only after we had made several critical accommodations in our schema to take account of the unique aspects of the career patterns of women. Most women in the early post–World War II decades married and had children, responsibilities that they had to balance with their jobs and career goals. Once again we enlarged our perspective not only to assess their work and life-styles as of the time of our investigation but also to look at shifts over time since the completion of their graduate studies and to explore their plans for the future.

The major difference in the work patterns of talented men and talented women is revealed by our finding that only slightly more than one-third of the total group of 311 women had a "continuous" work history; about one in four had stopped working at some point in the past (usually with marriage or the birth of their first child) or had never been regularly attached to the labor force. The remaining two out of five were more or less evenly divided between those with "minor breaks," and those who worked "intermittently."

Another categorization that we developed distinguished the women among those who saw themselves primarily as workers, combination (work and home), or homemakers. The single women and those who married but had no children tended to work more or less continuously; in contrast, only a small minority of those with more than one child were continuously in the labor force. Slightly less than half of those with a single child worked continuously. One of the striking findings related to the women's reported degrees of satisfaction with the two major dimensions of their lives, their work and their personal lives. About three in four indicated that they were satisfied with both areas; the remaining one in four were almost equally divided between those who reported being dissatisfied with both areas and those who were satisfied with one and dissatisfied with the other.

Our society has made significant moves in the past two decades to alter its attitudes and behavior with respect to the development and utilization of women of potential, but at the same time it has been reluctant to make many necessary and desirable adjustments within the family, the educational system, and the world of work. Many overt barriers of discrimination have been lowered or removed, and the number of women in college now exceeds the number of men. Moreover, many educated women are now promoted into positions that were formerly closed to them. Nevertheless, so far our society has not been willing to make basic adjustments that would contribute to a higher level of societal well-being even though more and more educated women are making a commitment to their careers and consider their childbearing, child-rearing responsibilities as episodes they can manage without withdrawing for an extended period from the world of work.

## Macro-Studies

In the late 1950s I made a first halting effort (*Human Resources: The Wealth of a Nation*, 1958) to pull together some of the strands of our empirical research, but the result omitted many critical elements and I could not develop a broad synthesis. Since then, I have made several such forays aimed at integrating and synthesizing various facets of our empirical research. The first was entitled *The Pluralistic Economy* (1965). In seeking the source of new job creation, my associates and I recognized that much of the dynamism of the U.S. economy was coming from the not-for-profit sector, that is, from government and nonprofit organizations, which as noted above, we calculated were responsible for between one-third and two-fifths of all payroll employment. Aerospace, education, health, and state and local government were large industries and were providing a high proportion of the new jobs. In a country where the bias of neoclassical economists and business leaders is to view government as "nonproductive," the expansion of the not-for-profit arena had been ignored, as were our findings about its growth and critical scale.

Partly as a result of what we learned in writing *The Pluralistic Economy* and partly as a result of external stimulation—the New York City Planning Commission had requested our help in developing the human resources inputs into its master plan—our attention moved away from the macrodeterminants of employment and began to center on a subunit, in this instance, the New York metropolitan area. Mainline economists had long recognized the relationships between residence and work but had paid relatively little attention to them. These economists postulated that the relocation of some workers would bring about the adjustments required to assure that different labor markets would be in proximate equilibrium. The U.S. worker is certainly mobile, but this does not mean that differences in employment and wages in local labor markets do not persist. As we became acquainted with the unique aspects of the New York metropolitan area, we came however to recognize more clearly that competition among localities would in large measure determine the future prospects for New York City's remaining the nation's leading economic center.

In early 1973 my colleagues and I published a volume entitled *New York Is Very Much Alive: A Manpower View* in which we reviewed what we had been learning over the larger part of a decade about the changing contours of the city's labor supply and the critical role played by key public and private institutions that mediated between the two, particularly the changing family, the educational system, migration, and the welfare system. Although we knew about the many dire forecasts of the city's economic future, we were reasonably upbeat. Our conclusions were predicated on the belief that New York City was still attractive to much of the nation's young talent and continued to lure many ambitious migrants and immigrants, potent contributors to its continued dynamism. But we did not give adequate weight to the deterioration in the city's financial position and to its distorted cost structure, making it less competitive with important metropolitan centers in the South and West. Within two years, the city was in a major crisis; but by 1978 it had begun to recover.

The timing of our 1973 study may have been off by a few years, but the underlying analysis was sound. New York's future depends on its ability to stay out front in its transformation into an advanced service economy and as part of this process must continue to attract and retain a large pool of talent. Although there are in the city in 1986 several hundred thousand persons of working age with only marginal skills and marginal attachments to the labor force, and more than a million persons on the welfare rolls, such disabilities can be borne if the rest of the economy remains vibrant—which has been the case since the late 1970s.

In 1964, I began to travel on behalf of the U.S. State Department to a large number of developing countries in Africa and Asia and also to Eastern Bloc countries and some of the developed nations in Western Europe to advise and consult on the role of manpower in their economic development plans. Within less than a decade, I had visited thirty countries on five continents.

In *Manpower for Development: Perspectives on Five Continents* (1971), I sought to summarize and synthesize the important findings from my field investigations. In the concluding chapter, "Lessons for Development," I identified the following:

1. *Development policy must be unique.* Each country must fashion policies appropriate to its own history, traditions, goals.
2. *Manpower represents the key constraint on growth.* This is the central theme of the book and its most important lesson.
3. *Rapid economic growth is an illusion.* Rewriting this a decade and a half later, I would make a distinction between relatively small countries, Taiwan and South Korea, and China, India, and Indonesia and apply the stricture only to the large countries.
4. *Political stability comes first.* I would place even more stress on the political dimension and would make more explicit its interrelationships with economic growth.
5. *Government bureaucracies have limited capabilities.* The evidence keeps accumulating that this is a truism and nowhere more so than in Africa.
6. *Trained manpower is important, but capital cannot be ignored.* I was seeking to formulate a counterweight argument to the conventional wisdom at the time that held that physical capital is the limiting factor in growth.
7. *The neglect of agriculture is costly.* Another dominant view held that the best prospects for developing countries was to speed their industrialization, which I challenged.
8. *Talent is the key to enhancing the quality of life.* The removal of barriers to the fuller development of human potential holds the key to progress; most of the responsibility rests with the indigenous population and facilitating organizations—political, economic, social—which must be built and strengthened before development can be transformed from a dream into a reality.

It was not until 1976 that I carried through a major effort to synthesize what we had learned about human resources since the onset of our empirical research in 1939, almost four decades earlier. *The Human Economy* (1976) set a series of ambitious goals. It discriminated between the conventional approaches of economists who treat labor as if it were a commodity and our alternative schema that took off from the concept that labor is embodied in human beings who have values and goals, who acquire competences and skills over many years of education and work experience, and who live in a society with institutions that help shape and give direction to their activities, although these institutions frequently are left behind by the changing times. Although change can be costly and dangerous, "The highest cost of all would follow an attempt to maintain the status quo in a world of never ending change" (p. 244).

A decade later, in 1985, I published two related volumes. The first, written with George J. Vojta, elaborated my earlier analysis of "The Employing Organization" in *The Human Economy*. We looked at the large corporation from the vantage point of its use of its managerial resources and discussed major shortcomings between its conventional organizational and management structure and the use of its people. A simplified version of the message of *Beyond Human Scale: The Large Corporation at Risk* (1985) is that the economies of scale are often cancelled out by diseconomies of coordination.

## A Half-Century
## of Human Resources Research

At the suggestion of Clark Abt, I selected about fifty publications from my research efforts over the past half-century that provide an overview of our findings about the many facets of human resources (*Understanding Human Resources*, 1985). The rereading and selection of these pieces led me to recognize more clearly than before the directions of this cumulative effort, its strengths as well as its weaknesses. I shall outline below what I believe to be the most important differences between our efforts at the Conservation of Human Resources Project at Columbia and mainline economics as it relates to labor market issues.

First and most important, our research has explicitly raised a host of objections to the underlying treatment of labor as a commodity, bought and sold in competitive markets, in which the assumption of workers' seeking to maximize their income and other benefits (including leisure) are postulated as the driving forces.

Second, the predilection of mainline economics to assess the relative forces tending toward and away from equilibrium largely ignores the powerful role of institutions in shaping worker competences and skills. Family structure and income, access to the educational system, the influence of discrimination on value formations, self-image, and motivation are often ignored or treated as peripheral by mainline economists.

During the quarter-century after 1940, the employment expansion of developed economies, and to a lesser extent, of developing economies, led many economists to believe that the Keynesian macroapproach provided an answer to the most difficult of all human resources problems— an inadequate number of employment opportunities relative to the number of job seekers. The period since 1970 has provided powerful and repeated evidence that a continuing high level of employment remains an elusive goal.

We have not addressed directly this overriding analytic challenge. We have, however, directed attention to the dangers of overconcentration on the dynamism of the private sector in an advanced economy in which the not-for-profit sector accounts for more than one-third of all jobs and also for much of the innovation on which private job creation ultimately depends. Moreover, we have insisted that a democracy confronting a continuing shortfall in jobs must continue to experiment with public job-creation efforts because the permanent disemployment of a significant minority can jeopardize a nation's future.

We have also addressed a number of critical human resources issues from the perspective of developing economies, subnational areas, and large organizations. In each instance we found the conventional wisdom wanting, particularly as we delved into the underutilization of managerial personnel in large corporations. We concluded from *Beyond Human Scale* that the future of developed economies is at risk unless large organizations become more adept at developing and utilizing their pools of talent.

## Human Capital Versus Human Resources

One way of assessing the alternative approaches that we have developed and that we consider halfway theories is to contrast them with those of the "human capital" theorists led by Gary Becker of Chicago. Becker, his colleagues, and his students, working within the main corpus of neoclassical economics, have been able to illuminate a great many important dimensions of the labor market, in particular the extent to which workers' earnings are related to their prior investments in education and training, and the ways in which married women allocate their time between work in their households and in paid employment. We shall note but not discuss their more esoteric efforts directed to applying the human capital methodology to such wide-ranging issues as crime, marriage and divorce, the rearing of "quality children," conscription, and discrimination.

The human capital school has surely demonstrated what was more or less implicit in the economics of Adam Smith and Alfred Marshall—that the investment/future returns mechanism could be applied to the study of human as well as to financial and physical capital. In a world characterized by the ever larger accretion of bodies of statistical data bearing on employment and earnings, the human capital approach has enabled investigators to go through their econometric paces and ferret out many interesting facts and findings. But in the present context, I shall limit myself to highlighting a few of the major differences between the human capital and the human resources approaches.

The human capital approach conceives of the labor market in much the same manner as it deals with the market for commodities or for any other scarce resource. The underlying assumptions are two: First, employers want to buy labor as cheaply as possible; workers want to get the best deal they can in terms of wages, fringe benefits, and other desiderata—such as safe and easy work in a pleasant environment where there are reduced prospects of their being laid off. Second, in most large urban markets, there are so many competing employers and workers that no company and no union is able to dominate and determine the outcome of the bargaining.

The human capital theory calls particular attention to the importance of firm-specific skills and points out that employers are willing to invest in their work force and add to their skills because those skills will be of value to the workers only if they remain with their present employer.

The human capital school also argues against the pervasiveness of racial discrimination in the labor market, insisting that employers acting in accordance with their self-interest would be inclined to hire the best worker irrespective of race for the lowest possible wage. When it comes to explaining the markedly lower wages and earnings of women workers, the human capital school emphasizes the smaller investments that most women in comparison to men have made in their education and in accumulating skills on the job because of their intermittent work record.

Clearly there is something to each of these observations and conclusions, but the critical question is whether the human capital school, by squeezing the analysis into the framework of neoclassical economics, has not done violence both to history and to the institutions that help to shape the labor market.

In the human resources approach we have found it essential to widen the angle of vision and to take into account the differences in the developmental experiences of individuals and groups, differences that largely determine the amount of "human capital" that young people are able to accumulate prior to their reaching working age. Next we have, in the case of women, emphasized the truly revolutionary changes that have been and that still are under way in altering their relationship to the world of work. As late as 1941 a woman civil servant in Massachusetts who married had to resign her position. Today about half of all married women with children under one year old are in the labor force. Furthermore, the oligopolistic companies that had to negotiate with strong unions in the U.S. heartland during the halcyon period of 1945–1970 and that anticipated that their booming markets were invulnerable surely bargained differently than the human capital school postulated.

I could go on and call attention to many other differences between us in point of departure, in lines of analysis, in policy conclusions—differences that led us to emphasize the striking changes occurring in the labor market as the U.S. economy shifted toward services, particularly business and professional services; the mounting evidence of segmentation in the labor market as it affects minority youth who fail to complete high school; the disturbing increase in the number of households headed by women, who carry responsibility for raising a high proportion of the nation's children; the unexplained disappearance from the labor market of so many black men of working age; the causes and consequences of the large stream of immigrants, including illegal entrants.

We are reasonably sure that the explanations for these and still other major developments in the labor market cannot possibly be captured by any single paradigm and surely not by the human capital approach. In fact convinced that reality is changing more rapidly than academics can study the changes, we have opted for halfway theories in the hope that we can capture at least in broad outline some of the significant new trends and point directions for public policy. The premise of our work in human resources has been the recognition that important as is the challenge of preparing for and making a living, paid employment is only one facet of a person's life.

# 9

## The Policy Arena

The formulation has been advanced repeatedly in the foregoing chapters that one measure of the relevance and success of economic analysis is its contribution to policy. Accordingly, in this chapter I shall select from my long experience—from President Roosevelt's second administration to President Reagan's first administration—a number of instances where economics and policy met face to face, and I shall extract some lessons about their interaction. All of the cases are drawn from the public (governmental) arena not because I believe that this is the only sphere for policy action, but because issues addressed in that arena provide an opportunity to consider the role of other sectors. Such a consideration would not necessarily obtain if the illustrations were from the corporate, trade union, or nonprofit arenas.

### Women and the World of Work

The first case relates to enlarging the scope of female participation in the labor market during World War II. Early in 1942, as a by-product of my consulting for the Executive Office of the President (the Committee on Scientific and Specialized Personnel), I was asked to speak at several conferences around the country about emerging manpower problems incident to the rapid buildup of the armed forces and the conversion of U.S. industry to war production. Stimulated by my earlier research interest in the relation of educated women (college graduates) to the world of work, I had informed myself about the utilization of women in Great Britain, which at the time was well into its third year of war. I found that the British were exercising tight controls over their civilian human resources and that women in the younger age groups were screened for essential defense service and assigned to specific jobs. The German experience did not parallel that of the British; Nazi Germany apparently had no interest in a more effective utilization of its female labor force.

After making a number of projections, I concluded that although millions of men were still unemployed, it would not be long before the United States would run out of male reserves and that early federal action was therefore indicated. My recommendation was to start a voluntary or compulsory registration of women with baccalaureate degrees in the twenty- to forty-four-year-old group. This recommendation was considered to be so outlandish by the staff director that he would not even forward it to the committee. When I reported for work in the Pentagon some months later as a manpower consultant attached to General Bretton B. Somervell's staff in the War Department's Services of Supply, I discovered that senior military personnel were addressing various women's groups throughout the United States, pleading with them to take defense jobs.

Each of the armed forces was building up a woman's corps so that women in uniform could take over support services and thereby free servicemen for combat duty. Colonel Oveta Culp Hobby was the head of the Women's Army Corps (WACs). Prospective changes in personnel policies and procedures were routinely sent to the WACs for comment. In many instances, the WACs' replies pointed to major shortcomings in the proposed regulations and contained constructive alternatives. After a while, the evidence indicated that the Office of the Assistant Chief of Staff for Personnel was the beneficiary of many insights and good advice from the WACs for drafting policies that affected men as well as women. In fact, one of the long-term gains resulting from the removal of all forms of discrimination in the hiring, assignment, and promotion of individuals belonging to different groups is the elimination of misconceptions and errors that are entrenched in organizations that deal with a more homogeneous group of employees.

As the end of hostilities approached in the late fall and winter of 1944–1945, the army sponsored a number of opinion surveys to assess the present attitudes and potential behavior of the troops once they returned to civilian life. The vast majority of those queried anticipated that married women would leave the work force and return to housekeeping and childrearing. It was my view that the large-scale entrance of women into the labor force represented a discontinuity in U.S. experience and that the former pattern whereby men worked out of the homes and women were restricted to the home had been permanently altered.

The United States won the war without having registered college women and with only modest direct controls over the civilian labor market. On balance, that was probably wise because of our limited capacity to operate with even modest controls. At one point, the army discovered that it had 600,000 more personnel on active duty than its authorized congressional ceiling of 7.7 million. When Under Secretary of War Robert Patterson, angered by a number of strikes in 1944 that delayed the shipment of ammunition to men at the front, recommended the introduction of a National Service Act to control the civilian labor market, he was unable to obtain the support of the Pentagon and was turned down by the Congress.

Four decades later, with the labor participation rates for women approaching the levels for men, the public still remains uneasy and ambivalent about the preferred work roles for married women. We have expanded opportunities for women to be hired into and promoted in many occupations, professions, and organizations from which they were formerly excluded, but overt and covert barriers remain. The buildup of support for and subsequent failure of the passage of the Equal Rights Amendment is only one recent illustration of our ambivalence.

Little attention has been paid to the strategic role that women have played in recent decades to help institutions of higher learning maintain their total enrollments and particularly the enrollments in their major professional schools. In the absence of steeply rising admissions on the part of women, institutions of higher education would have entered a period of major decline. What is more, medical, law, and business schools would have been confronted with a Hobson's choice: to scale down dramatically or to reduce their admission requirements. Only the large pool of qualified women applicants saved them.

What lessons can be extracted from this abbreviated account? First, if the market had been left to its own devices, it would have done little to open job and career opportunities for women and then only at a snail's pace. The major reason for women's greater acceptance in the workplace was the demands created by World War II. The powerful restraints of the preexisting structure once they had been loosened, could not be reinstituted. But adaptation to the new was slow in coming. Even with legislative and judicial support, the old patterns of behavior show great resilience. Furthermore, society has been remarkably slow to consider and even slower to put in place the range of innovations that are required now that most families have two wage earners and more than a majority of all women with minor children are in the labor force.

## Educational Preparation for Work

The second policy case that we will inspect relates to the extension of the educational preparation of successive cohorts of young people entering the labor force. Education and science gained prestige as a result of the development of the atomic bomb during World War II.

Moreover, the millions who enlisted or were inducted into the armed forces came to appreciate that their assignments, training, and promotions were greatly influenced by their prior educational status. Clearly, educational achievement was not an incidental matter when it determined who would be placed in a combat unit and who would be assigned to a clerical job in the rear.

We called attention in the last chapter to the horrendous manpower waste as a result of the pervasiveness of illiteracy among a significant minority of selectees, affecting one in four among blacks in the southeastern states. With differing motives, but primarily because it had come to believe in the value of education, in 1944 Congress passed the GI Bill, which represented the largest single intervention of the federal government to expand the educational (and occupational) opportunities available to young people who had been honorably discharged. The combination of federal assistance for both tuition expenses and living expenses enabled millions of veterans to return to school to complete their studies and led many others to reassess their career plans and enter and graduate from college or professional school.

College and university faculties are not particularly astute observers of the changing scene; they anticipated that the returning veterans would prove to be indifferent students, more interested in recuperating from their military service than in applying themselves seriously to their studies. No forecast could have been further from the truth. Older, more mature, often married, the veterans who returned to the campus were determined to make the most of the opportunities to which the GI Bill entitled them.

Just as Congress had spent only a short time discussing the GI Bill before passing it, the same haste characterized the next major Congressional move on the educational front in the late 1950s. The public and Congress were shocked that the USSR was the first nation to launch a satellite into space. They interpreted Sputnik's success as a threat to U.S. technological preeminence, a threat that they were determined to counter. Congress passed the National Defense Education Act (NDEA) in 1958. Although President Eisenhower indicated his belief that the federal government had no legitimate role to play in the support and direction of higher education, he signed the bill because federal support for higher education could strengthen the nation's defense.

NDEA expenditures were aimed at enlarging and improving the nation's pool of scientific and engineering personnel. Furthermore, it made funds available to support the expansion of foreign language courses and foreign area specialists. Small amounts of money were also made available to strengthen the preparatory process (high school) so that the pool of college and graduate students in the defense-related subjects could be rapidly increased. The new legislation also removed the financial barriers that had blocked many able young persons from low-income families from continuing with their studies.

The post–World War II era saw an increasing number of states act to establish and expand junior colleges in areas of population concentration; open branches of their state university system in urban centers; convert underutilized teacher-training institutions and add new campuses to their state university system; and finally, establish and enlarge scholarship and fellowship support for qualified students.

The third national effort on the educational front occurred in 1965 in connection with President Johnson's launching of his Great Society programs, which were focused primarily on improving the opportunities of the poor, the disadvantaged, and the elderly. Despite almost a century of effort, Congress had never been able to appropriate funds for basic education because of the opposition of religious groups that insisted that some of this money go to the support of parochial schools; the fear of southern Congressmen that federal money would be accompanied by federal interference with the South's separate system of public education; and conservatives of many stripes who were opposed on principle to weakening local control of schools.

The recital of these objections indicates the political determination and skill of President Johnson in reversing a century of opposition and in winning congressional approval for significant amounts of federal funds for public schools, primarily to enable them to improve the quality of education available to low-income, hard to educate youth.

The White House Conference on Education in 1965 was led by John Gardner, secretary of the Department of Health, Education and Welfare (HEW). The speakers and the delegates were enthusiastic about the new federal breakthrough on funding, but they made at best modest contributions to illuminating the causes and the cures for the low productivity of many schools, particularly those in metropolitan areas with large enrollments from low-income families.

To keep the issues in perspective, one must recall that shortly after World War II an increasing number of southern states, fearing that a Supreme Court decision would find that their racially segregated schools were not equal, substantially enlarged their appropriations for black schools. Moreover, state equalization efforts were also under way in other regions of the country to assure that schools in districts with a small tax base would not be seriously disadvantaged in providing an acceptable educational experience.

The two decades of 1950–1970, despite the much expanded total pupil population, saw an increase in real per pupil expenditures of about 100 percent. The widespread discontent of the early 1980s with the quality of basic education must not obscure the sizable efforts during this earlier era to improve quality and broaden equity.

A few concluding observations on these several efforts of educational reform. It was distinctly easier and less costly for the federal government through the GI Bill and NDEA (and later student grant and loan funds) to expand the opportunities for high school graduates to continue with higher education than it was for government at all levels to provide an adequate educational experience for large numbers of minority children from low-income homes. Once the school has to serve as an effective counterweight to an oppressive environment characterized by anomie, crime, segregation, discrimination, drugs, prostitution, and widespread unemployment, it is set up for failure. Moreover, even with good preschool opportunities (Headstart and similar programs), the deadweight of the environment is often too much for most schools to overcome. In a study of Harlem schools in New York City in 1980, we encountered fifteen year olds who did not know a single high school graduate who had secured a regular job. Under such circumstances and in the face of powerful peer pressures, it is not surprising that a high percentage of youngsters do not become seriously engaged in their studies and drop out before obtaining a diploma.

## The Challenge of Race

In 1966, President Johnson appointed a "secret" task force on the urban ghetto with George Shultz as chairman. The membership included a number of senior business executives, leaders of the black community, and academics (including myself). The staff official from the White House was William Kolberg, who later became assistant secretary of labor. Our assignment was to look at all aspects of the ghetto and to outline a program that held promise of accomplishing fundamental improvements in the lives of the people who were growing up under such distressful conditions.

Howard Rosen, the longtime director of research and development for the U.S. Department of Labor, suggested, only partially in jest, that the best way for the federal government to proceed was to dynamite the major ghettos and redistribute the people who had been living there. He did not believe that any halfway measures would succeed. One of the most intense of the task force members, a leading industrialist, kept insisting that the beginning and end of all the problems in the ghetto were directly related to the large number of illegitimate births, particularly to teenagers. In his view, no significant gains could be achieved until this problem was solved. His constant harping on illegitimate births led me to inquire of another task force member, a distinguished constitutional lawyer, how long it would be before the Supreme Court might rule that carrying or not carrying a fetus to term is a matter of choice for the woman and not subject to regulation by the state. His answer was that an abortion case might get to the Supreme Court in the early 1980s when the court would probably find an excuse to send it back for findings of fact and that the court might rule on the subject in the late 1980s or early 1990s. At that point it might decide that abortion was a matter of personal choice. In point of fact, the Supreme Court so ruled in *Roe v. Wade* in 1973.

One of the effective techniques employed by the task force was to arrange for small groups of members to spend a day or two visiting the people who lived in the ghettos and talking directly with them about their problems and their aspirations. There is little doubt that the immediacy of these experiences contributed greatly to the structuring of a unanimous report despite the wide range of opinion among the members. No one who had spent two days in the ghettos of New York, Philadelphia, Cleveland, or Chicago had serious reservations about recommending major interventions by the federal government. Our final recommendations were for an annual expenditure level of between $13 billion and $18 billion.

The escalation of hostilities in Vietnam placed all new large federal expenditure programs beyond the pale. We were called together by Joseph Califano acting for the president; our draft reports were sequestered, and we were asked not to talk about the task force and surely to avoid publicizing our emerging findings and recommendations. From the time that he steered the Civil Rights Act of 1958 through the Senate and particularly after he became vice president and then president, Lyndon Johnson was the nation's first, and possibly its only, chief executive who was so deeply committed to improving the condition of the blacks that he was willing to commit a large part of his political capital to that end. The tragedy of Vietnam went far beyond the loss of life in Southeast Asia. The blacks, as Martin Luther King, Jr., so clearly perceived, were victimized by that horrendous blunder of a war with little purpose and no goal.

This calls to mind an earlier assignment. Secretary of the Army Frank Pace asked me to assist in the desegregation of the army in 1951–1952 when President Truman decided that the time had come to implement the recommendations of the Fahey report that had called for early action on this front. A few points stand out clearly. I went to SHAPE and sought General Eisenhower's help before proceeding to Heidelberg (U.S. Headquarters, Europe) to talk with General Thomas Handy and members of his staff. Eisenhower was sympathetic, but he offered neither advice nor assistance; he explained that the issue was a matter of concern solely to the United States, not to NATO.

In my discussions at Heidelberg, I made it clear that the time schedule for total desegregation was twelve months, at the expiration of which field units, living quarters, recreational facilities, in short, every aspect of the army, had to be fully integrated. Handy's staff insisted that the program could not be carried out in less than two, or at least one, decade. Only Lt. Gen. Manton Eddy, the commanding general, Seventh Army, whose headquarters were in Stuttgart, accepted the challenge and raised no serious objections.

After my return to the Pentagon, I discovered that, true to the ways of the army, Heidelberg had written informally to Lt. Gen. Anthony C. McAuliffe, assistant chief of staff for manpower and personnel, to inquire whether I was *really* speaking for the secretary and the chief of staff. When Heidelberg learned that the top staff was determined to desegregate within the stated time period, they fell in line. When the under secretary of the army, Earl Johnson and I visited Heidelberg the following summer, General Handy spent an hour after dinner recounting the great success of *his* efforts to desegregate all U.S. forces in Europe. And he had good reason to be proud of how smoothly the entire desegregation effort had been carried out. A determined leadership can accomplish a great deal in a short period to alter organizational attitudes and behavior.

Eisenhower believed that recourse to the law and administrative fiat were ill advised in the area of race relations. He looked to education, the leadership of the churches, and voluntary efforts rather than to the coercive use of government power. I read the army's successful desegregation efforts of 1951–1952 as powerful support for the application of power to change encrusted structures and folkways.

One more illustration in support of recourse to the law. In 1963, President Kennedy sent a civil rights bill to Congress that lacked an employment provision. The president, always a cautious politician, had decided that the prospect was better for passing a bill limited to public accommodations than an expanded bill that also addressed discrimination in employment. Senator Joseph Clark of Pennsylvania asked whether I thought that a number of prominent academics could be persuaded to testify in favor of an amendment that would add an employment section to the bill. I assured him that such testimony could be elicited, and in 1964 an amendment was added before the bill was put to a vote and passed. It is possible that if President Kennedy had not been assassinated and Judge Howard W. Smith of the House Rules Committee had not added sex discrimination to race discrimination in the belief that the addition would torpedo the bill, the Civil Rights Act with an employment section might have been doomed. But success in politics, as in business, goes to the risk taker.

To complete these observations about desegregation, I will comment briefly on the Kerner Commission, which reported in 1966 after extended hearings at which I had the opportunity to present evidence about the large gaps that remained between the job and income profiles of whites and blacks. The commission's report was analytically sound, but its strident tone and ambitious goals were out of step with the nation's willingness and capacity to respond.

## Health Policy and Programs

In addition to manpower and employment issues, my longest exposure in the policy arena relates to health policy and programming. From 1943 to 1946 I served as chief logistical advisor to the surgeon general of the army and had oversight over the policy and plans for all patients, hospital beds, and medical personnel. I carried away from that wartime experience some important conclusions: Ample resources without a sound organizational structure do not permit the delivery of quality care; patients are at risk from overtreatment as much as from lack of treatment; patterns of treatment differ greatly among competently trained physicians with respect to both procedures and length of hospital stays; allied health personnel, properly deployed, can add greatly to the effective utilization of physicians; the attitudes of patients toward their recovery is a major factor in determining their health outcomes; and simple statistical reporting systems can provide useful guidance to those who have the responsibility to oversee the use of resources and to assure quality.

After the end of hostilities, the then secretary of war, Robert R. Patterson, with the prompting of some of his advisers, established the secretary of war's Medical Advisory Committee (of which I was a member) under the chairmanship of the distinguished Harvard thoracic surgeon, E. D. Churchill, to help the army maintain close linkages to civilian medicine, which had been a major contributor to the high level of performance that military medicine had had been able to achieve during the extended two-front war. As the years passed and civilian physicians were increasingly able to shape their practices and their lives according to their preferences, the armed forces experienced more and more difficulties in attracting and retaining the numbers and quality of specialists they needed to operate a first-class medical service. Even after Congress funded an armed forces medical school, the services encountered difficulties in attracting and retaining specialists. In recent years, a growing number of shortcomings have become public. Moreover, no secretary of defense has ever been successful in bringing about significant cooperation, including the joint use of hospital facilities, among the three services.

One of the major accomplishments of the federal government in the post–World War II era was the thorough overhaul of the Veterans Administration including its inadequate medical service, an accomplishment achieved through the leadership of General Omar Bradley, and aided by successive medical chiefs who were able to elicit the support of the deans and faculties of most of the nation's medical schools. But an independent medical system for veterans, most of whom do not suffer from service-connected disabilities, has been periodically attacked by federal officials and by leaders of civilian medicine who have questioned the need and the cost of operating a system solely for veterans.

In 1977, a prestigious committee of the Assembly of Life Sciences of the National Research Council under the chairmanship of Dr. Saul Farber recommended to Congress that the Veterans Administration's health care system be radically and rapidly reduced and that veterans should increasingly receive their care in civilian institutions. In writing about the report in *The New England Journal of Medicine* (1978) in a piece entitled "How Not to Offer Congress Advice on Health Policy," I called attention to the fact that the committee had not adequately addressed the full range of political as well as health care issues that had to be weighed before making such a radical recommendation. But the problem will have to be faced some time soon now that the federal government is under increasing fiscal pressure to control its total outlays for health care and more and more veterans are reaching an age when they become eligible for Medicare. With evidence mounting that the nation's civilian hospital system has a sizable surplus of beds and that the surplus is likely to worsen in the years ahead, it would make little sense for Congress to appropriate new funds to expand the large veterans hospital system. There are better ways to assure that indigent veterans have access to treatment. Farber's report may have been premature and extreme, but we are entering a period when at a minimum, the federal government must consider anew how it can make use of two federally supported systems—for veterans and for the elderly—to provide an acceptable level of care for both without embarking on a new veterans hospital construction program.

In 1959–1963 I served as a member of the National Mental Health Advisory Council at a time when the National Institute of Mental Health (NIMH) was still a part of the National Institutes of Health. (It now belongs to the Alcohol, Drug and Mental Health Administration.) During my four-year term I made the following observations about federal policy in the arena of mental health. First, there was a powerful alliance between the civilian leadership and the Congress that was able repeatedly to bypass the administration on critical issues including budget. Mrs. Albert Lasker played a leading role in organizing the proponents for more research and better care and saw to it that one of her representatives was appointed to the advisory council, which for the most part consisted of leading professionals with a few laymen for ballast. The director and the staff of the NIMH saw their principal task as extracting more money from the Congress and insuring that it go to those civilian institutions that submitted the best proposals.

When I joined the council, the NIMH was receiving about $50 million in annual funds; four years later the figure was approximately $180 million. I kept pointing out, but to little avail, that a significant proportion of the funds were going to academic psychologists who knew how to prepare sophisticated research proposals that impressed the peer review committees, but that held little or no promise of adding to psychiatric knowledge or improved patient care. I often told Dr. Robert Felix, the dedicated director of the institute, that there was a danger in his pursuit of ever larger appropriations. At some point, Congress would take a closer look at his budget and would be likely to ask difficult questions about what its earlier appropriations had accomplished.

There were two policy initiatives in particular that made little sense to me. Because of the shortage of psychiatrists in state mental hospitals, the NIMH had persuaded Congress to fund a sizable retraining program whereby physicians, both general practitioners and specialists, could receive substantial financial aid while they pursued psychiatric training on the assumption that they would eventually add to the small pool of available psychotherapists. It seemed to me that these newly trained psychiatrists, as soon as they had completed their training, were likely to start private practices in affluent neighborhoods where they would treat ambulatory patients with minor neuroses and would not be available to oversee and treat the seriously mentally ill confined in state hospitals. This was my first encounter with poorly conceived, poorly executed health manpower policy.

Felix and his staff had also become impressed with what they were learning about the "successes" of the British in treating more and more of their mental patients within the community, thus avoiding the need for prolonged hospitalization. Because new programs must compete for congressional patronage and funding with existing programs that have staunch supporters, they have little chance of winning approval and funding unless their sponsors make exaggerated claims on their behalf. But in doing so the sponsors fall into a trap. Several years down the road they will often be unable to impress their friends and even less their opponents that they have accomplished what they originally promised to do. And that is what happened to the community mental health center program.

The two most important dimensions of health planning and policy that I shall identify and briefly discuss are the supply of physician personnel and the passage of Medicare and Medicaid. By the early 1960s, because of the decision of the the American Medical Association (AMA) to use all of its resources to fight Medicare, the federal government was finally able to take initial steps to expand the supply of physicians. During the next eight years the federal government intervened many more times to the same end. In the early and mid-1960s, Washington bureaucrats talked of a shortage of physicians of 50,000 or 100,000, without providing much support for their estimates. But opinion leaders, inside and outside of American medicine, were generally supportive of a forced expansion in the supply of physicians. Drawing on my World War II experience, I spelled out my doubts and fears and stressed that broadening the access of the elderly and the poor to the health care system—surely desirable objectives—did not necessarily require a vast expansion in the supply of physicians. Improved organization and new financing together with greater reliance on allied health workers could lead to improved access. By 1971, Congress, realizing that the large additions to the supply of physicians still left a minority of the population with inadequate coverage, redefined the problem in terms of specialty and geographic maldistribution, again stipulating rather than specifying the causes of maldistribution. Despite sizable new congressional appropriations for training for family practice residencies and for enrollments in the National Physician Health Service Corps, the residual problems of access did not disappear.

With the advantage of hindsight, it is clear that the unwillingness of the AMA to take a position on the issue of enlarging the physician supply after 1963 and the powerful forces in and out of Congress that supported strong federal action overshadowed the few dissenters who questioned the rationale of an expansionary policy. Even after the dissemination in 1980 of the prestigious Graduate Medical Education National Advisory Committee (GMENAC) report, which projected large surpluses of physicians for 1990 and for 2000, the issue was not addressed either by the leaders of medicine or others. Most economists, convinced that an increased supply will reduce price, were strong supporters of an enlarged supply, ignoring or ignorant of the many ways in which the unit price of physician services could be reduced while total costs would nonetheless expand.

As noted above, the AMA fought hard to stave off the passage of Medicare in the early 1960s but lost the battle when Wilbur Mills, chairman of the House Ways and Means Committee, decided that the elderly had to have financial protection against large hospital bills. Through the astute legislative liaison of Wilbur Cohen, the assistant secretary of HEW, the administration also secured the passage of Medicaid. From being a minor partner in the financing of health care, government (with the federal government accounting for almost three-quarters of the total) quickly became the largest payer, accounting today for about 40 percent of all outlays. Despite the radical change in financing, President Johnson, seeking to mollify the AMA, promised that the government would not seek to alter the basic relationships between physician and patient. By this single promise, Johnson set the stage for the accelerated increase in health care expenditures, which rose absolutely and relatively; in 1964, total dollar outlays were $41 billion and accounted for 6.5 percent of GNP. The figures for 1985 totaled about $420 billion and approximated 10.5 percent of GNP. Broad entitlements without budgetary controls was an invitation to financial instability, a condition that Congress began to recognize in the early 1970s but for which we still have no effective remedy. The one error that we have not made, at least up to the present, is to pass sweeping new legislation under the rubric of "national health insurance" (NHI), which some believe would bring health care costs under control and still provide the public with the type of health care to which it has been accustomed. Because Jimmy Carter, as a presidential candidate, had committed himself to NHI, I wrote a monograph, *The Limits of Health Reform* (1977), and I asked a member of the cabinet to put it in Carter's hands in the hope of restraining his enthusiasm for this particular solution. It turned out that budgetary restraints sufficed to derail the president's interest.

## Technical Assistance Overseas

Another arena of policy that I shall address is that of technical assistance. In 1953, the Government of Israel asked the U.S. State Department to have me consult on matters affecting manpower policy and programming. Although the department had avoided sending American Jews to Israel, it agreed in my case, probably because of encouragement from the White House. This was my first trip to the Middle East. The previous year I had accompanied the undersecretary of the army on an extended trip to army and air force bases that took us from Lybia to Thule, just below the North Pole. But Israel and the Middle East were new.

My early tie to Israel resulted from my diplomatic assignment on behalf of the United States in 1946 when I negotiated for and on behalf of nonrepatriable refugees the second Reparations Agreement involving

German reparations including nonmonetary, gold, and heirless funds in Switzerland. About 85 percent of what eventually turned out to be approximately $60 million was allocated to the Jewish Agency and to the Joint Distribution Committee to assist in the resettlement of Jewish refugees. In connection with that assignment, I visited in London with David Ben-Gurion, who later attended my wedding. He had been a longtime friend of my father-in-law, Robert Szold.

Despite this earlier contact I had great difficulty in the summer of 1953 in orienting myself to Israel. More than 100,000 recent refugees were housed in temporary shelters; agricultural production was low, and Israel had to import much of its food; it had no real industry, just some small work shops around Haifa and Tel Aviv; the borders were not fully secure; and the U.S. Treasury had sent two experts, Raymond Mikesell and Gardner Patterson, to instruct and assist the Israelis in controlling their inflation so that the country would need less aid from the United States.

I knew from long discussions with Mikesell and Patterson that they were even more at sea. They kept insisting that because the Arabs had been able to live off the land by cultivating olives and oranges and tending sheep, the Israelis should be able to do the same. With tens of thousands of unemployed and underemployed immigrants, they strongly opposed expenditures for farm machinery. Moreover, they had a pessimistic assessment of Israel's capacity to become a center for even selected manufacturing because the country had no energy, raw materials, or access to regional markets. I saw the point of their skepticism and pessimism, but I knew that they were leaving out several critical factors— the strength of the Zionist dream, the quality of the leadership, the willingness of Diaspora Jewry (especially Jews in the United States) to help, the human capital of many immigrants, and the potential of governmental assistance from abroad, particularly from the United States and also possibly from some European governments.

I finally found the key to the riddle: The only reasonable perspective on the Israeli economy was to assess the present and the future in terms of where the economy had been some years earlier. All cross-national assessments were beside the point. When I left after an intense eight weeks of activity, I was willing to bet that Israel would make it, although I had no idea of how it would solve its existing, not to mention its future, problems. Over the next decades, I returned for many more field visits, but despite phenomenal gains in modernization, per capita wealth, research and development, a much strengthened military posture, and many more remarkable achievements, I always left with some degree of unease, less because of unresolved economic problems and more because of social tensions. The major challenge that Israel faces in 1987 is to speed the process of accommodation and assimilation between the children and grandchildren of older settlers from Europe and families and descendants of the new settlers from the Arab world.

When we left Israel in 1953, we took the plane to Cyprus and another plane to Ankara. Some months later, when Secretary of Labor James P. Mitchell arranged that I make a presentation to the president and his cabinet on "The Skills of the U.S. Work Force," I was able to intrigue the Cabinet with the following story about our technical assistance to Turkey. On a Saturday afternoon, the U.S. Agricultural attaché took me out to the countryside. At one place we ran into a large group of Turkish farmers walking around a tremendous U.S. combine, which stood inert. The explanation was as follows: The Turks had relatively little difficulty in learning to drive the machine, but when it hit a large rock or encountered some other impediment, it stopped working. It remained out of commission until the British mechanic whose territory covered an area of 500 square miles came back to fix it, which was once a month. It would then be operational for a week or so before the next breakdown. The attaché estimated that it was operational one week in four—low utilization for a piece of equipment that cost at the time $125,000. The points I stressed to the cabinet were that we were sending too many high-priced capital goods abroad and that we could do more to help the third world and at a much reduced cost by providing more vocational and technical training on less sophisticated equipment.

In 1966, the State Department asked me to undertake a manpower survey of Ethiopia that also gave me an opportunity to spend a little time in Egypt, both in Cairo and in the Delta. After a morning in the incomparable Cairo museum, which had many artifacts from two and three thousand years before the common era, I visited the Delta in the company of the minister of agriculture. On several occasions during that drive, I was convinced that the farmers in the fields were using exact replicas of the plow that I had just seen in the museum. But there was one difference: Some farmers were listening to portable radios!

In discussions with the younger members of the civil bureaucracy, I found little interest and less concern about Egypt's relations to Israel. Land maps of the Middle East simply left the territory that was Israel's blank. This was before the war of 1967, but the civilian bureaucrats appeared preoccupied with other problems and didn't want or need renewed fighting with their neighbor. My recollection of this pervasive attitude made me an optimist during the long-drawn-out Camp David negotiations.

I visited Ethiopia in January and again in June of 1966, spending a total of about five weeks in the country, primarily in and around Addis Ababa. I had arranged with the State Department to have a highly experienced manpower specialist, Herbert Smith of Jerusalem, spend six months collecting the information needed for our comprehensive report. Ethiopia, according to our best estimates, was a country of about 25 million, overwhelmingly illiterate (more than 90 percent), overwhelmingly rural, in the lowest per capita income category, where the emperor's horses in their daily exercise routine had the right of way on the sidewalks of the capital. Much of the cattle was seriously diseased, internal communications were often possible only by plane because of the rugged terrain, and the outlying provinces barely acknowledged the emperor's sovereignty.

The United States was trying to be helpful, but in the key agricultural project sponsored by Oklahoma State University, the U.S. experts were largely isolated on their experimental farm; there were exchanges of military favors, including gifts of equipment to the Ethiopian military from the United States for opportunities to monitor communications; we were helping the university get on its feet. But Smith and I made a calculation in *Manpower Strategy for Developing Countries: Lessons from Ethiopia* (1967) that highlighted the immensity of the task of speeding modernization. With substantial foreign assistance and good internal management, both of which were highly problematic, it would take until the year 2000 for Ethiopia to turn 10 percent of its economy into manufacturing (handicrafts). The near- and middle-term prospects for Ethiopia were tied to improvements in productivity in agriculture, and the prospects looked bleak.

Over the following years, I traveled to the Far East (Indonesia, Singapore, and Vietnam), Southeast Asia, Central Asia (Afghanistan and Pakistan), Iran, and also to the Eastern Bloc countries, all on behalf of the State Department, with occasional additional assignments from the U.S. Army. My major duties were to consult with and advise government manpower planners and to lecture to university, business, and occasionally, trade union audiences. I am listing below some of the more important lessons that I extracted from these extensive travels abroad, particularly in the highly populated Asian countries.

In the late 1950s, Saburo Okita, at the time chief economist in the Office of the Prime Minister of the Government of Japan, visited me at Columbia University to discuss the future of manpower policy in his country, which I had visited only once some weeks after V-J day, when it lay prostrate. I had followed from afar Japan's remarkable recovery, and when we spoke, it appeared to me that Japan's best chance to continue its progress lay in the enhancement of its human resources; to extend the basic educational system to high school graduation; and to increase the flow of students into institutions of higher learning. Okita translated my early volume, *Human Resources: The Wealth of a*

*Nation* (1958), and many of my subsequent books have been translated into Japanese, presumably because my emphasis on the human resources factor in economic development has struck a responsive note among Japanese leaders. When I visited Japan in 1967, I noted a paradox: Japanese management was clearly aware of and alert to the importance of skill development and utilization among all levels of its work force, but it had demonstrated only modest flexibility when it came to "womanpower." Two decades later, that continues to be a challenge that the leadership—and the society more broadly—still must confront and resolve. It is amazing that the Japanese have been able to do so well at home and abroad while they continue to underutilize half of their human potential. One of these days, and probably quite soon, Japan will have to change its ways with respect to the improved utilization not only of its womanpower but also of its older population (fifty-five and over) whose early retirement is extracting a horrendous cost.

Although I would have been hard-pressed to believe in 1967 that South Korea would soon enter a period of accelerated economic development, I was impressed by the advances it had made since my earlier visit in December 1945. Major contributors to the process of economic development were the sizable investments in education, particularly in urban areas, reinforced by the advantages of a homogeneous population stimulated by its gaining national independence. In addition, the Koreans accelerated their acquisitions of skills and capital as a result of the large U.S. military presence and liberal U.S. aid and had a strong, if autocratic, government that could and did pursue the goal of accelerated development.

Singapore—with its dominant Chinese population in the midst of a Malay world, under an autocratic but efficient government that knew where it wanted to go and how to get there—was also impressive. The ruling cadre recognized that Singapore had to exploit its producer services—banking and transport—and add a significant manufacturing component. In talks with the then minister of finance, I was impressed to learn that the Singapore government had sent several groups of workers to Australia for skill training.

The conventional interpretation of the Indonesian troubles of 1965 was that an attempted Communist coup was repressed with heavy loss of life. The interpretation provided by one of the senior military officers was pure Malthusianism: Many migrants from the land had moved into urban areas, but when the urban economy worsened, they returned home, after which there was a life and death struggle between the returned owners of the land and the temporary tenants. Only the winners would eat. Although the U.S. embassy and other foreign experts talked about a quarter of a million deaths resulting from the conflict, my informant put the figure above 1.5 million!

Two visits to India in the late 1960s and early 1970s yielded many conflicting observations and impressions of the subcontinent. A quasi-Western metropolis such as Bombay contrasts sharply with Calcutta, with its quarter million or more street people and a total metropolitan population of 9 million, characterized by great vitality but also abysmal poverty. Agricultural regions such as the Punjab were responding to the Green Revolution, but in other areas, the birds and weather caused a loss of one-third of the crops.

One point emerged with clarity. Western concepts of labor force and employment were ill suited to assess what was transpiring in the Indian economy. Useful concepts had to be related to the extended family's ability to feed its members; the number of days that individuals were able to engage in productive labor; and the amount of cash income that a family could earn during the course of a year. Taking the long view, it appeared that India had been able to increase its productivity to support a more than threefold increase in its population since 1920; the majority of the population since independence in 1947 had enjoyed some modest gains in its standard of living, particularly when allowance was made for its increased access to schooling and health services; but a sizable minority, possibly as many as one in three, were living at or below the ragged edge. The government planners, especially the more optimistic among them, appeared to be mesmerized by their models of socialism and ignored the many reality factors—economic, political, human resources—that stood between the nation's goals and their realization.

Two visits to Iran during this same period provided some understanding of the fiasco that overtook the United States in its Iranian policy at the end of the decade. The conspicuous U.S. role in this rigidly controlled but unstable country should have been seen as an unacceptable risk. In my 1969 debriefing, I asked the specialists in the State Department to consider the dilemma the United States would face if the shah were assassinated or otherwise lost power.

Here was a ruler who did not trust his own ministers and who kept reassigning them to new posts so that they could not develop a power base of their own. Here was a ruler bent on forced modernization whose students in his own university at Shiraz went on strike to protest mixed dancing. Here was a country where many of the best educated and most successful professionals went abroad and refused to return even when highly attractive offers were dangled before them. Here was a country in which bribery and corruption were a way of life for the royal family, their hangers-on, and most of the multinationals that had contracts with the government. In turn, many of these contracts were ill conceived; others had little prospect of being successfully completed, and only a few promised long-term benefits to the population.

One more illustration: In the late 1960s, after I had published *The Pluralistic Economy* (1965), several of the Eastern Bloc countries indicated that they would welcome a visit from me on a cultural exchange program under the auspices of the U.S. Department of State to talk about the role of "producer services" in economic development. I came away from a two-month visit to all of the COMECON countries except Poland—which cancelled my visa when they discovered that I had long-standing ties with Israel—with a few simple conclusions. Marxist theory weighed heavily on these controlled economies because banking, domestic and international, was viewed askance. State control of agriculture was highly dysfunctional. Bureaucracy exacted a heavy toll in the use and misuse of resources. Each of the COMECON countries had impressive manufacturing plants with modern machinery in place, but many were operating at 30 or 40 percent of capacity. I learned that the service infrastructure was largely missing. Many factories had to wait for a month or two for essential raw materials or a critical piece of machinery. The supply of consumer goods represented in retail stores, even in the capital cities, was pitiful in quantity, quality, and variety.

But for all these shortcomings most people looked reasonably healthy, wore appropriate clothing, and much new housing was going up. Those at or near the top had many privileges and were able to enjoy such luxuries as were available: from seats at the opera to meals in the best restaurants. There was little or no recorded unemployment, but labor productivity was abysmally low. Once there, I understood why I had been invited: Many of the state planners had realized that a modern economy, even one run on socialist principles, had to make more use of "services" than Marx had allowed for in *Das Kapital*.

## The Armed Services

With the exception of my continuing involvement in training and employment policies, there was one further policy arena, the Pentagon, that had long engaged my interest and attention. My involvement with the Pentagon was primarily with the War Department, later the Department of the Army. However, I served a four-year term as a member of the Scientific Advisory Board, U.S. Air Force; my last major assignment was as chair of a manpower advisory committee to the Defense Science Board in 1970–1971, and I served for many years as a member of the faculty of the Industrial College of the Armed Forces. I had reported for work in the Control Division, Services of Supply, in September

1942, and my last direct exposure to the problems of the Pentagon was in 1981 when I was a member of a special review committee established by the comptroller general, Elmer Staats, to assess the readiness posture of the armed forces. Throughout these four decades, my interest and responsibility was human resources, military and civilian, officer and enlisted men and women, white and black, combat and noncombat.

World War II had demonstrated the tremendous capability of the armed forces to expand from a small poorly equipped and unsophisticated organization into the most powerful military machine that the world had ever known. Certainly much of the success reflects the capabilities of the more than 14 million Americans who volunteered or were drafted. But a large part of the credit must go to the professional military leadership of the army, navy, and air corps, which had the responsibility to recruit, train, equip, transport, and deploy the troops successfully in combat with the enemy. Much that happened between Pearl Harbor and V-J Day, both at home and abroad, did not reflect favorably on the efficiency with which the armed forces carried out their difficult missions. But their accomplishments should not be underestimated.

We have no analogue in our nation's history where such a huge task of mobilizing human resources was ventured and carried out successfully. Although one of my first assignments for General Bretton B. Somervell was to reduce the Army Service Forces by 180,000 civilians and to transfer 60,000 soldiers from service to combat assignments—all within a period of ninety days—the fact that the ASF was a functioning organization, before and after, was more impressive than its overstaffing and other shortcomings.

I called attention earlier to the striking success of the army in pushing through a program of desegregation in the 1950–1951 period, against the initial opposition of many senior officers. But once these officers understood that the president, the secretary of the army, and the chief of staff were committed to achieving this goal, they fell in line and performed this difficult task quicker and better than anybody could have anticipated.

Building on their experience in World War I and on later advances in psychometrics, the military services in World War II and subsequently devoted considerable resources to perfecting their personnel assessment techniques, particularly screening devices that helped them to judge whether selectees would be able to perform effectively in uniform. Faced with the challenge of large numbers, the military early developed a number of standardized tests. Selectees who scored in Armed Forces Qualification Test (AFQT) categories I, II, or III were much more likely to make the grade on active duty than those scoring in category IV or particularly, in category V. A high school diploma was viewed as a good indicator of potential socialization to a military organization dependent on strict discipline. The military looked askance at potential recruits who had had run-ins with the criminal justice system.

Additional screening criteria were also employed, such as height, weight, emotional stability, and heterosexuality, but because of the limitations of the total pool, the military could not set them at the norms the services would have preferred. Each of them wanted only the best, but the total numbers of recruits required made this impossible. Moreover, the services were in constant competition with each other for a preferred allocation of the available manpower. In the midst of the Korean War, the secretary of the army called a meeting of his senior advisers at which I tried to convince the chief of staff, General Lawton Collins, that the army's personnel screening policies were dysfunctional. My final argument went as follows: Would the general prefer to take out a night detail in Korea consisting of young men who had grown up in the Tennessee mountains who had failed to graduate from elementary school or a group of PhDs from Columbia University? He maneuvered around the question, but the army continued to adhere to a relatively high educational cutoff point.

During the Great Society program, President Johnson enlisted Secretary of Defense Robert McNamara's cooperation to reduce selection standards and to monitor the outcomes. The Pentagon accepted about a quarter of a million "substandard" men. Although the follow-up findings were never publicized, they showed that over 90 percent of the group performed satisfactorily or better. The military's desire for high cutoff points on selection tests was predicated on an exaggerated, but not totally mistaken, belief that the less-educated, low-scoring men were more likely to prove ineffective. But it also reflected racial prejudice: Blacks were overrepresented in groups IV and V.

Racial prejudice was not the only prejudice that characterized the armed services. The services were reluctant to enlarge the numbers and proportion of women in uniform; to increase their reliance on civilians, even for work on domestic bases; to make more use abroad of indigenous labor; or to expand opportunities for reservists. In this respect, the armed services shared with other large organizations the belief that they could operate best with their own employees, preferably male uniformed personnel, over whom they could exercise tight control and who provided the best base in the event of mobilization. It should be observed in passing that the larger the uniform base, the more opportunities for officers to be promoted.

The constant advances in technology reinforced the determination of the armed services to be more selective in their manpower policies because the services had a steadily increasing need for specialists to operate their more sophisticated equipment and systems. But it was by no means clear that the trade-offs they continued to make were optimal. First, the new weapons systems were almost always late; contractors promised more than they could deliver; learning to operate and maintain the new equipment often proved more complicated than had been anticipated; troops in combat sometimes preferred to use older models that they could handle easily and keep operational rather than take a chance with the newer and more sophisticated equipment. The imbalance between the U.S. technology and manpower was never more sharply demonstrated than in Vietnam where we fought a war in which we could use only a small part of our advanced technology, and often, not very well.

The Vietnam conflict revealed another major shortcoming—our excessively long "tail" that provided only small numbers of soldiers for front line duty. Supply lines admittedly were stretched from reception centers on the East Coast of the United States to Saigon and the combat zones. But our military organization used inordinately large numbers of soldiers to support those in the front lines.

In 1971, President Nixon appointed the Gates Commission to review the future of the draft, and the Department of Defense sent my name to the White House for possible membership. Fortunately, I was not appointed because I was opposed to shifting to a voluntary force even though I recognized the difficulties of selecting only a portion of the age-eligible group. The president and the public were ready to abandon selective service in favor of a voluntary force, and Milton Friedman offered his fellow commissioners all the rationales they needed to support a unanimous report that advocated a free market solution—pay servicemen what they are worth.

The Defense Science Board decided at the beginning of the 1970s, with the changes pending in manpower procurement and the war in Vietnam winding down, that the time was opportune to have a task force of civilian consultants take a hard look into the personnel policies and practices of the armed forces. I was the chair of the task force and after almost a year's deliberations its report was completed, *Manpower Research and Management in Large Organizations: A Report of the Task Force on Manpower Research* (1971).

In preparing the draft of the report, I reflected on my almost thirty years of continuing exposure to the manpower policies of the armed forces—with an aim of distinguishing the "doable" from the desirable. This is where I came out: The armed services were going to go their own ways, largely independent of one another and paying attention only occasionally to the larger manpower issues facing the nation. There was little or no likelihood that any secretary of defense, even with help from senior civilian and military advisers, would be able to bring about more than marginal changes in the behavior of each of the services. The control of its personnel system was critical to each of the services, for the personal system was the guardian of the service's tradition and the key to its future. For better or worse, and it was an admixture of both, the services should be encouraged to manage themselves better. The best leverage to assure such an outcome was for the president and the Congress to scrutinize closely their annual budget for personnel and to encourage each of the services to pursue a modest but sustained program of research focused on military manpower issues, preferably in association with the Department of Defense and a few civilian specialists from outside the Pentagon.

The unsolved problems of military manpower have to be seen in perspective. They loom large, but they are of the same genre as the other policy areas that I have reviewed—women, education, blacks, health funding, and technical assistance. Any distinction that military manpower can claim derives from their being deeply embedded in each of the armed services, which in turn operates largely under its own momentum, subject only to fiscal controls set by the president and the Congress.

# 10

## Toward Realistic
## Economic Policy

### The Reality of Change

It may be useful to start this penultimate chapter with a few references
to the great economists' conceptions of the relations between theory
and policy. Adam Smith, a believer in free trade, noted that if a foreign
nation were to place restrictions on trade with Great Britain, it would
be desirable, nay necessary, for Parliament to answer in kind to protect
British interests. Unless all nations adhere to a policy of free trade, no
nation can follow its dictates.

Smith introduced some additional caveats. In a world characterized
by nationalistic rivalries, which often led to blockades and war, he noted
that a nation that valued its freedom, security, and survival had to
adopt certain regulatory and expenditure policies. These could not be
justified if they were predicated solely on the principle of the most
efficient allocation of resources.

Despite Smith's generally negative view of the performance capabilities
of government and the bureaucracy and his clear preference for enlarging
the scope and scale of decisionmaking for the individual, he favored
public funding for education because he knew that without it, many
children from poor families would not be able to attend school, thereby
reducing the nation's pool of competences and skills.

When John Stuart Mill published *Principles of Political Economy and
Taxation* in 1848 (Mill, 1909), he insisted that the classical laws of
production—the theory of diminishing returns, and so forth, as worked
out by his predecessors—were natural laws in the same sense and
commanding the same authority as Newton's theory of gravity. But with
respect to the laws of distribution, he insisted the outcomes could be
modified. What society had once introduced, he believed, it could later
decide to modify, change, or even eliminate. Accordingly, Mill raised
questions about the ownership and use of the Crown lands and about

public policies aimed at encouraging emigration; he particularly advocated special efforts to establish producer cooperatives so that the working population could participate not only in the creation but also in the distribution of profits.

The doyen of modern British economists, Alfred Marshall, whose engine of partial equilibrium analysis dominated the Anglo-Saxon world from 1890 to World War II, was by temperament and intellect a conservative in the best sense of the term. He saw the family and religion as the two most powerful forces influencing how men and women thought and acted. Another hallmark of his conservatism was his cautionary views about the rise of trade unionism and his skepticism about their contributing to the well-being of the working man. In his definitive work, *The Principles of Economics* (Marshall, 1890), this cautious, conservative Cambridge professor concluded that the state should consider removing children of the most disadvantaged urban families from their homes—in contemporary terminology, the underclass—and rear them in public institutions so that they could acquire the socialization and skills that they needed in order to become self-reliant workers and citizens. Marshall used the term *residuum* to describe the underprivileged, who he estimated accounted for about one-sixth of the urban population.

Smith, Ricardo, Mill, and Marshall, the major architects of mainline economics, were aware that efforts to improve the production and distribution of goods and services, important and compelling as these activities are in the lives of individuals and nations, could never be the exclusive goal of a civilized society. Such a society must protect its defenses, respond to claims of equity, and provide opportunities for each new generation. This intellectual heritage cannot be ignored or belittled. No amount of sophisticated theorizing or econometric calculations can substitute for the shared values that alone can assure societal continuity.

When Alfred Marshall died in 1924, Calvin Coolidge was president of the United States. Coolidge held the view that the business of America is business. In the succeeding six decades the American people have faced a series of challenges and experiences that have altered the reality they had known and that altered their views of themselves and their future. A short list of these untoward events would have to include at a minimum the Great Depression of 1929–1933, the major era of social and economic reforms spearheaded by the New Deal, World War II, the atomic bomb, the emergence of the United States to a position of world leadership, the Cold War, the Korean War, the decolonization of Africa and Asia, the golden age of U.S. capitalism (1945–1970), the Civil Rights revolution, the Great Society programs, Vietnam, the onset of inflation and the volatility of the world economy after the first oil crisis, Watergate, the Iranian crisis, the political shift to the right exemplified by the election of Ronald Reagan, the accelerated changes in the U.S. and world economies that have led to the decline in U.S. smokestack industries, budgetary deficits, the inflated dollar, and even more unanticipated concomitants.

The challenges listed above can be regrouped into the following schema: The economy underwent wide swings from the prosperity of the 1920s to the deep depression of the 1930s, to the recent prolonged period of growing volatility, rising unemployment, and a weakened competitive role in the international arena. On the political front, the transformational process moved the country slowly out of its historic isolationism into becoming the arsenal of democracy in World War II and catapulted it into the role of world leader in the immediate postwar era, a position that the USSR began to challenge when it became a nuclear power in the 1950s. Vietnam, Iran, and Lebanon attest to the speed with which the United States was challenged—and successfully— by minor powers.

On the domestic front, these sixty years have seen the rise and decline of the trade union movement, the marked increase in social welfare legislation, the rapid economic development of the South and West, the Civil Rights movement of the 1960s and its subsequent weakening, the women's revolution, the challenge to conventional values by college students, Yuppies, and others, the vast expansion in higher education, the long success of the Democratic party through forging a coalition of diverse aspiring groups, and the dissolution of that coalition in the 1968 presidential election.

This abbreviated recapitulation underscores several major themes: the United States, a major democracy, was forced to confront and respond to a series of major challenges, internal and external, over the past six decades. The country could not rely on history and experience alone to determine its responses, for instance, to the Great Depression of the 1930s, to its short monopoly of the atomic bomb, to its unique position in the international markets in the early decades after World War II, when Germany and Japan were rebuilding their economies.

Because the United States had to find its way in responding to each of the challenges cited above and to other major events, it is not surprising that many of its responses were less than satisfactory. There is simply no way for a democratic society, or for that matter any society, to develop the knowledge and understanding necessary to respond effectively to a flood of new problems. It can only hope to limit and constrain the dangers and the damage that the new brings in its wake, and through time and experience develop more effective responses.

I shall now address the theme of this chapter: economic policy, particularly as it relates to human resource issues in the arenas of education, training, and work. However, I shall first call attention to the major lessons that I have extracted from the policy arena. These lessons speak to the strengths and weaknesses of the political process through which American democratic society responds to challenges and opportunities.

### The U.S. Political Process:
### Some Lessons

The governmental system is structured to assure that innovations are debated before they are put to a vote and institutionalized. The U.S. electorate is continually forming and dissolving special interest groups along many different axes—economic, geographic, political, demographic, ideological—that coalesce in favor of or in opposition to specific proposals. Unless there is a crisis that demands a speedy response, the development of a political consensus is a time-consuming, energy-absorbing undertaking.

In the almost six decades since the end of the New Era in 1929, I can identify only six years during which a president and his administration had broad public support for large-scale innovative federal programming—Franklin Roosevelt's first administration (1933–1937) and the first two years of Lyndon Johnson's incumbency (1964–1966). The American people gave repeated evidence of their support for Roosevelt as he pressed Congress to pass a large number of recovery and reconstruction measures. That was not the situation in the mid-1960s. Johnson pulled and dragged the nation to support his Great Society programs, drawing on the public's guilt about the murder of Kennedy and making full use of his own expertise in the legislative arena. The only reasonable deduction from this retrospective view is to recognize the existence of powerful structural constraints in the federal system that favor a conservative approach to policy and program innovation.

A related phenomenon, all too often neglected or misunderstood, is the restricted arenas within which the federal government interacts directly with the citizenry. What the government does best is to send out on time Social Security checks to beneficiaries and to provide medical care for designated groups of veterans. But it is no longer directly responsible for delivery of the mail; it relies on a special public corporation to accomplish that particular service. Because of the size and diversity of the country and the ways in which power was allocated in the Constitution between the federal and state governments, the federal government must work through subsidiary levels of government, as well as through nonprofit institutions and the private sector to carry out most basic federal missions from defense to unemployment benefits; from loans and grants to college students to the financing of research and development; from Medicare and Medicaid to such programs as Aid to Families with Dependent Children.

This dependency of the federal government on intermediaries has several implications. First, new federal initiatives should be weighed not only in terms of their potential dollar costs and returns, but also in terms of the existing implementing capacity, governmental and nongovernmental. Furthermore, in the event that states fail to carry out their duties effectively, the federal government faces difficulty in obtaining compliance. In the absence of egregious nonperformance, neither Congress nor the administration is likely to cut off the flow of funds that were initially allocated. This means that in most programs financed by the federal government but implemented through other governmental agencies and nongovernment organizations, the level of performance will be heavily dependent on the capacity and competencies of the intermediaries.

The national political arena is influenced by styles and fashion. Even popular programs that initially elicit strong support for a period of years, such as strengthening national defense, expanding medical care, financing higher education, improving the nation's highways, are not able to continue at center stage. Part of the explanation lies with the public's belief that the initial problem should have been solved, or at least eased, by several years of strong governmental support. The other force working to undermine the original support comes from the changes in the external world. New problems come to the fore, and they need to be addressed. This requires that Congress shift its attention and redistribute its resources.

Although the United States has responded to trends on the international scene by building up and maintaining its regular military and naval personnel at approximately the 3 million level (including 1.1 million civilian employees) and by providing for large numbers of trained reservists, it has continued to keep the mission of the Department of Defense apart from the predominant civilian activities of the federal government. There is a strong tradition in Washington that the armed services should attend to the defense of the country and should not be asked or required to assume civilian functions. The outstanding exception is the Corps of Engineers, which has had long-term responsibility for planning and development of river and harbor works.

The insistence on a distant relationship between the Department of Defense and the rest of the federal government was not significantly modified even during the two decades (1949–1971) when the National Training and Service Act (the draft) was in force. The law required that every young man on reaching the age of eighteen register for military service; it resulted in approximately two out of three enlisting or being drafted for active or reserve service. The strong preference of politicians not to enlarge the scope of responsibility of the Department of Defense and the resistance of the military leadership to take on additional duties that would deflect them from their principal responsibility help to explain the civilian sponsorship and operation of the new federal youth programs in the 1960s and 1970s.

The long tradition of keeping the military and the civilian spheres of government sharply separated, according to President Eisenhower's farewell address, was more sentimental than real. The president spoke at length about the intermingling of the two as the result of the rise of the "military-industrial" complex. He called attention to the new linkages that had been fashioned among the Pentagon, the major aerospace corporations, and members of Congress. With billions and tens of billions of annual appropriations at stake, new interest groups are formed to influence the flow of federal appropriations to their states and districts. Vice President Lyndon Johnson's role in locating NASA field headquarters at Houston was but one of many illustrations of the new, interlocking relations between the flow of federal dollars and the state and local pursuit of them. Another illustration has been the voting record of former Senator Barry Goldwater, whose conservative ideology has not interfered with his strong advocacy of and support for all federal spending programs for the state of Arizona.

The continuing growth of the federal government in the post–World War II era, which brought the federal budget for 1986–1987 close to the trillion-dollar mark, presented the American people and its political leaders with a Hobson's choice. If the federal government were not to grow to gargantuan size by undertaking to perform more and more functions on its own behalf, it had to secure the goods and services it needed through reliance on intermediaries, particularly from the private sector and nonprofit organizations. Once it decided to follow the latter route, it inevitably encouraged the creation and strengthening of new interest groups such as the military-industrial complex, the medical-industrial complex, the university-federal government complex, and many old and new interest groups involving farmers, trade unions, cooperatives, public housing, highway construction, exporters, as well as a host of others that are dependent in whole or in part on federal legislation and federal financing.

Recent decades have witnessed an increase in the level of federal expenditures, from $92 billion in 1960 to close to $1 trillion in 1985–1986, with federal expenditures rising from 18 to 24 percent of GNP. Despite these much larger outlays, there is never enough money available to the Congress to fund all of the competing programs on the agenda. Sooner or later, and usually sooner, Congress has been forced because of a stringency in financing, to prune and discard programs of merit. Since 1972 for instance, after six years of relatively open-ended financing for Medicare and Medicaid, Congress has avoided expanding entitlements and has attempted with only limited success to slow the flow of its health care outlays. A more striking example has been the radical cutback in the administration's proposed outlays for defense in its 1985–1986 budget proposals. It initially sought average annual increases of 5.7 percent in real dollars. It had to settle on 2.3 percent with some potential increases in later years, increases that may not materialize.

A final lesson to be extracted from a review of these past six decades are the limitations of presidential leadership in moving the country toward any important domestic or foreign policy initiative. As suggested earlier, the latitude for presidential leadership in periods of crisis has been considerably enlarged, but aside from the Great Depression and its immediate aftermath, the nation has fortunately escaped major economic turmoil. As a consequence, presidents have had more opportunity to leave an impact on foreign affairs, but even here, as the disengagement from Vietnam made clear, a powerful and committed president such as Lyndon Johnson can be forced by public opinion to give way and alter his policy. President Eisenhower, the most popular of the post–World War II presidents, invested much of his capital to achieve one overriding objective—to bring the isolationist wing of the Republican party into the twentieth century so that the United States could pursue a foreign policy based on a close alliance with the nations of Western Europe. The aim of this policy was keeping the peace through a balance of armed strength and political negotiations with the USSR.

In recapitulation, seven critical political parameters set the frame within which the United States has moved in the past and is likely to move in the future to adjust its dynamic economy so that it can respond more effectively to the needs of the American people. I stipulated earlier that if the basic needs of significant groups are neglected, aberrant and destructive behavior, which can weaken the social fabric and the consensus on which the continued progress of our society depends, may follow. Here are the seven propositions:

1. The U.S. Constitution has an inherently conservative structure; the political system favors tradition and the status quo over innovations and reforms.
2. The federal government is dependent on subsidiary levels of governments for implementing new programs; instituting major changes is difficult because of the weaknesses in these mechanisms.

3. The electorate is fickle and unwilling to stay committed to achieving important new national goals, especially when these require considerable time and continuing large outlays.
4. The civilian and military departments of the federal government are differentiated; the public, the Congress, and the military leadership prefer to respect this separation.
5. For reasons of ideology, efficiency, and practicality, the federal government has relied on private and nonprofit institutions to produce most of the goods and services it requires. The large federal funds appropriated for this purpose become the target of interest groups that seek alliances with legislators and bureaucrats.
6. Despite the steeply rising federal outlays during the last quarter century, Congress has never had sufficient resources to fund all existing programs and even less to finance new programs on a scale commensurate with the public's and its own preferences. Budget constraints are a continuing reality.
7. Finally, I have observed that except in periods of crisis, the ability of a president to move the public toward a new consensus or to avoid dissolving an existing consensus is more constrained than most critics realize. Since the midterm elections in 1946, the incumbent president's party has controlled both houses of Congress in ten elections, with nine of the ten under Democratic presidents.

I turn now to one substantive area where the economy and society should be restructured so that the needs of the entire population can be more effectively met. I have neither the knowledge nor the experience to offer a full agenda for economic reform. But my lifetime of research and consulting leads me to advance some modest proposals in the area of my specialty, human resources.

## Earned Income and Income Transfers

Most Americans agree about the broad responsibilities of the individual and society with regard to the upbringing of children, education, work, self-support, and the circumstances under which income transfers should be made available to individuals who have inadequate earnings or none at all. These understandings include the following: The nuclear family is responsible for the nurturing of children; local and state governments are the principal societal agencies with oversight for and financing of basic education; and individuals are responsible for finding a job that will provide them with the income required to support themselves and their dependents. When there is short-term unemployment, the federal-state unemployment insurance system provides up to about one-half the individuals' previous earnings, usually for twenty-six weeks, a period extended to thirty-nine weeks in a severe recession. If individuals or families exhaust their unemployment insurance, they may be eligible for welfare in the state in which they reside. The principal welfare program, Aid to Families with Dependent Children (AFDC), is federally financed, although operated by the states and localities. It provides income for female heads of households with minor children. In about half the states, the presence of an unemployed father makes the family ineligible for support under this program; in the other half it does not. Many permanently disabled persons receive benefits under the disability provisions of the Social Security system, and most persons with work histories are eligible at age sixty-two for Social Security benefits.

To complete this overview, there are a significant number of low-income persons, circa 19 million, eligible for food stamps, an exclusively federal program. A much smaller number receive one or another type of housing asistance, and there are many additional in-kind federal, state, and local benefit programs, usually means-tested. Of these, Medicaid is the largest and others cover such diverse services as Headstart, day care, home care, free or subsidized school meals, and Supplemental Security Income, which provides federal support for the blind, the low-income elderly, and other disabled groups. The foregoing sketch is not complete, but it identifies the most important sources of transfer income and in-kind benefits available to groups that society recognizes as unable to support themselves and their dependents.

There has been much discussion and argument about President Reagan's concept of the "truly needy" and congressional attitudes and actions with respect to the size of the pool of recipients and the appropriate level of benefits. However, the gap between the administration and the Congress is narrower than the gap between the more generous and less generous states in defining the needy and in assisting them.

For the better part of twenty years the subject of income transfers has been framed by the statistical data about the size, distribution, and flow of individuals and families into and out of poverty. There are several issues here. Many families are in poverty because their principal wage earners are unable to earn enough from their low-paying, and often intermittent, jobs to meet the minimum requirements of their large families. The growth of the off-the-record economy suggests that many of the poor and near-poor may be somewhat better off than the official data suggest, but how much is unclear. One reason is that so many heads of households are employed at minimum wages, that is, they earn between $6,000 and $7,000 a year, and welfare benefits in the more liberal states often equal or exceed this level. The overlapping between earnings and income transfers contributes to communal dissonance because many of the employed resent the "free ride" of persons on welfare. And conservative economists worry that income transfers discourage the labor market participation of unskilled persons, many of whom will opt for welfare over a job.

Many years ago George Wiley, the president of the League of Welfare Mothers, and I were waiting to talk to the members of the executive committee of the National Council of Churches. I asked Wiley what he planned to say; he told me that he would seek support for a $6,500 minimum for families on Aid to Families With Dependent Children. I told him that although I did not consider the target figure unreasonable, I could not support his position. Too many workers earned only slightly more, and they, among others, should not be asked to pay additional taxes to bring the welfare group up to the $6,500 level.

The United States has walked up to radical reforms of its welfare systems on three occasions: the explorations of the Heinemann Committee in the late 1960s; Nixon's abortive effort in the early 1970s; and Carter's stillborn effort. The explanations for these failures are many and diverse; even at this late date there is no agreement among the experts. I believe that the key to the failure is embedded in the problem. There is no simple way, in fact, there is no way to square the following: to provide a decent minimum income for every needy person/family in the United States, given the differentials in living standards, public attitudes, and state taxing capacity, and at the same time avoid serious distortions in basic value and incentive systems that expect people to be self-supporting through income earned from paid employment. Accordingly, I would like to shift the focus from welfare to work, from income transfers to the opportunity to compete, from dependency status to participation in society. In advocating this shift toward jobs and earned income and away from unemployment and income transfers, the planners must focus on two fundamentals: the developmental experiences that young people need in order to be prepared to enter and succeed in the world of work; and the level of employment opportunities that a society must provide so that everybody able and willing to work, at least at the minimum wage, will be able to do so.

## Unprepared for Work

Economic theorists are skillful in explaining why economic reality frequently differs from their model of self-clearing markets, including the labor market. There are academic economists, primarily those with close ties to the Chicago School, who contend that much or most of the reported unemployment is "voluntary" in the sense that many unemployed persons choose to delay looking for and accepting a job, preferring to use their transfer money or to engage in nonpaid work or leisure activities (home repairs, vacations, etc.). A related group of analysts argues that once one takes account of the altered composition of the labor supply (more women and younger persons in the labor force), the unemployment rate has not really been rising in recent years. Finally, some analysts see the galaxy of interventions from the side of federal and state governments and trade unions as raising wages to levels that prevent the market from clearing. These "new neoclassicists," as they are called, believe that the way to reduce and eliminate unemployment is to give the market its head.

The neo-Keynesians do not accept this analysis, for they see the high unemployment rates as directly linked to recent efforts of governments to run their developed economies with considerable slack so as to prevent a recurrence of rapid inflation. The excessively high rates of unemployment in the United States and in Western Europe date from the first oil crisis in 1973, and to make matters worse, most experts see little prospect of any significant decline in the immediate years ahead.

Although the U.S. economy ended its post–World War II era of rapid growth in 1970 or shortly thereafter, after which serious inflation, a severe recession, and lowered productivity took over, the United States nevertheless added 20 million *net* new jobs during the unspectacular 1970s. Some of these new jobs were part-time; many were low paying, but the majority were jobs that differed little from those extant at the beginning of the decade. In a discussion in the spring of 1981 with Raymond Barre, the French premier who had been a professor of economics before he entered politics, I had occasion to mention the U.S. growth in service-sector jobs. He was nonplussed—the entire French economy at that time had a total employment level of only about 25 million. And France had done somewhat better in new job creation than either Germany or the United Kingdom. Germany experienced major productivity gains, but not job gains, as a result of large capital investments in the 1970s; the British lagged on both fronts.

The large job creation that characterized the U.S. economy in the 1970s made it possible for most young people to find work and start their careers. Those who experienced trouble were heavily concentrated among poorly educated minority youth. A Nobel laureate, when challenged with the steeply rising rates of unemployment among minority youth, brushed the issue aside on the ground that time would take care of the problem. He emphasized the striking declines in unemployment rates once young people enter their twenties. I suggested that the figures pointed to a less sanguine outcome: Many minority youth would get into trouble with the criminal justice system and be put in jail; many others would be the victims of homicide or suicide; still others would never become permanently attached to the labor force and would live a marginal existence on the periphery of the economy, moving between short-term, poor-paying jobs and illicit and illegal activities. Clearly, there are different ways to read the same figures. Analysts have called attention to the startling fact that it was impossible to account for half of all black males as a result of an undercount by the U.S. Census and their nonparticipation in the labor force.

So far I have identified minority youth of both sexes and black men as two groups that experience differentially high levels of unemployment. A third group consists of female heads of households on AFDC, particularly those with children of school age who do not require full-time care. A significant proportion of these women are not at work for one or more of the following reasons: They cannot find jobs; they cannot earn enough from a job to support themselves and their dependents; they may conclude that they are better off if they remain on welfare because they can, in many urban localities, earn additional money from unreported employment. About 42 percent of black and 13 percent of white female-headed households are on AFDC.

Still another group with serious employment problems are "displaced workers," mostly white males, especially those in the higher age groups of fifty or more, who have been regularly attached to the work force since their late teens or early twenties and who have recently been permanently discharged by their employers. Because of their age, education, experience, residence, home ownership, and other characteristics, they are often at a severe disadvantage in finding new jobs, even if they reconcile themselves to working for less pay and fewer benefits than in the past.

Still another large, heterogeneous category, best characterized as "handicapped" persons, are the mentally retarded, the emotionally disturbed, the physically impaired, ex-offenders, ex-addicts, and other groups that encounter great or insurmountable difficulties in locating work. In 1943–1944 at the height of the war boom when the unemployment rate fell to 1.2 percent, some state mental hospitals decided to release their stabilized long-term patients, a significant proportion of whom were able to find jobs in the overheated economy—only to lose them when the veterans returned. Another illustration from that same period: The army accepted a sizable number of felons from federal prisons. Follow-up studies revealed that they performed on average as well as any random group of selectees. The army offered them a second chance, and most of the felons were able to take advantage of it and straighten themselves out.

The earlier references to minority youth, black men, and black women on AFDC suggest that race discrimination plays a large role in the

differentially high unemployment rates of these groups. It is not immediately clear, however, whether it is race alone, or the correlates of
race, such as poverty, single-parent households, ghetto living, and even
other disabilities frequently associated with race.

For the purposes at hand, I need merely stipulate that in a society
such as ours, racial discrimination continues to affect both the development and utilization of human resources and reduces the opportunities
of minorities as they seek jobs and advancement in their careers. Black
youngsters from early childhood have their self-esteem undermined and
find it difficult to develop the self-confidence required to set and pursue
ambitious goals. And black adults are repeatedly rebuffed in the labor
market on the basis of their color. Discrimination continues to take a
heavy toll.

But race alone is a minor, not the major, handicapping factor. The
frequent correlates of race are reflected in the following: 44 percent of
all black children live with only one parent at some point in their lives;
48 percent of all black children are reared in families that live in poverty;
34 percent of all black children at age fourteen are below grade level;
21 percent of all blacks between the ages of twenty-two and twenty-
four have failed to graduate from high school. As early as 1968, my
colleague Dale Hiestand and I wrote a report for the U.S. Civil Rights
Commission, *Mobility in the Negro Community*, which called attention
to the growing differences in the circumstances and the life prospects
of the members of the black middle class compared to those who were
at the bottom of the income distribution. This differentiation has become
even more prominent in the past two decades. There has been growing
concern on the part of both the black and white leadership about the
large numbers of unmarried teenagers who become pregnant, decide to
have their babies, and then go on AFDC. Despite a variety of inter-
ventional programs, none has proved particularly effective. Whereas the
psychodynamics of early parenthood are many and complex, there is
considerable agreement among those who work in this arena that many
young women, particularly young black women, do not believe that
having a baby will make their lives worse. Rather, the reverse. Disliking
school, without employable skills, living in the midst of poverty and
family tension, they hope and expect that having a baby may provide
them with some significant source of satisfaction.

Since World War II the U.S. economy has experienced a radical
reduction in the number of unskilled jobs in both agriculture and
manufacturing, a trend that is currently appearing in the service sector.
Increasingly, the rapidly growing business services—the source of employment growth in metropolitan centers where such a high proportion

of minorities live—are hiring only individuals with high school diplomas and preferably those who have attended junior college. The high drop-out rate among black youth in their high school years foreshadows major employment difficulties for them.

The combination of racial discrimination, poverty, single-parent households, neighborhood pathology, the substantial absence of a communal infrastructure of supporting religious and other institutions create a mockery of our national ethos of "equality of opportunity." Moreover, there is little basis for believing that the nation has the knowledge, the resources, and the will to attempt to reduce and eradicate these pervasive pathological conditions. We can expect, however, that society will continue to provide many of these young people who are growing up under such adverse conditions "second-chance" opportunities to add to their education and skills so that they have a better prospect of becoming self-supporting and self-reliant adults. The Job Corps has been one such effort. And amid the array of other youth programs, there have been a number of exemplary efforts that have succeeded in combining remedial education, work experience, skill training, and transitional supports into regular employment.

Based on more than two decades of experience, we are in a better position today to understand the preconditions for successful intervention: a much larger and sustained level of federal-state financing for job training and job creation; the active participation of local employers and trade unions; the involvement of community groups for outreach and other assistance; the support of municipal government and its multiple agencies, particularly the schools; and much strengthened placement services. At the same time that these second-chance opportunities are being strengthened, longer-term reforms aimed at reducing the pathology of ghetto life and improving the efficiency of the urban school system require continuing attention.

A serious and sustained commitment directed to expanding second-chance opportunities for disadvantaged youth along the foregoing lines would give some substance and support to the doctrine of equality of opportunity. It is unreasonable and wrong in an advanced urban society to continue to place all of the responsibility for employment on the individual and the family.

## The Shortfall in Jobs

Important as it is for society to make an increased commitment toward young people to assure that they are better prepared to assume self-supporting roles as adults, it is equally important that it recognizes the urgency of addressing the shortfall of jobs that contributes so much to individual, family, and community pathology. The difficulty that many black men encounter in finding jobs, especially regular jobs that pay a living wage is surely closely linked to the large number of female-headed households that are characteristic of so many families living in the ghetto. It should be emphasized that the significant reduction of marginality and ineffectiveness among many disadvantaged families requires congruent intergenerational efforts, directed at both parents and their children. To raise the employability potential of children requires that more of them grow up in families where one or both parents are regularly attached to the labor force and are self-supporting.

Just as reality has mocked the ethos of equality of opportunity for many minority children, the counterpart doctrine that adults are responsible for their own support and that of their dependents has been undermined by the continuing shortfall in jobs. The existence of high unemployment rates make it socially callous, even reprehensible, for a society to continue to affirm the doctrine that all adu s who need income should work and then not to provide adequate opportunities for many of them to fulfill this imperative.

Although the United States experimented with federally financed job creation in the 1930s and again in the 1970s, the record in retrospect must be viewed as equivocal. Most students believe that on balance the New Deal was right to put large numbers of the unemployed to work on governmentally financed programs rather than to keep them on the dole as the British did.

Even though during the 1960s and 1970s, I chaired the national committee and commissions that had oversight over the galaxy of employment and training programs, the total expenditures for which approximated $100 billion, I find it difficult to reach a clear-cut evaluation on their performance and effectiveness. A temperate assessment would have to note the following pluses and minuses: On the plus side, many disadvantaged persons who needed income had an opportunity to get a public service employment (PSE) job where they usually performed useful work. Some of them were able to build up a work record and to acquire skills that enabled them to make the transition into a regular job in the private or public sector.

On the downside, the 1975 amendments to CETA made it possible for many persons with only a week's unemployment to get a PSE job, many of which paid considerably more than the minimum wage. In 1977, President Carter decided to use the large-scale expansion of the PSE program as the principal device to stimulate the economy, with the result that the administrative infrastructure became overloaded.

Furthermore, Congress insisted (after 1976) that PSE jobs should be reserved for the most disadvantaged, but its failure to provide opportunities for remedial education or skill acquisition made it impossible except for a small number to move thereafter into regular jobs. With Congress increasingly dissatisfied with the PSE program, President Reagan in 1981 encountered relatively little difficulty in phasing it out. The president remains strongly opposed to public job creation, convinced that the private sector can provide jobs for everybody who wants to work.

There has been remarkably little support for a permanent program of federally financed jobs for the long-term unemployed, although when Arthur F. Burns, a trusted adviser of Nixon, Ford, and Reagan, was chairman of the Federal Reserve Board in 1975, he spoke out in favor of the federal government's becoming the employer of last resort, offering jobs at 10 percent below the minimum wage, to all who were willing to work whenever private-sector jobs were insufficient to meet the needs of job seekers.

If such an entitlement program were not to draw excessive numbers into the labor force from among students, married women, the elderly, the early retired, as well as to encourage many others to shift out of self-employment into publicly financed jobs, its design would have to take account of family income, prior work experience, age, and location. For instance, public jobs in distressed communities might be offered to workers who are over fifty years old, but care would have to be taken not to discourage the relocation out of the area of younger workers who had reasonable prospects of securing permanent employment in other locations. Similarly, effective liaison would have to be established between local employment services and public job-creation projects to assure that as the local labor market strengthened, an increasing number of workers on federally financed jobs could move into private-sector jobs. Moreover, it would probably be desirable to set a maximum term of two years on public-sector jobs to discourage individuals from considering them as permanent, but to provide them with the opportunity to reapply after they had engaged in a designated period of job search.

The federal government currently has been spending about $20 billion annually (to be increased in the future) to assist fewer than half a million farm families to improve their incomes. It is incomprehensible that the government has not seriously contemplated a program of comparable magnitude to enable the most disadvantaged of its urban citizens to work to support themselves and their dependents. Another contrast: We spend close to $30 billion annually to enable young people to attend college. Clearly the noncollege group is entitled to more consideration than it has elicited up to this time.

Additional complexities have to be faced and solved, such as the need to supplement the incomes of large families that could not subsist on the earnings of one worker on a public job; the need to provide remedial education to enhance the prospects of public job holders to move into private-sector employment; and provision of adequate supervision and work discipline so that public support for the program could be assured.

A publicly financed job creation program is not being advanced as a panacea. Crime, drugs, prostitution, and extortion will not disappear and may not even be significantly diminished with the establishment of publicly financed jobs to enable the long-term unemployed to work and support themselves. Advocacy for such a program rests on a few compelling societal values and judgments: It is wrong, in fact indecent, for a society to hold up the virtue of self-reliance and self-support and not provide the jobs that people need in order to support themselves; the gross and net costs of even a large publicly financed job program on the order of $2 billion is well within the capabilities of federal and state budgets that together total about $1.5 trillion annually; the costs of not acting come high, particularly when we consider the intergenerational effects of unemployed parents on the development and aspirations of their children.

Some economists and other social scientists believe that any additional efforts of the federal and state governments to enlarge their scale of activities and their share of the national income will inevitably weaken the fabric of American society by shifting responsibilities from the individual and the family to politicians and bureaucrats. But the thrust of this book has been to demonstrate the extent to which prevailing economic and other theories have failed to grasp fully and assess correctly many of the characteristic changes of developed economies that require and demand governmental action.

I began this chapter with an account of the difficulties and limitations of government to perform effectively; then I called attention to the dissonance between the nation's belief in and commitment to individual responsibility and the reality of inadequate preparation and a continuing shortfall in jobs; and I end with a plea for a renewed and enlarged government effort to provide work, rather than income, for large numbers of disadvantaged persons who otherwise will remain dependent on income transfers.

We know that many investments in physical capital turn out poorly or result in total loss. But we also know that large-scale investments in plant and equipment have brought the developed economies to an unparalleled level of output of useful goods and services that have made life much better and less brutish. We are slowly learning that the future of advanced economies lies primarily in raising the potential and capacity of all of its people. It does not follow that every investment that we make in our human resources will prove successful, but it is hard to see how improving the life chances of disadvantaged youths and adults can fail to strengthen the social fabric.

# 11

## The Value of Skepticism

What findings, generalizations, or lessons can we extract from this broad inquiry into economic theory, economic policy, and social welfare? No two students would agree about the conclusions that should be drawn from more than a half-century of experience, especially because during the period, the United States and the rest of the world were challenged by major and minor crises and enjoyed intermittent periods of tranquility and well-being. Moreover, even if observers agree about the major forces that shaped these tumultuous decades, it is likely that they differ as to the lessons that should be emphasized.

Any investigator is likely to be more certain about some than about others of his findings and conclusions. Accordingly, I shall set down in this concluding chapter only those precipitations that have become part and parcel of my belief structure.

The major corpus of economic thought that in the jargon of the profession is called Marshallian neoclassical theory appeared flawed to me early in my studies because of first, its basic assumption that competition characterizes most markets and second, its premise that all economic actors—farmers, workers, investors, employers, professionals, retirees—in fact everyone who makes, buys, or sells anything seeks to maximize material gains, although most men and women are in no position to know what would necessarily yield them the best outcome. I had no difficulty understanding and acknowledging the fact that the market is a powerful human invention and that it contributed to widening the scope of consumer choice, allocating resources, reducing prices, encouraging savings, and furthering innovation. The fact that the market had considerable potency and potential to add to human well-being was not the same as endowing it with supernatural powers. I knew of no human institution that could claim that order of efficiency—not religion, government, the law, science—and I could not credit the market with such powers.

Within the same year that I acquired my doctorate in economics at Columbia University, Edward Chamberlin of Cambridge, Massachusetts, and Joan Robinson of Cambridge, England, published major works that argued the predominance of imperfect competition or monopolistic competition across a broad area of developed economies, particularly in markets where large industrial corporations dominated (Chamberlin, 1933; Robinson, 1933).

Only three years after the Chamberlin-Robinson attack came an even more devastating onslaught, this one by Marshall's favorite pupil, John Maynard Keynes, who argued formidably in *The General Theory of Employment, Interest, and Money* (1936) that advanced economies operate with inherent tendencies toward underutilization of human and physical resources because of the inflexibility of wages during depressions, a general tendency to oversaving, and periodic shortfalls in effective demand. Keynes insisted that the only way to compensate for the indirect flaws of the market was government investment to counterbalance shortfalls in private investment.

Whether the old competitive market, the new imperfect competitive market, or the Keynesian theory was the most reliable became moot with the outbreak of World War II. And the quarter-century that followed the outbreak of the war was dominated by what came to be designated as the "Samuelson synthesis," in which the old competitive micro price-theory was stitched to the neo-Keynesian macroeconomics without much attention to the organic relationship between the two. An occasional warning was raised that rampant Keynesianism could generate inflation, but such warnings were largely ignored. The world's economy was strongly expansionary in developing as well as in developed countries, among the defeated as well as among the victors. Most academic economists were able to explore the frontier problems that interested them. They had a captive audience of peers and students, and they were able to pursue their intellectual interests with little pressure or interference from outside the academy.

The steep inflation that got under way in the United States in the mid-1960s and that continued unabated until the early 1980s refocused attention to the state of economic theory, which led to the recrudescence of old as well as the formulation of new doctrines. The recrudescence of the old involved a reformulated monetarism that argued that the principal cause of economic instability derives from the mishandling of the money supply by central bankers as well as a new neoclassicism that held that deviations from the competitive market were systemic errors of moment. A major new esoteric doctrine that was called "rational expectations" held that governments were impotent to affect the business cycle because smart traders would become wise in the ways of government and discount them in advance.

Mainline economics has gone through a series of major gyrations over the past five decades. Today its practitioners belong to a number of schools—new neoclassicists, monetarists, neo-Keynesians, post-Keynesians, the school of rational expectations, neo- and post-Marxists, and the "share" economists. Each purports to offer a comprehensive view of the same phenomenon—the changing contours of modern developed economies. It is not possible to judge the validity of such discordant models of the same reality. A discipline that does not permit its competing theories to be tested and proved or disproved may have many virtues, but it cannot claim the status of a science.

If many of the factors that determine output and employment originate from outside the boundaries of the discipline, that is, in the political arena (defense) or in the realm of mass psychology (speculation), if economists generally tend to ignore these extraterritorial forces, and if the excluded forces are significant, as they appear to be to most noneconomists and even to a few within the profession, their neglect will result in flawed conclusions and inferences.

There are further difficulties, easier to recognize than to correct. In fact, correction may not be possible. Most economists work with the conventional model that is insensitive to changing institutions that characterize a dynamic economy. But a model that is not in accord with reality sooner or later will yield flawed results.

The dilemma facing modern economics can be formulated thus: Economics can deepen and strengthen its analytic schema only by ignoring the changing economic realities that continue apace. But in proceeding in this way, economists ensure that their theories will be subject to neither proof nor disproof through recourse to the facts of economic life.

Another way of exploring the potential and limitations of economics as a system of thought is to consider whether and to what extent it has been able to provide guidance to politicians and the public. I can draw up the following balance sheet. The Marshallian neoclassical synthesis that dominated the Anglo-American academic scene in the 1920s and for most of the 1930s was unable to provide much insight into the long stretch of post–World War I prosperity in the United States (1922–1929) just as it was unable to explain the below par performance during this decade of Great Britain as it sought to restructure itself after the long and costly war. The dominant economic theory, as Keynes correctly insisted, was even less helpful when the Great Depression struck in 1929; its ravages were still present when the United States entered World War II in December 1941.

The relationship of economics to the New Deal is somewhat equivocal. Many analysts argue that Keynes's reformulation, with its emphasis on public spending in periods of depression, speaks well for the relevance of the new economics. Possibly, but the evidence is not definitive. As I have noted earlier, Roosevelt's New Deal proceeded with little attention to academic economics; the recession of 1937–1938 occurred in the face of the new Keynesian wisdom. With unemployment still above 10 percent as late as 1940, one can conclude that Roosevelt was surely not a convinced Keynesian, but a cautious pragmatic politician determined to assist the victims of the malfunctioning economy. There are no accolades for economics, hardly a passing grade, for its performance in the 1920s and the 1930s.

What can one say about the relations of economics to economic development during the four decades since the end of World War II? First I must distinguish the following periods: the era of rapid economic growth (1941–1970); the decade and a half of stagflation (1970–1985); and the discordances and volatility that characterize the international economic scene in 1987 and that will probably continue.

The first period, the good years of strong economic growth, was considered at the time and later in retrospect as the untrammelled victory of Keynesian economics as a guide to public policy. The economics profession gained self-confidence to a point where, in the late 1960s, U.S. government advisers set forth the claim that they had learned to fine-tune the economy.

But it is far from clear that the new economics was entitled to the credit that the economists claimed for their handiwork or that business leaders and the public were willing to acknowledge. It is true that Bretton Woods was a major achievement because it fit the political goals of Pax Americana. The best bulwark against communism was the speedy recovery of Germany and Japan and rapid economic growth at home and in the developing world. In the pursuit of these goals the United States was both able and willing to commit large resources and to follow a long-range policy.

On the domestic front, the Eisenhower years witnessed a determined effort to keep inflation in check, which was hardly a lesson drawn from Keynes. And when President Kennedy and President Johnson in turn decided to bring the economy closer to full employment, they finally persuaded Congress to pass the tax reduction bill of 1964, a move definitely dictated by their acceptance of Keynesian doctrine. But the following years were shaped much more by the inflationary commitments of the Johnson doctrine to both "guns and butter" than by the Keynesian advice of adjusting government spending as the economy approached full employment.

The long sad sequel of stagflation that accelerated in the 1970s with a strong boost from OPEC and that engulfed almost all of the developed world found the Keynesian economists in disarray about what had gone wrong and even more perplexed about how to design alternative policies. The proposals advanced by the anti- and post-Keynesians, which spanned the gamut from rigid monetarism to an incomes policy, had little to commend them either intellectually or otherwise. Most developed countries were forced to bring their inflation under control and recognizing the crisis in economics, decided to muddle through after proclaiming adherence to one doctrine and pursuing another (witness Mrs. Thatcher's commitment to sound money and President Reagan's repeated admiration for balanced budgets).

The muddling through carried high costs but has had some good results. As of early 1987, however, the United States has no clear-cut answers, possibly no answers at all, for the following array of major economic challenges: the persistence of unemployment at heretofore unacceptable levels that foreshadow the quasi-permanent disemployment of large numbers of poorly educated persons, especially minorities; a federal budget out of control today and as far as one can see ahead; an unfavorable balance of payments of record proportions that has the potential to reduce the U.S. standard of living; excessive debts in third world countries that could lead to defaults that would jeopardize the solvency of the U.S. (and world) banking system; the impending bankruptcy of many U.S. farmers and an economic environment that augurs ill for those who survive; a dollar that despite recent corrections is still misaligned with several currencies; the continuing lag in U.S. productivity, together with the weakened competitive position of many U.S. industries; stock market speculation associated with an ever-increasing number of acquisitions, mergers, and takeovers based on questionable logic except for high profits for investment bankers and arbitragers.

The aforementioned list of pressing problems places economists in a double bind. On the one hand, their analytic schemas are not sufficiently potent to provide the illumination needed to shape responsive policies. And to make matters worse, it is difficult to see the major developed nations, each pursuing its own short-term objectives, cooperating to a point where comprehensive reforms can be fashioned and implemented.

I recognize that most of the leaders of the economics profession would not accept this pessimistic assessment of the current state of economics nor its limited potential to contribute to economic policy. But this is my reading of the record of the last six decades.

There is an additional reason to challenge the imperialistic claims of many in the academy who believe that economics is not only a science, or well on the way to becoming one, but also that it is well positioned to provide guidance to governments on how to shape and implement their economic policies to assure rapid growth and the diffusion of its benefits.

Men and women who participate in an economy have a multitude of social connections, from families and neighborhoods to municipalities, states, nations, and even international bodies. They differ along a great many axes such as gender, race, education, occupation, income, and marital status. Every community, small or large, has a past that constrains it and a future whose shaping remains a spur. In many respects, the present is the arena for modifying the part of a society's inheritance of the past that is no longer functional and to allocate resources to help speed its vision of the future.

Some economists hold that the public will be better off if it does not seek to accomplish through collective action what it can achieve through the efforts of individuals. Looking to the state to accomplish ends that can be achieved by individual or corporate action can jeopardize freedom and liberty. In fact because of faulty governmental policies we may soon enjoy less income and less wealth. In a world that has seen the unfulfilled promises of controlled economies in their many variations, fascism, Nazism, Russian communism, Chinese communism, and the many other varieties of state oligarchy, the libertarian position cannot be dismissed out of hand.

Nevertheless, it must be dismissed, as must the dominant belief of most economists who, following Max Weber, see their "scientific" economics as value-free. To put it simply and directly: In a world where nuclear energy and nationalism abound, nations unable or unwilling to act collectively may increase their income in the short term but at the risk of sacrificing their future.

Even in the absence of nationalism and the threat of war, economists err when they contend that theirs is a value-free science or that it can ever become one. As long as people must live together in large aggregations; as long as the dice of history have created great discrepancies among them; as long as men and women are sensitive to the shortfalls in equity, just so long will they seek to alter the marketplace in directions that they hope will result in greater equity. They may falter as they pursue reforms aimed at enhancing justice and equity, but their errors will be insignificant, compared to adopting and pursuing a policy of nonintervention. As long as people strive collectively to improve their lot, they remain a viable society seeking a better future. In the absence of such striving, they are a brutish lot, concerned with protecting what they have, indifferent to the needs and claims of others.

The value of skepticism looms large. First and foremost, skepticism is a corrective against the arrogance of scholars who are convinced that they have succeeded in gaining a corner on the truth. Skepticism is a reminder that truth, surely in the social and economic spheres, is always time conditioned. Whatever lessons individuals and nations extract from their experience will inevitably lose some of, and with time a great deal of, their relevance, as the world that gave rise to such experiences recedes and disappears.

Skepticism can also be a spur to social experimentation. No sensible people will uproot its basic institutions in the expectation that what will replace them will prove that much better. But skepticism should help to remind even a cautious and conservative people that they have a right, even a duty, to seek to improve their institutions in order to increase their effectiveness.

Finally, skepticism can help assuage the hunger of those who seek certainty, who look to the day when economics will join the natural sciences and be recognized as their equal—able to pursue the truth according to the canons of logic and evidence, able to test its findings by recourse to the realities of the marketplace. But that day is far off and it may never arrive. Skepticism is a powerful reminder that there are many types of truth and that science, despite its potency, cannot claim exclusive dominion over the minds of men.

An economics in a lower key may not be able to provide a powerful engine of analysis that will yield unequivocal interpretations of a constantly changing reality. That may be too much to expect. But it should be able to illuminate facets of the changing reality that can contribute to both understanding and policy.

A skepticism that can accomplish this much, or even some part of such a broad agenda, is surely not to be denigrated. In a world beset by extremists in the realm of ideas and action, a skepticism that promises modest gains in understanding and policy is to be valued above rubies.

# References

Arrow, Kenneth, "General Economic Equilibrium: Purpose, Analytic Techniques, Collective Choice," Nobel Prize Lecture, December 1972, *American Economic Review*, Vol. 64, No. 3, June 1974, pp. 253–272.

Barro, Robert J., *Macroeconomics*, New York: Wiley, 1984, p. 446.

Bennett, Harry, *We Never Called Him Henry*, New York: Fawcett, 1951.

Brandeis, Louis D., *The Curse of Bigness*, Port Washington, N.Y.: KENNIKAT Press, 1965.

Chamberlin, Edwin, *The Economics of Monopolistic Competition*, Cambridge, Mass.: Harvard University Press, 1933.

Clark, John M., *Preface to Social Economics*, Fairfield, N.J.: Kelley, 1935.

———, *Alternative to Serfdom*, New York: Knopf, 1948.

Debreu, Gerard, "Economic Theory in the Mathematical Mode," Nobel Prize Lecture, December 1983, *American Economic Review*, Vol. 74, No. 3, June 1984, pp. 267–278.

Drucker, Peter, *The End of Economic Man*, New York: John Day, 1939.

Friedman, Milton, "Inflation and Unemployment," Nobel Prize Lecture, December 1976, Stockholm: Nobel Foundation, 1977.

Ginzberg, Eli, *Studies in the Economics of the Bible*, Philadelphia: Jewish Publication Society, 1932.

———, *The House of Adam Smith*, New York: Columbia University Press, 1934.

———, "Customary Prices," *American Economic Review*, June 1936, p. 276.

———, review of "An Economic Program for American Democracy," *Saturday Review of Literature*, March 11, 1939.

———, *The Illusion of Economic Stability*, New York: Harper, 1939.

———, *Grass on the Slag Heaps: The Story of the Welsh Miners*, New York: Harper, 1942.

Ginzberg, Eli, Ethel L. Ginsburg, Dorothy Lynn, Mildred Vickers, Sol W. Ginsburg, M.D., *The Unemployed: 1. Interpretation, 2. Case Studies*, New York: Harper, 1943.

Ginzberg, Eli, Sol W. Ginsburg, M.D., Sidney Axelrad, and John L. Herma, *Occupational Choice: An Approach to a General Theory*, New York: Columbia University Press, 1951.

Ginzberg, Eli, Douglas W. Bray, *The Uneducated*, New York: Columbia University Press, 1953.

Ginzberg, Eli, *The Negro Potential*, New York: Columbia University Press, 1956.

———, *Human Resources: The Wealth of a Nation*, New York: Simon and Schuster, 1958.

Ginzberg, Eli, James K. Anderson, Sol W. Ginsburg, M.D., John L. Herma, *The Ineffective Soldier: Lessons for Management and the Nation*, Vol. 1, *The Lost Divisions*, Vol. 2, *Breakdown and Recovery*, Vol. 3, *Patterns of Performance*, New York: Columbia University Press, 1959.

Ginzberg, Eli, John L. Herma, *Talent and Performance*, New York: Columbia University Press, 1964.

Ginzberg, Eli, Dale L. Hiestand, and Beatrice G. Reubens, *The Pluralistic Economy*, New York: McGraw, 1965.

Ginzberg, Eli, Ivar Berg, Carol Brown, John Herma, Alice Yohalem, Sherry Gorelick, *Life Styles of Educated Women*, New York: Columbia University Press, 1966.

Ginzberg, Eli, Alice Yohalem, *Educated American Women: Self-Portraits*, New York: Columbia University Press, 1966.

Ginzberg, Eli, Herbert A. Smith, *Manpower Strategy for Developing Countries: Lessons from Ethiopia*, New York: Columbia University Press, 1967.

Ginzberg, Eli, Dale Hiestand, *Mobility in the Negro Community*, Washington, D.C.: U.S. Commission on Civil Rights, 1968.

Ginzberg, Eli, *Manpower Research and Management in Large Organizations: A Report of the Task Force on Manpower Research*, Washington, D.C.: U.S. Department of Defense, 1971.

———, *Manpower for Development: Perspectives on Five Continents*, New York: Praeger, 1971.

Ginzberg, Eli, and the Conservation of Human Resources Staff, *New York Is Very Much Alive: A Manpower View*, New York: McGraw, 1973.

Ginzberg, Eli, *The Human Economy*, New York: McGraw, 1976.

Ginzberg, Eli, Jerome Schnee, James W. Kuhn, Boris Yavitz, *The Economic Impact of Large Public Programs: The NASA Story*, Salt Lake City: Olympus, 1976.

Ginzberg, Eli, *The Limits of Health Reform*, New York: Basic Books Inc., 1977.

———, "How Not to Offer Congress Advice on Health Policy," *The New England Journal of Medicine*, Vol. 298, No. 11, March 16, 1978, pp. 623–625.

Ginzberg, Eli, George Vojta, *Beyond Human Scale: The Large Corporation at Risk*, New York: Basic, 1985.

Ginzberg, Eli, *Understanding Human Resources*, Lanham, Md.: Abt, 1985.

Hayek, F. A., *The Road to Serfdom*, Chicago: University of Chicago Press, 1944.

Horney, Karen, *The Neurotic Personality in Our Time*, New York: Norton, 1937.

Keynes, John Maynard, *The General Theory of Employment, Interest, and Money*, New York: Harcourt, 1936.

Klein, Lawrence R., "Some Economic Scenarios for the 1980s," Nobel Prize Lecture, December 1980, Stockholm: Nobel Foundation, 1981.

Knight, Frank, *The Ethics of Competition*, Chicago: University of Chicago Press, 1935.

Koopmans, Tjalling C., *Activity Analysis of Production and Allocation*, New York: Wiley, 1951.

———, "Concepts of Optimality and their Uses," Nobel Prize Lecture, December 1975, *American Economic Review*, Vol. 67, No. 3, June 1977, pp. 261–274.

Kuznets, Simon S., "Modern Economic Growth: Findings and Reflections," Nobel Prize Lecture, December 1971, *American Economic Review*, Vol. 63, No. 3, June 1973, pp. 247–258.

Leontief, Wassily, "Structure of the World Economy: Outline of a Simple Input-Output Formulation," Nobel Prize Lecture, December 1973, *American Economic Review*, Vol. 64, No. 6, December 1974, pp. 823–834.

Lindbeck, Assar, "The Prize in Economic Science in Memory of Alfred Nobel," *Journal of Economic Literature*, Vol. 23, March 1985, pp. 37–56.

Lucas, Robert E., Jr., "An Equilibrium Model of the Business Cycle," *Journal of Political Economy*, Vol. 83, No. 6, December 1975, pp. 1113–1144.

Marshall, Alfred, *Principles of Economics*, London: Macmillan, 1890.

Marx, Karl, *Capital*, New York: Modern Library, 1936.

Mill, John Stuart, *Principles of Political Economy and Taxation*, Fairfield, N.J.: Kelley, 1909.

Mitchell, Wesley C., ed., *What Veblen Taught*, Fairfield, N.J.: Kelley, 1936.

——— , *The Backward Art of Spending Money and Other Essays*, Fairfield, N.J.: Kelley, 1937.

Modigliani, Franco, "Life Cycle, Individual Thrift and the Wealth of Nations," Nobel Prize Lecture, December 1985, Stockholm: Nobel Foundation, preliminary release.

Muth, John, "Rational Expectations and the Theory of Price Movements," *Econometrics*, Vol. 29, No. 3, July 1961, pp. 315–335.

Okun, Arthur, *Prices and Quantities: A Macroeconomic Analysis*, Washington, D.C.: Brookings Institution, 1981.

Phillips, A. W., "The Relationship Between Unemployment and the Rate of Change of Money Wage Rates in the United Kingdom, 1861–1957," *Economica*, Vol. 27, November 1958, pp. 283–299.

Robinson, Joan, *The Economics of Perfect Competition*, London: Macmillan, 1933.

Samuelson, Paul, *Economics*, New York: McGraw, 1967.

——— , "Maximum Principles in Analytical Economics," Nobel Prize Lecture, December 1970, *Science*, Vol. 173, September 10, 1971.

Schmidt, Louis Bernard, *Topical Studies and References on the Economic History of American Agriculture*, Philadelphia: McKinley, 1923.

Schultz, Theodore, "The Economics of Being Poor," Nobel Prize Lecture, December 1979, Stockholm: Nobel Foundation, 1980.

Simon, Herbert, *Administrative Behavior*, New York: Macmillan, 1947.

——— , "Rational Decision Making in Business Organizations," Nobel Prize Lecture, December 1978, *American Economic Review*, Vol. 69, No. 4, September 1979, pp. 493–513.

Smith, Adam, *The Wealth of Nations*, London: Methuen, 1904.

Stigler, George J., "The Process and Progress of Economics," Nobel Prize Lecture, December 1982, Stockholm: Nobel Foundation, 1983.

Thorp, Willard, *Business Annals*, New York: National Bureau of Economic Research, 1926.

Tobin, James, "Money and Finance in the Macro-Economic Process," Nobel Prize Lecture, December 1981, Stockholm: Nobel Foundation, 1982.

Veblen, Thorstein, *The Theory of Business Enterprise*, New York: Scribner, 1904.

# About the Author

Eli Ginzberg is director, Conservation of Human Resources, and A. Barton Hepburn Professor Emeritus of Economics, Columbia University. He is the author or editor of numerous books on manpower economics, including *From Physician Shortage to Patient Shortage* (Westview, 1986), and coauthor of *Technology and Employment* (Westview, 1986).

# Index

Abraham, David, 23
Abramovitz, Moses, 16, 18, 20, 30, 46, 47
Abt, Clark, 121
*Administrative Behavior* (Simon), 74
AFDC. *See* Aid to Families with Dependent
    Children
AFQT. *See* Armed Forces Qualification Test
Agricultural Adjustment Act, 27
Agricultural sector, 88–89, 90, 94, 99, 100,
    163
Aid to Families with Dependent Children
    (AFDC), 156, 157
*Alternative to Serfdom* (Clark), 30
AMA. *See* American Medical Association
American Medical Association (AMA), 136,
    137
Angell, James Waterhouse, 13, 16
Armed Forces, 143–147, 152, 155
    manpower policies, 131–132, 144–147
    personnel assessment, 144–145
    women in, 126
Armed Forces Qualification Test (AFQT), 144
Arrow, Kenneth, 65–66, 67–68, 70, 78, 86,
    88, 101, 102, 104, 105
Automation. *See* Technology, effects of
Automobiles, 89, 90, 91

*Backward Art of Spending Money, The*
    (Mitchell), 18
Banking system, 40
    reconstruction of, 92, 102
    regulation of, 93
Barre, Raymond, 158
Bean, Louis, 35
Becker, Gary, 103, 122
Bell System, 90
Benedict, Ruth, 12, 19
Ben-Gurion, David, 138
Bequests, 80
Bergson, Abram, 68
*Beyond Human Scale: The Large Corporation at
    Risk* (Ginzberg), 121, 122
Blaisdell, T. C., 18
Boas, Franz, 12
Bonbright, James C., 13
Bradley, Omar, 134
Brandeis, Louis, 30, 50–51
Brazil, 91
*Breakdown and Recovery* (Ginzberg et al.), 113,
    115
Bretton Woods system, 91, 92, 169
Brookings Institution, 39
Brumberg, Richard, 80
Bühler, Charlotte, 112
Bühler, Karl, 112
Burns, Arthur F., 18, 39, 54, 56, 76, 81, 163
Business cycles, 15, 28, 51, 62, 73, 74, 81,
    102, 167–168

*Capital* (Marx), 12, 143
Capital
    export of, 55
    markets, 9, 78–79
Carter, Jimmy, 41, 42, 57–58, 137, 157, 162
Central Bank of Sweden, 64
Chamberlin, Edward, 29, 167
Chicago School, 46, 54, 102, 104, 105, 157.
    *See also* Friedman, Milton; Schultz,
    Theodore; Stigler, George
Churchill, E. D., 133
Citicorp, 93
Civil Rights Act, 131
Clark, John B., 12, 17
Clark, John M., 4, 7, 12, 13, 15, 16–17, 18,
    20, 30, 31, 36, 76, 84
Clark, Joseph, 132
Cohen, Benjamin V., 15
Cohen, Wilbur, 137
Collins, Lawton, 145
COMECON countries, 143
Commission on Automation, 54
Committee for Economic Development, 51
Communications, 90
Competition, 4, 101–102, 104, 166, 167
Computers, 37, 95. *See also* Technology
Conservation of Human Resources Project,
    The, 113, 121
Constitution, 154
Consumer behavior, 29, 44, 67, 68, 79–80,
    89, 103. *See also* "Rational expectations"
    doctrine
Coolidge, Calvin, 149
Corps of Engineers, 152
Council of Economic Advisers, 52, 53, 54–55,
    60
Credit, 89, 91, 100, 102
*Curse of Bigness, The* (Brandeis), 51

Dantzig, George, 70
Davenport, Herbert J., 67
Debelius, Otto, 11
Debreu, Gerard, 65, 66, 68–69, 86, 88, 105
Debt, 79. *See also* Deficits
Decision theory, 74–75, 101
Defense Science Board, 146
Deficits, 41, 53, 58, 80
Demand, 4, 44. *See also* Consumer behavior;
    "Rational expectations" doctrine
Demographics, 43–44
Department of Defense, 38, 152–153
Department of Health, Education and Welfare
    (HEW), 38
Department of Labor, 38
Deregulation, 41
Development economics, 37, 119–120, 137–
    143
Director, Aaron, 36

Displaced workers, 159
Distribution, 68, 95–96, 148–149. *See also*
    Resources, allocation of
Disturbances, 73
Drucker, Peter, 23
Dupont, 90

*Economic Impact of Large Public Programs, The*
    (Ginzberg et al.), 45
*Economics* (Samuelson), 47
Economics
    consensus, 39, 41
    institutionalization of, 35–49, 50
    as science, 83–84, 99, 107, 170
*Economics of Monopolistic Competition*
    (Chamberlin), 29
Economists, 49
    education of, 47–48
    government, 36–38, 51–55
    nonacademic, 46, 48
    proliferation of, 46
    as scientists, 84
Eddy, Manton, 132
*Educated American Women: Self Portraits*
    (Ginzberg and Yohalem), 116
Education, 94, 98, 113, 127–130, 148, 163–164
Efficiency, 68, 70, 101, 102
Egypt, 139
Einstein, Albert, 4
Eisenhower, Dwight D., 52, 53, 54, 55, 113,
    128, 131–132, 153, 154, 169
Empiricists, 4, 12, 83–84
Employment Act, 52
*End of Economic Man, The* (Drucker), 23
Energy prices, 72–73. *See also* Oil crisis
Engels, Friedrich, 35
Entitlements. *See* Income, transfers; Medicaid;
    Medicare; Social Security; Unemployment
    insurance
Environmental protection, 43, 69, 105
Equal Rights Amendment, 127
Equilibrium, 4, 67–68, 119, 121
Equilibrium theory, 66, 67–69, 72, 78, 101,
    102
Equity, 95–96, 101, 104, 171
*Ethics of Competition, The* (Knight), 16
Ethiopia, 139–140
Eurodollar market, 40, 93
Exchange rates, 39, 55, 56. *See also* Bretton
    Woods system
Ezekiel, Mordecai, 35

Farber, Saul, 134
Federal Reserve Act, 12, 92
Federal Reserve Board, 40, 58
Federal Reserve system, 40, 60, 62, 92–93
Federal spending, 45–46, 53, 54, 98–99, 148,
    153–154, 155. *See also* Intervention;
    Public sector
Feis, Herbert, 35
Feldstein, Martin, 61
Felix, Robert, 135
Financial markets, 93
Fiscal policy, 98, 102, 103
Fisher, Irving, 60
Flows, 78–79. *See also* Input-output analysis
Ford, Gerald, 57, 163
Ford, Henry, 88
Forecasting, 37, 46, 72–74
Foreign aid, 91, 98
France, 39, 158
Free-trade policies, 41, 69–70, 148
Freud, Sigmund, 19

Friedman, Harry, 14, 15
Friedman, Milton, 16, 17–18, 40, 76–77, 84,
    86, 102, 103, 104, 105, 146
Fromm, Erich, 19
Full Employment and Balanced Economic
    Growth Act, 42
Full Employment Bill, 51–52

Galbraith, John Kenneth, 53
Gardner, John, 129
Gates Commission, 146
General Electric, 28, 90
General Motors, 29
*General Theory of Employment, Interest, and
    Money, The* (Keynes), 6, 16, 20, 33, 51,
    53, 62, 167
Germany, 22–24, 125, 138. *See also* West
    Germany
GI Bill, 128, 130
Ginsburg, Sol W., 19
Glass, Carter, 12
GMENAC. *See* Graduate Medical Education
    National Advisory Committee
Gold standard, 39, 91
Goldwater, Barry, 17–18, 153
Goldweiser, E. A., 35
Goodrich, Carter, 13
Goodyear, 28
Government services, 151–152, 154, 155. *See
    also* Medicaid; Medicare; Social Security
Graduate Medical Education National
    Advisory Committee (GMENAC), 136
*Grass on the Slag Heaps: The Story of the
    Welsh Miners* (Ginzberg), 110
Great Britain, 26, 39, 42, 61, 110, 125, 135,
    158, 168
Great Depression, 8, 14–15, 18, 21, 22, 26–30,
    33, 53, 90, 113, 154, 168
Great Society programs, 38, 48, 55, 95, 129,
    145, 151
Growth, 57, 73, 81–83

Haig, Robert C., 13
Handicapped persons, 159
Handy, Thomas, 131, 132
Hansen, Alvin, 18
Hayek, F. A., 30
Headstart, 156
Health care, 133–137
Heinemann Committee, 157
Heller, Walter, 53
Herma, John L., 112
HEW. *See* Department of Health, Education
    and Welfare
Hicks, John R., 66, 68, 78
Hiestand, Dale, 97, 160
Hitler, Adolf, 23–24
Hobby, Oveta Culp, 126
Hoffman, Paul, 51
Hoover, Herbert, 13, 26, 35
Horney, Karen, 19
Hotelling, Harold, 13, 20, 76
*House of Adam Smith, The* (Ginzberg), 13
"How Not to Offer Congress Advice on
    Health Policy," 134
Human capital, 44–45, 84–85, 103, 122–124
"Human capital" school, 103
*Human Economy, The* (Ginzberg), 120, 121
Human resources, 93–95, 98, 100, 103
    performance studies, 115–118
    postwar, 113–116, 117
    research, 109–124

*Human Resources: The Wealth of a Nation* (Ginzberg), 118, 140–141
Humphrey, George, 52

Illiteracy, 113–114, 128
*Illusion of Economic Stability, The* (Ginzberg), 15, 17
Immigration, 93–94
Income, 56, 90, 155–157
  savings and, 79–80, 103
  transfers, 95, 104, 111, 155–157
Income accounting, 37, 82
India, 142
Indonesia, 141–142
Industrialization, 50, 88
Industrial policy, 41, 70
Industry, 41, 90
  decline of, 61
  internationalization of, 91–92
  protection of, 70
*Ineffective Soldier: Lessons for Management and the Nation, The* (Ginzberg et al.), 113, 114–115
Inflation, 10, 15, 167
  deficits and, 53
  under Johnson, 56
  under Kennedy, 55
  Keynesianism and, 20
  under Nixon, 56–57
  under Reagan, 58
  unemployment and, 54, 61–62, 77
Information theory, 83, 84
Input-output analysis, 71–72, 101, 105
Inputs, 71–72. *See also* Human resources
Institutions
  growth and, 81, 82
  labor quality and, 121
International Harvester, 29, 90
Internationalization, 90–92, 100–101
Intervention, 104–105
  social, 95–97
  *See also* Policy
Investment, 103
Iran, 142–143
Israel, 137–139, 143

Japan, 4, 38, 57, 91, 95, 98, 140–141, 169
Jaspers, Karl, 11
Jellenick, George, 11
Jewish Agency, 138
Job Corps, 161
Job creation, 158, 161, 162–163, 164
Johnson, Earl, 132
Johnson, Lyndon, 53, 54, 56, 129, 130, 131, 137, 145, 151, 153, 154, 169
Joint Distribution Committee, 138
Jones, Thomas, 110

Kahn, Richard, 13–14
Kantorovich, Leonid V., 70
*Kapital, Das* (Marx), 12, 143
Kennedy, John F., 53, 54, 55, 77, 97, 132, 151, 169
Kerner Commission, 133
Keynes, John Maynard, 3, 4, 6, 13, 15, 16, 20, 23, 29, 33, 47, 49, 50, 51, 53, 60, 78, 79, 81, 86, 103, 167, 168, 169
Keynesian theory, 8–9, 18, 20, 38–39, 46–48, 50–63, 78–79, 121, 158, 167, 169, 170
Kindleberger, Charles, 18
King, Martin Luther, Jr., 131

Klein, Lawrence, 70, 72–73, 86, 88, 100–101, 102, 104
Knight, Frank H., 12, 16, 76
Kodak, 90
Kolberg, William, 130
Koopmans, Tjalling, 65, 70–71, 86, 100, 102, 104, 105
Korean War, 52, 145
Kuznets, Simon, 37, 65, 80, 81–83, 85, 86, 99, 100, 103, 104, 105

Labor
  agricultural, 89, 94, 99, 100
  demographics, 43, 45
  force alterations, 45, 89, 99–100
  management, 95, 122
  markets, 42, 43, 45, 54, 60–61, 111, 119, 121–122, 123–124, 157–158, 161–165
  migration, 90, 100, 119
  organized, 28, 29, 89, 95, 99
  specialization, 30
  unskilled, 160–161
  *See also* Human resources; Training; Unemployment
Laffer Curve, 40, 59
Lasker, Mrs. Albert, 135
LCH. *See* Life Cycle Hypothesis
Lederer, Emil, 11
Lehman Brothers, 36
Leontief, Wassily, 65, 70, 71–72, 86, 101, 105
Lever Brothers, 29
Lewis, Arthur, 84
Libertarians, 98
Life Cycle Hypothesis (LCH), 80–81, 103
*Life Styles of Educated Women* (Ginzberg et al.), 116
*Limits of Health Reform, The* (Ginzberg), 137
Lindbeck, Assar, 64, 65, 74, 82
Linear model, 70
Linear programming, 37
*Lost Divisions, The* (Ginzberg et al.), 113, 115
Low, George, 45
Lucas, Robert, 62
Ludendorff, Erich, 23

McAuliffe, Anthony C., 132
McCracken, Paul, 39
McCrea, Roswell C., 16
McGovern, George, 57
MacIver, Robert, 12, 13
McNamara, Robert, 145
Macroeconomics. *See* Keynesian theory
Malthus, Thomas, 85
Management, 95, 122
Manhattan Project, 38
Mannheim, Karl, 4
Manpower Development and Training Act (MDTA), 54
*Manpower for Development: Perspectives on Five Continents* (Ginzberg), 119–120
Manpower economics, 38
*Manpower Research and Management in Large Organizations: A Report of the Task Force on Manpower Research* (Ginzberg), 146
*Manpower Strategy for Developing Countries: Lessons from Ethiopia* (Ginzberg and Smith), 140
Markets
  adjustment, 39
  extension of, 101
  labor, 42, 43, 45, 54, 60–61, 111, 119, 121–122, 123–124, 157–158, 161–165
  self-equilibrating, 72

Marshak, Jacob, 11, 79
Marshall, Alfred, 20, 35, 47, 66, 85, 103, 122,
    149, 167
Marshallian economics. *See* Neoclassical
    theory
Marshall Plan, 91
Marx, Karl, 4, 12, 35, 143
Marxism, 26, 31, 143
Mathematics, 19–20, 47, 66–69, 75
MDTA. *See* Manpower Development and
    Training Act
Medicaid, 136, 137, 154, 156
Medicare, 134, 136, 154
Mental health, 135–136
Mikesell, Raymond, 138
Mill, John Stuart, 4, 35, 148, 149
Mills, Frederick C., 13
Mills, Wilbur, 136–137
Milton, Rose, 17
Mincer, Jacob, 103
Minimum wage, 162, 163
Minorities, 43–44, 45, 89, 100, 110–111, 113,
    114, 128, 129, 130–133, 145, 158–161,
    162
Mints, Lloyd, 76
Mitchell, James P., 139
Mitchell, Wesley C., 12, 13, 15, 16, 18–19, 20,
    21, 27–28, 51, 76, 81, 109
*Mobility in the Negro Community* (Ginzberg
    and Hiestand), 160
Model building, 4, 47–48, 73, 78, 99, 105
Modigliani, Franco, 65, 76, 79–81, 86, 88,
    102, 103, 105
Moley, Raymond, 26
Mondale, Walter, 41
Monetarism, 62
Monetarists, 40, 60
Monetary policy, 98, 102, 103
Monetary theory, 78
Money markets, 39–40
Money stock, 78
Monopoly, 29, 50–51
Moore, Henry, 12
Morse, Marston, 19–20
Muth, John, 62
Myrdal, Gunnar, 4


Napoleon, 22
NASA. *See* National Aeronautics and Space
    Administration
Nathan, Robert R., 37
National Aeronautics and Space
    Administration (NASA), 153
National Bureau of Economic Research, 73–74
National Defense Education Act (NDEA), 128,
    130
National health insurance (NHI), 137
National Institute of Mental Health (NIMH),
    134, 135
National Physician Health Service Corps, 136
National Recovery Act, 27
National Research Council, 134
National Science Foundation, 38, 44
National Training and Service Act, 152–153
Natural gas, 69
"Nature of work," 117
Nazis, 23. *See also* Germany
NDEA. *See* National Defense Education Act
*Negro Potential, The* (Ginzberg), 113, 114
Nelson, Donald, 29
Neoclassical theory, 8, 21, 22, 30, 31, 47–48,
    50, 51, 60, 74–75, 101, 103, 118, 158,
    166, 167, 168

*Neurotic Personality of Our Time, The*
    (Horney), 19
New Deal programs, 8, 15, 17, 27–28, 30, 31,
    33, 36, 38, 46, 48, 93, 95, 98, 151, 162,
    169
New Era, 14, 15, 28, 88–90, 92
Newton, Isaac, 148
New York City, 118–119
*New York Is Very Much Alive: A Manpower
    View* (Ginzberg), 119
NHI. *See* National health insurance
NIMH. *See* National Institute of Mental
    Health
Nixon, Richard, 39, 53, 54, 56, 57, 91, 146,
    157, 163
Nobel prize, 64–65
Norton, John DeWitt, 19
Not-for-profit sector, 97–99, 118, 122. *See also*
    Public sector


Occupational choice, 112–113
*Occupational Choice: An Approach to a General
    Theory* (Ginzberg et al.), 113
Oil, 69
Oil crisis, 39, 57, 58
Okita, Saburo, 140
Okun, Arthur, 42
OPEC. *See* Organization of Petroleum
    Exporting Countries
Organization of Petroleum Exporting
    Countries (OPEC), 42, 57, 58, 170
Output, 28, 71–72. *See also* Input-output
    analysis; Productivity


Pace, Frank, 131
Pahlavi, Riza Mohammed, 142
Palmerston, Lord, 26
*Patterns of Performance* (Ginzberg et al.), 113,
    115
Patterson, Gardner, 138
Patterson, Robert, 127, 133
Pearson, Frank A., 26
Phillips, A. W., 61–62
Phillips curve, 62, 77
Piaget, Jean, 112
Pigou, A. C., 70
Piore, Emanuel, 17
Piore, Nora, 17
Pius XI (pope), 13
*Pluralistic Economy, The* (Ginzberg et al.), 97,
    118, 143
Poland, 143
Policy, 86, 98, 102–103, 125–147
    agricultural, 85
    demand and, 80
    fiscal, 98, 102, 103
    models for, 73
    monetary, 98, 102, 103
    postwar, 51–52, 53–59
    theory and, 69–70, 170–171
    trade, 41, 50, 69–70, 148
Population quality, 85
Potofsky, Jack, 17
Poverty, 85, 101, 149, 156
Poverty Institute, 38
*Preface to Social Economics* (Clark), 16
Prices
    control of, 56, 69
    experimentation with, 29
    federal emphasis, 55
    supply and demand and, 4
*Prices and Quantities: A Macroeconomic
    Analysis*, 42

*Principles of Economics, The* (Marshall), 20, 149
*Principles of Political Economy and Taxation* (Mill), 148
Private sector, 97, 98. *See also* Business cycles
Procter & Gamble, 29, 36
Productivity, 44, 73, 98
Project LINK, 72, 73
Protectionism, 70
PSE. *See* Public service employment
Psychology, 74
    business and, 28
    economics and, 18–19
    of workforce, 115–118
    *See also* Consumer behavior
Public sector, 97–98, 104, 118, 122, 155, 162–163, 164
Public service employment (PSE), 162–163

Radbruch, Gustav, 11
Rathenau, Walter, 10
"Rational expectations" doctrine, 21, 62, 74, 105, 167–168. *See also* Consumer behavior
Reagan, Ronald, 40, 41, 44, 46, 58–59, 63, 97, 98, 125, 150, 156, 163, 170
Reaganomics, 9, 63. *See also* Supply-side economics
Recession, 39
Reconstruction programs. *See* Foreign aid
Redistribution, 95–96. *See also* Resources, allocation of
Regulation, 41, 83, 84, 97, 148
Research and development, 37–38, 44, 45, 46, 95
Resources, 60
    allocation of, 70–71, 100, 148
    *See also* Capital; Human resources; Labor
Retirement, 43, 80
Reubens, Beatrice, 97
Reuther, Walter, 54
Ricardo, David, 12, 35, 85, 149
Rickert, Heinrich, 11
*Road to Serfdom, The* (Hayek), 30
Robinson, Joan, 167
*Roe v. Wade*, 131
Roosevelt, Franklin D., 8, 15, 26, 27, 31, 33, 66, 125, 151, 169
Rosen, Howard, 130

Sachs, Alexander, 20, 36
Samuelson, Paul, 18, 47, 65, 66, 67, 68, 81, 104
Samuelson synthesis, 167
Savings, 79–81, 103
*Schechter Poultry Corporation v. U.S.*, 27
Schultz, Henry, 76
Schultz, Theodore, 81, 84–85, 86, 99, 101, 102, 103, 104, 105
Schumpeter, Joseph, 4, 19, 20
Seager, Henry, 12
Search theory, 42, 61
Sears Roebuck, 29, 30, 90, 92
Self-expression, 117
Seligman, E.R.A., 12, 13, 89
Sherman Antitrust Act, 50
Shultz, George, 56, 130
Simkhovitch, V. G., 13, 14
Simon, Herbert, 70, 74–75, 84, 86, 101, 105
Simons, Henry, 60, 76
Singapore, 141
Skepticism, 171–172

Smith, Adam, 4, 12, 13, 16, 35, 67, 75, 83, 101, 103, 122, 148, 149
Smith, Herbert, 140
Smith, Howard W., 132
Social Security, 95, 156
Solow, Robert, 54
Somervell, Bretton B., 36, 126, 146
South Korea, 141
Soviet Union, 128, 154
Space race, 128
Special interest groups, 96
Staats, Elmer, 144
Stabilization, 52, 79, 80, 98
Stagflation, 8–9, 57
Stagnation theory, 18
Stalin, Joseph, 31
Statistical concepts, 47, 75. *See also* Mathematics
Stigler, George, 81, 83–84, 86–87, 99, 102, 104, 105, 106
Stock market, 31, 92–93
Structuralists, 54
Supply-side economics, 40–41, 58–59
Sweden, 39
Switzerland, 138
Szold, Robert, 138

*Talent and Performance* (Ginzberg and Herma), 116
Tariffs, 50
Taubler, Eugene, 11
Taxes, 40–41, 52, 53, 80, 169
    on income, 95
    under Johnson, 54–55, 56
    under Kennedy, 53
Taylorism, 95
Tead, Ordway, 15
Technical assistance, 137–143
Technology, 127
    changes in, 44
    effects of, 45, 54
    growth and, 81, 82
    military, 146
    models and, 71
Teenage pregnancy, 160
Tennessee Coal and Iron, 28
Thatcher, Margaret, 170
*Theory of Business Enterprise, The* (Veblen), 28
Thorp, Willard L., 12
Tobin, James, 76, 77–79, 86, 88, 101, 102, 103, 105
Trade
    barriers, 50
    policy, 41, 50, 69–70, 148
Trade unions. *See* Labor, organized
Training, 94–95, 98, 123. *See also* Education
Transfer payments. *See* Unemployment insurance
Transportation, 89, 90
Truman, Harry S., 52, 131
Turkey, 139

*Understanding Human Resources* (Ginzberg), 121
Underutilization, 60, 167
*Uneducated, The* (Ginzberg and Bray), 113
*Unemployed, The* (Ginzberg et al.), 111
Unemployment, 39, 41–42, 43, 51–52, 54, 60–62, 109–112, 161–164
    long-term, 110–112
    segments, 157–159
    voluntary, 157–158
Unemployment insurance, 61, 95, 155–156

Unions. *See* Labor, organized
Urbanization, 90, 100
U.S. Steel, 28
Utility maximization, 84

Values-added, 71–72
Value theory, 83
Veblen, Thorstein, 4, 12, 17, 19, 28, 67
Veterans Administration, 134
Vietnam war, 55, 131, 146
Villard, Henry, 18
Viner, Jacob, 26
Vojta, George J., 121
Volcker, Paul, 58, 59

WACs. *See* Women's Army Corps
Wage controls, 56
Wages
  rigidity of, 60
Wales, 110
Wallis, Allen, 54
Walras, Léon, 66
Walras' Law, 78
War Department, 36

Warren, George F., 26
*Wealth of Nations, The* (Smith), 4, 12, 16, 83
Weber, Max, 11, 171
Weimar Republic, 10, 12
Welfare system, 95, 104, 111, 156–157
*We Never Called Him Henry* (Bennett), 29
Westermann, William L., 12
West Germany, 39, 91, 158, 169
Wharton model, 72, 73
*What Veblen Taught* (Mitchell), 19
White House Conference on Education, 129
Wiley, George, 157
Willis, H. Parker, 12, 14
Wolman, Leo, 13, 14
Women, 43–44, 45, 46, 61, 89, 90, 94, 99,
  116, 117, 118, 122, 123, 125–127, 145,
  159
Women's Army Corps (WACs), 126
Wood, Robert E., 30
Woodbridge, Frederick J., 12
Workforce. *See* Labor
Work patterns, 117
World War II, 113–116, 125–127, 167

Young Plan, 22
Youth, 61, 160